A NEW VIEW OF DORSET

An Exploration of Dorset's Landscapes and Guidance for their Future Management

by Richard Burden and Gordon Le Pard
of the Coast and Countryside Policy Unit,
Dorset County Planning Department
based on the
Dorset County Landscape Assessment (1993
by Landscape Design Associates

First published in Great Britain in 1996 by Dorset Books

British Library Cataloguing in Publication Data
A CIP Catalogue Record for this book is available from the British Library

ISBN 1 871164 30 3

DORSET BOOKS
Official Publisher to Dorset County Council

Halsgrove House
Lower Moor Way
Tiverton EX16 6SS
Tel: 01884 243242
Fax: 01884 243325

Printed and bound in Great Britain by Ebenezer Baylis & Son Ltd., Worcester

CONTENTS

ILLUSTRATIONS

The photographs are by Richard Burden and Gordon Le Pard. All the modern drawings were originally produced for the *Dorset County Landscape Assessment* by Kate Collins of Landscape Design Associates. Drawings of this type are an integral part of a landscape assessment enabling a surveyor to pick out the key features of a particular view. For each drawing the National Grid Reference of the viewpoint is given. In addition several older drawings have also been used. The majority are by Joseph Pennell and were originally drawn to illustrate Sir Frederick Treves' *Highways and Byways in Dorset* (1906).

The other drawings are by Heywood Sumner: *Grim's Dyke* was published in 1910. *The View from Dudsbury* and *The View from Ramsdown* were never published in the artist's lifetime and are reproduced by permission of the Bournemouth Natural Science Society. These older drawings both add variety and also illustrate the antiquity of many of the county's landscapes. It is a tribute to the enduring qualities of the Dorset landscape that drawings made over ninety years ago can still be used to illustrate a contemporary study.

PREFACE

A New View of Dorset is for everybody who has an interest in the Dorset Landscape. For those who simply enjoy it and want to understand it, there is an account of what makes up the landscape, an outline of those forces which have changed the landscape in the past and will continue to do so in the future, and a detailed description of the differing landscape areas which comprise the county.

For those people who have a hand in managing the landscape, and these range from county and district planners, across farmers and land managers to community groups working to improve their local environment, there are guidelines for each of the landscape character areas. These indicate those actions which would help to maintain the character of the Dorset Landscapes, and actions which would alter or change the local landscape. *A New View of Dorset* is both the first detailed description of the landscapes of Dorset, and is also a guide to sustaining them for future generations.

A New View of Dorset builds on the work of Professor Robert Tregay, Colin Goodrum and Kate Collins, of Landscape Design Associates, that was jointly funded by Dorset County Council, Purbeck District Council, and the Countryside Commission in 1993. The consultants' report described and assessed the landscapes across the county of Dorset. A 1:100,000 scale map of the Landscape Character Areas is separately available. Using their work, the Countryside Commission has published booklets on the Dorset Area of Outstanding Natural Beauty, and on the Cranborne Chase and West Wiltshire Downs. The regional context has been considered in the Commission's pilot project for the New Map of England, and discussed in 'The Landscape, Coast and Historic Environment of the South West' produced by the South West Regional Planning Conference.

Over recent decades information has been gathered in a variety of ways on various aspects of Dorset's landscapes. In 1948 Ronald Good, in his study of the Dorset Flora, identified some fourteen 'Natural Regions' in Dorset. In the 1970's the County Council supported graduate studies from University College London on Chalk Downland, Heathland, Woodland, the River Systems, and Agricultural Landscapes. It joined with the Manpower Services Commission and West Dorset District Council in sponsoring a detailed ecological survey of the whole of West Dorset in 1978, and co-operated closely with the landowners in the production of *The Historic Landscape of the Weld Estate* in 1987.

A New View of Dorset looks at the whole of Dorset. The landscapes of the county are described and a reproduction of the Landscape Character Map is included.

FOREWORD

By Hugh Clamp, Past President of the Landscape Institute

This book brings together the Landscape Character Map and the Dorset Landscape Assessment which are both innovative and valuable contributions to a deeper, and broader, understanding of the county of Dorset. The fact that these are the products of a partnership – County Council, District Council, Government Agency, and private consultant – reinforces the range and scale of interests in sustaining the landscapes of Dorset. The professional descriptions deserve consideration by a wider audience, and this book strives to put them into a readable and readily comprehensible form. It draws together the range of elements that constitute the concepts of landscape, the links that exist between land use, form, geology, drainage, ecology, history, culture, and aesthetic appreciation. Leading as it does from descriptions of the landscapes, identifying the key features, to the issues to be considered and the opportunities for management, it provides timely guidance. The inclusion of management topics and principles that apply across the county, in addition to advice on particular areas, extends the survey work by the consultants and moves the emphasis towards practical activities.

Sustainability of the environment is fundamental to quality of life in Dorset, and guidance that can help, encourage, and focus effort and resources to landscape management obviously makes a positive contribution. The changing national and international agricultural policies, and fiscal support, indicate there will be resources for the management of landscapes in their own right rather than, as previously, as by-products of agricultural and forestry activities. Furthermore, there is a positive role in both the strategic and local planning processes. The character, local distinctiveness, and 'sense of place' of a locality are crucial to good landscape planning and design. The county scale landscape character areas can, with more detailed assessment, be divided into smaller, more local units that provide the context for the appraisal of the impact of individual projects or the evaluation of particular sites.

The earlier publication by Cambridgeshire County Council, again based on a landscape assessment by Landscape Design Associates, provided innovative design guidance in a largely flat landscape. I believe this Dorset book is equally innovative, concentrating more on landscape management activities in a county with a great variety of landscapes and with some of the finest coast in the country.

Hugh Clamp

THE LANDSCAPE INSTITUTE

HUGH CLAMP
Yetminster,
Dorset.

LANDSCAPE APPRECIATION

What are Landscapes?

Practically everyone is conscious of the character and state of the environment around them now, be it in town or country. Perceptions of 'landscape' have, however, evolved and grown over centuries. The great landscape artists of two and three hundred years ago painted classical events and romantic idylls set against a countryside or coastal scene, as well as carefully composed and framed 'natural' and picturesque views for their patrons and benefactors. At that time, those pictures were for a select and privileged audience, as were those real areas of countryside where the landowner sought to control and enhance nature to create pleasing views or living paintings. Examples range from the grand and formal schemes of Le Notre, Brown, and Repton to the more domestic garden scale of planting, colours, and shapes of Jekyll. Design concentrated on visual and physical compartments, and these aspects are seen in designs today. Scenes were composed of curves, slopes, and reflections, with vertical and horizontal elements employed to guide, direct, and focus the eye along, over, and towards, as well as constructing and framing pleasing or inspiring views. Tracks and turns were used to lead and create surprises, whilst carefully located classical artefacts recalled a romantic past or an historical tale. Form, texture, structure, shape, siting, juxtaposition, and colour are major elements of these designed landscapes, and many were created at times when large and influential families managed big estates. Frequently they reflect the character and aspirations of the landowner just as much as that of the landscape architect.

The mid nineteenth century saw a much greater awareness and wider public appreciation of the extent of the semi-natural qualities of the countryside. Formality and the picturesque were no longer the criteria to gain 'landscape' status. Greater emphasis on, and recognition of, the working role of the countryside in the twentieth century have now brought us to a fuller understanding of the whole environment around us and the forces that have shaped it. Towns and villages have grown beyond previous expectations, and recent decades have witnessed both the intensification and extensification of agriculture with resultant changes impacting on virtually every aspect of the countryside. Although the emphasis has now moved from creating pleasing scenes, the land manager still has a profound influence on the character of the landscapes around us.

Today, landscapes are about space and character, and are considerably more than just the visual aspects arising from a combination of landform and vegetation. They are places where generations of people and wild creatures have sought food and shelter, set up homes, and lived solitary or communal lives. Landscapes embody the history, land use, human culture, wildlife and seasonal changes of an area. The local topography and geology, farming and forestry practices, plant and animal life, building styles and settlement form, together with infrastructure, combine to produce, within broad regional character areas, 'local distinctiveness'. The juxtaposition of materials, forms, and uses contributes towards the special 'sense of place' of a locality. This can be partially described visually, but the emotional responses, such as tranquillity, grandeur, enclosure and exposure, amongst many others, are crucial to a fuller appreciation of the 'local distinctiveness' and 'sense of place' of any individual landscape. In many cases these conjure up real examples of idealised pictures of traditional living landscapes, integrating people with the landform through villages and towns, grouped around a church spire or a tower of local stone, nestling, protected, into a fold in the landform. Moreover, landscapes are not static and their character can change as all landscapes are living, lived in, and dynamic. The rate of change varies with different components. The daily weather can influence the emotional response to a landscape whilst the colour, form and texture of the plant life and farm crops change with the seasons of the year. Trees and woodlands, however, mature and modify the scene over much longer timescales. Built development, on the other hand, has an almost instantaneous and long-lasting impact.

Apart from a few village surveys, passages in a few guide books, some photographic essays and descriptions of particular localities by authors such as Thomas Hardy and John Fowles, there is a dearth of accounts that include all elements of Dorset's landscapes. Earlier geographical, botanical, and planning studies have tended to restrict themselves to geology and landform. The last two decades have seen a focus on special interests, particularly wildlife, historic buildings, and archaeology. Nevertheless, the concept of landscape is wider, more embracing, more valuable than simply the sum of such vital individual topics.

Despite the previous lack of an overall co-ordinated and structured appraisal, the quality of the environment of Dorset has been both valued and recognised locally and nationally for a long time. However, there has been a certain wariness of formal designations in earlier decades for fear that locations without designation might be treated with less than the respect they deserved! In that sense it is still true that all the landscapes of Dorset are important to the inhabitants.

Of the individual interests there are 143 Sites of Special Scientific Interest, 9 National Nature Reserves, 861 Scheduled Ancient Monuments, and 224 Conservation Areas. It should be no surprise therefore that 53% of the county has the national designation as an Area of Outstanding Natural Beauty; the Dorset AONB dating from 1957 and Cranborne Chase AONB from 1981. In addition 91.3km, or 64.3%, of the coast is Heritage Coast, and the Purbeck Heritage Coast has held the coveted Diploma of the

Landscape elements diagram.

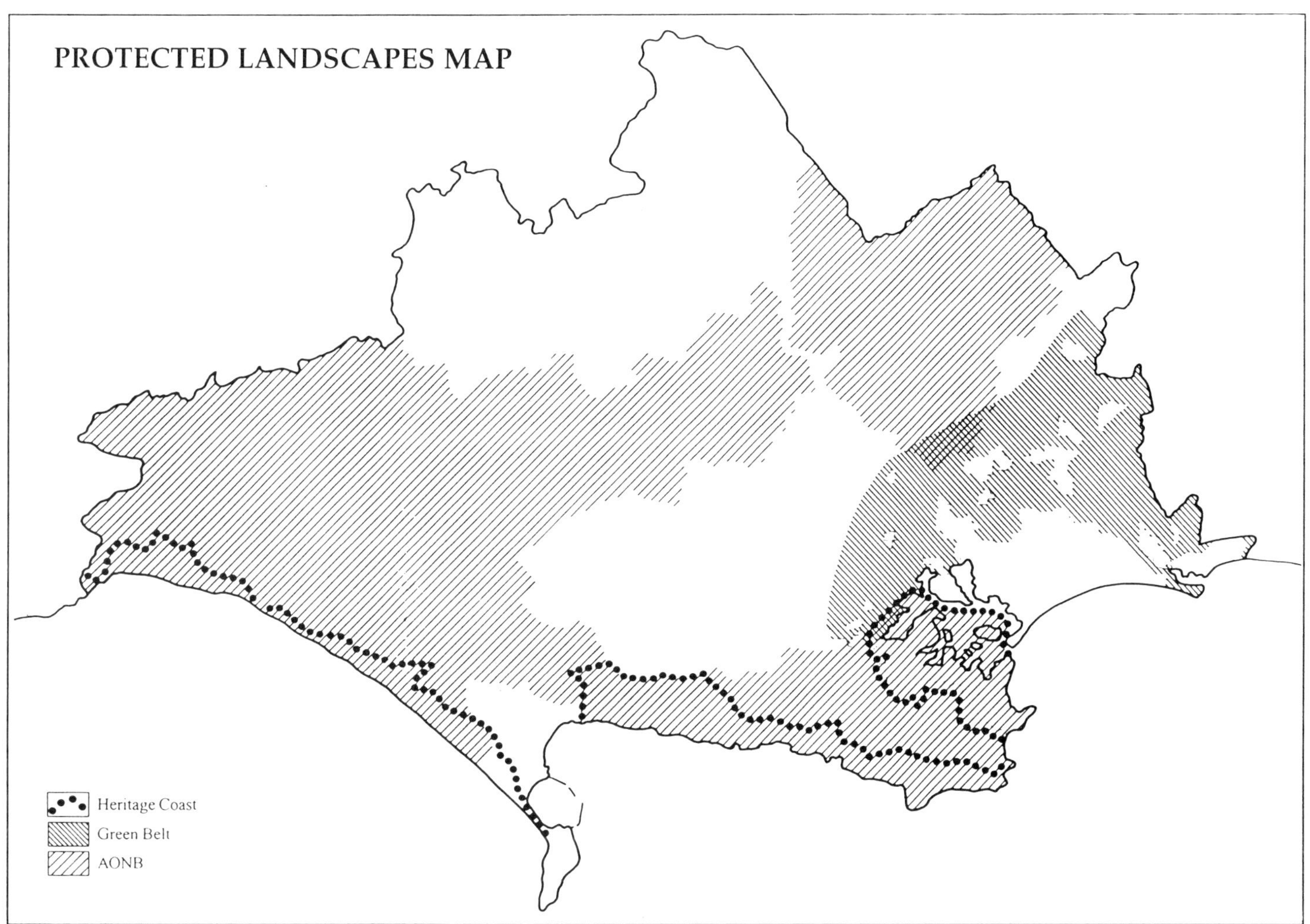

Council of Europe for Protected Landscapes since 1984. Whilst these simple statistics significantly exceed national averages, showing how important the Dorset landscapes are to the country as a whole, it is the combined effect of the individual elements that distinguishes their character and quality.

Furthermore Dorset is generally perceived as having an outstanding range of landscapes, with distinctive contrasts and many unique features. The 53% of Dorset classified as an AONB has national status as a scenic, valuable landscape, and this designation ensures some level of protection through the formal planning processes. However, visual and cultural character are often taken for granted and are as easily degraded by general trends in agriculture and tourism, for example, as by the sudden impacts of major developments. The other 47% of the county, which provides the setting for the AONB, includes extensive areas of fine landscape quality, and is particularly vulnerable to future change as development pressures are concentrated in a smaller area. As it is impossible to predict the future balance of forces for change with any certainty, so it is particularly important to recognise and understand the factors which influence landscape character so that policies, actions, and management guidelines can be geared to reinforcing the identity, character and quality of all landscapes.

Structured descriptions and assessments of landscapes are obviously a sound basis for identifying management strategies and activities to sustain those landscapes. They are also invaluable for preparing evaluations, either for the designation of areas for special status or for the impacts of change or developments. In addition they can provide the basis for area or site management plans. Moreover, at a time when quality of life and respect for the environment are taking an ever increasing profile, they have a significant role in strategic and local planning. Landscape assessment can therefore help us to understand how and why landscapes are important, promote an appreciation of landscape issues, and guide and direct landscape change.

The story we tell covers the formation of Dorset's landscapes, the current influences for change, and structured descriptions of the six major landscape zones and the twenty-three landscape character areas. For each, the key features are identified and management advice and guidance is provided to sustain the elements, characteristics, and quality of them. An overview of general principles of good practice in landscape management is also presented. The focus is on the landscapes as they exist in the first half of the 1990s. Whether particular landscapes should be changed significantly by design, management, or development is a part of another wider, strategic, debate. Nevertheless, the landscape assessments and their associated management should be fundamental elements in any deliberation on the future of the county's landscapes.

THE STORY BEHIND TODAY'S LANDSCAPES

Landscapes are frequently described as 'living', implying that the way in which they change over time parallels the growth, development and decay of a living organism. This metaphor can be taken a stage further, the landscape's structure can be compared to an animal's body; the geology forms the bones, the way in which these rocks have been shaped makes the skeleton, the soils are the flesh and the skin has been created by centuries of human activity.

Geology is a major influence in the creation of the county's landscapes since there is an obvious relationship between landscape character and the underlying geology which, in turn, has strongly influenced Dorset's varied topography and soils.

Overlaid upon this structural framework is a long history of human activities, principally agriculture and settlement, which has provided a substantial inheritance of distinctive landscape features. Fortunately the Dorset landscape is remarkably unspoilt and in places there is a sense that time has passed it by. Evidence of the successive chapters of history is scattered throughout the county and it is possible to appreciate much of the evolution of the landscape from its visual character and features.

Over the centuries Dorset's landscapes have inspired poets, authors, artists and musicians, many of whom have left their own rich legacy of cultural associations. The sheer number of physical and cultural landmarks is remarkable. This range and quality contribute to the distinctive identity of the county of Dorset.

Geology

The rocks supply the bones of the landscape. In Dorset they are all sedimentary in nature and were originally formed beneath seas or lakes, or laid down by rivers. The oldest rocks, the Lower Lias, were formed as sediments about 200 million years ago on the bed of the Jurassic sea. Over the succeeding 140 million years the rest of the Jurassic and Cretaceous rocks were deposited layer upon layer, culminating in the chalk. Later the sands, clays and gravels of eastern Dorset were deposited and finally the alluvial deposits of the rivers were laid down in comparatively recent times. In between times great lateral pressures buckled, bent and fractured the layers, changing their angles and aspects.

This geological variety gives rise to a wide range of landforms and soils. The quality and diversity of the landscape is enhanced by the broad changes in scale between the heathlands, the chalklands, and the ridge and valley landscapes of the farmlands. Looking at the maps of the geology and topography of the county a clear relationship can be seen between them and the mapped landscape character areas.

To geologists the importance of Dorset in the development of the science can be illustrated by the names it has contributed to the subject, for geological stages Kimmeridgian, Portlandian, and Purbeckian are used the world over. Nowhere else are these beds so fully developed and so ideally exposed to view, nor are their faunas so completed preserved. The diversity of the geology can be illustrated by the simple, but remarkable, fact that within the

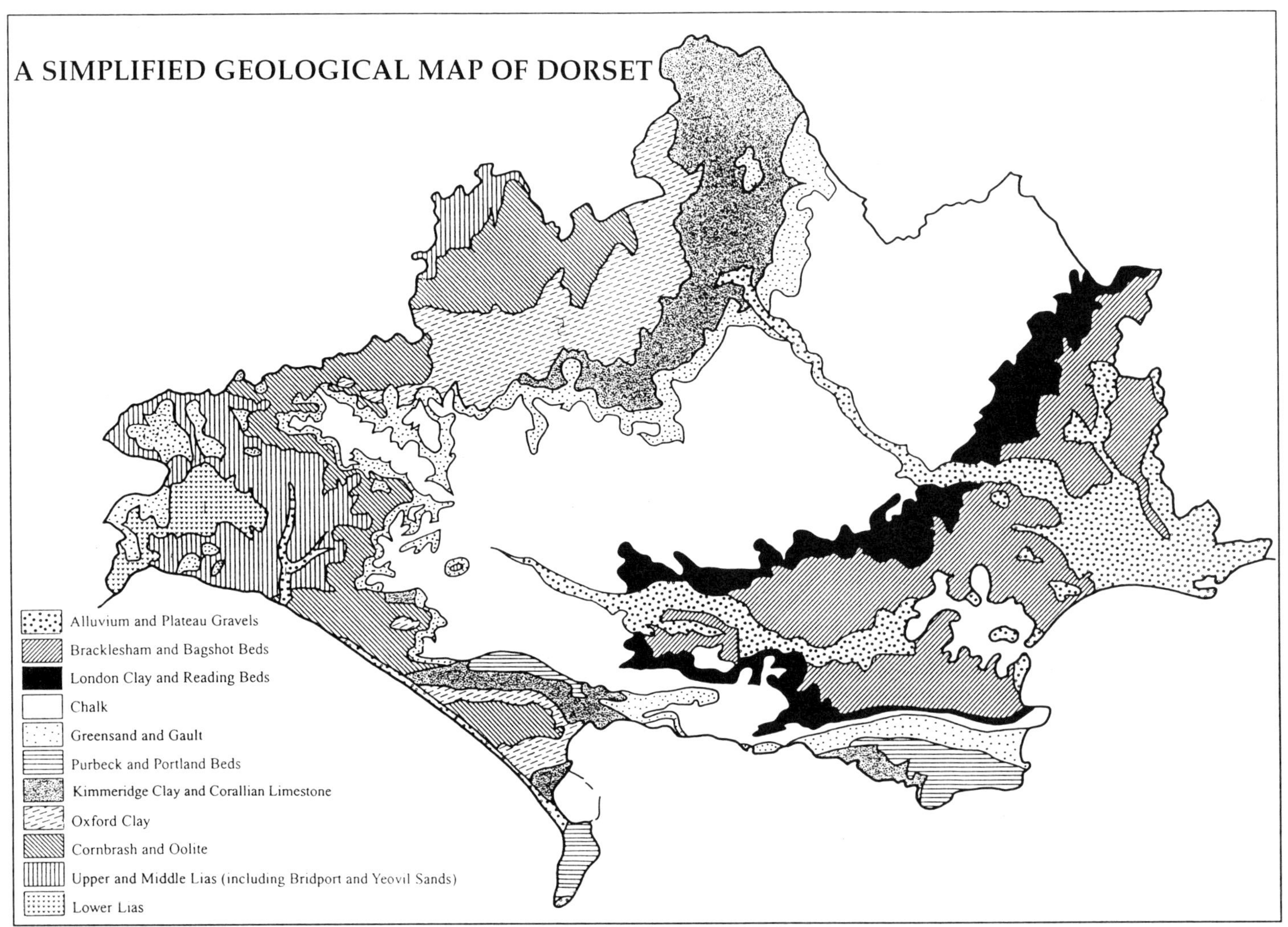

ninety-one kilometres of the Dorset Coast virtually all the rocks that are exposed along the east coast of England south of Teesside can be found.

The oldest rocks are to be found in the west of the county where, in the centre of west Dorset, the Marshwood Vale, formed on the Lower Lias, is a secluded bowl-shaped depression almost hidden by the surrounding landforms. These consist of distinctive Greensand ridges, separating clusters of deeply incised valleys which border the great mass of the chalk, which sweeps across Dorset in an irregular curve from the north east to the south west and back again to the south east. To the north of the chalk, the Blackmoor Vale is an extensive, flat clay vale bordered by limestone ridges to the north west and the undulating hills of the escarpment to the south and east. To the south of the chalk ridge lie the Weymouth lowlands and the prominent limestone peninsula of Portland. Further south east is the Isle of Purbeck, renowned for the variety and structural clarity of its rocks and landforms. A high chalk ridge, which once linked Purbeck to the Isle of Wight, separates the heathlands and the Poole Basin from the secluded valley of the River Corfe. North of the Isle of Purbeck lie the sands, clays and gravels of the Poole Basin. These rocks are the youngest in the county of Dorset, and support a gentler rolling landscape cut by several meandering river valleys. The heathland landscape continues to the county border along the River Avon and indeed goes beyond it into Hampshire and the New Forest.

The sequence of cliffs and bays along the Dorset coast clearly reveal the complex geological structure of the land and landscapes. The rocks have been carved by the powerful forces of coastal erosion and deposition, leaving a legacy of unique features such as Lulworth Cove, Durdle Door and Chesil Beach, examples which are used in textbooks the world over.

Topography and Geomorphology

Dorset is centrally placed on the south coast of England, and is usually considered to be the most easterly of the South Western counties. The variation in the types of landscape to be found within the comparatively small area of the county is particularly notable; indeed virtually all the landscape features of southern Britain can be found in Dorset. The chief exception being large areas of fresh water and the county only just misses out on this as its boundary with Somerset passes through the southern tip of Sutton Bingham reservoir.

The landform ranges from salt marshes at sea level to heights such as Golden Cap (191 metres) the highest point on the south coast of England, Bulbarrow (274 metres) and Pilsdon Pen (277 metres). In between are many variations, from the more level, rippling, ground of the Poole Basin at about 10 to 20 metres, to the higher ground of the chalk, above 100 metres, which forms the backbone of the county.

The chalk itself is dissected by various river valleys and on the northern and western escarpments produces impressive and substantial hills. Beyond the chalk the Blackmoor and Marshwood Vales are shallow bowls of less dramatic landform but even here small hills can produce remarkable images. Poole Harbour, one of the largest natural harbours in the world, is a dramatic backdrop to many views and certainly warrants the description as the 'Dorset Lakeland'. The Isles of Purbeck and of Portland have their own distinctive and unusual landforms. Few sites are more memorable than that of Corfe Castle and the Gap seen from Kingston, or Chesil Beach seen from Portland Heights.

The broad physical shape of the county's landscapes has mostly been created by natural forces starting some 25 million years ago. It was then that Africa, which had been gradually moving northwards for many millions of years, finally reached southern Europe. As it did so it pushed up the rock strata in front of it creating the Alps and Pyrenees. Further north the effect was less pronounced, but still noticeable, as chalk and limestone were pushed up to form high hills, then bent and twisted in places. The distorted rocks at Stair Hole near Lulworth bear testimony to the incredible forces at work. As soon as one force raised the chalk above sea level, different forces were wearing it away again. Gravel and clays from eroded rocks were deposited all over the chalk in eastern Dorset. Then, about two million years ago, the climate cooled and huge ice caps began to form in northern Europe. As they grew they pushed southwards, on one occasion reaching as far south as a line running across England between Bristol and The Wash. Four times the ice pushed south, then retreated again, the last time happening about 12,000 years ago. During the Ice Ages Dorset would have been subjected to tundra conditions, with a permanently frozen sub-soil, the permafrost, whilst the top soil would have thawed every summer. The lack of vegetation, together with the poor drainage caused by the permafrost (water cannot soak through ice) led to massive erosion. The dry valleys in the chalk were probably caused by this process which also sculpted many of the hills and valleys on the gravels of eastern Dorset.

Dorset – Contour Map

A contour map is one of the easiest ways of appreciating the diversity of Dorset's landscapes, giving at a glance the structure and topography, the valleys and hills, the troughs and ridges, and the plateaux and plains of a county. The distance between the contours is an indication of the slope, the closer they are the steeper it is. Here they are at 20 metre intervals, and the lower, flatter areas of the river valleys have least lines, while the coastal cliffs, the high chalk escarpments, and the intricate landscapes of western Dorset have many more contours, indicating both height and changes of slope.

The map shows the eastern boundary of the county is formed by the fairly straight valley of the river Avon. Moving north-westwards the land rises gently across the chalk lands until it reaches the edge of the escarpment, where it drops quickly into the Blackmoor Vale. Northward the higher land of the limestone hills can be seen around the county boundary, with ridges on either side of the Yeo valley to the west. The stour cuts through the chalk downland, and south-west of it the undulating heaths fall away to the valley of the river Frome.

The Frome valley can be seen rising on the chalk in the west, while south of its mouth in Poole Harbour the ridge of the Purbeck Hills forms a strong line across the map. The land then drops into the Corfe valley and climbs again to the ridges of the Purbeck coast. To the west the escarpment of the chalk shows as strong lines running north of Weymouth. South of the escarpment the contours pick up the east-west 'grain' of the landform and the wedge shape of Portland is clearly shown, rising dramatically and then falling gently to its southern tip.

The dense and convoluted contours of the numerous hills and ridges surrounding the bowl of the Marshwood Vale in the far west of the county reflect the truly complex topography and involved landform.

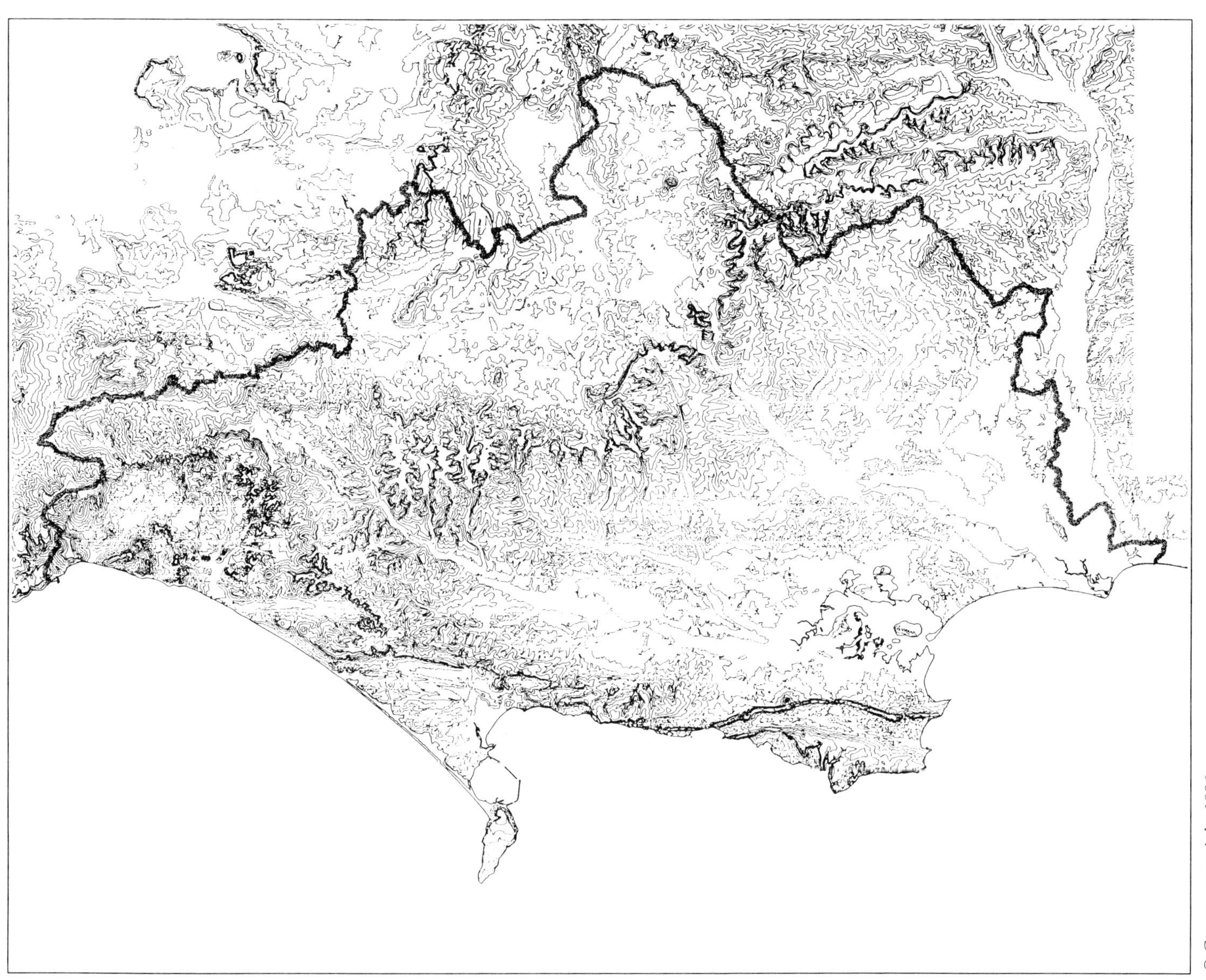

When the ice finally began to melt it triggered massive changes in the British landscape. The great weight of ice had depressed the land of northern Britain, causing southern Britain to rise like a see-saw. As the ice melted the pressure was released, and the land began to revert to its former position. This caused southern Britain to sink, the subsidence still continues to this day, though now at a very reduced rate. In addition the melting ice released a great flood of water and this, together with the subsidence of southern Britain, caused the sea level to rise in relation to the land. The chalk ridge that ran between Purbeck and the Isle of Wight was breached, and the valley of the ancient Solent river was flooded. Old Harry rocks, off Ballard Down, are relics of this ancient chalk ridge (as are the Needle rocks off the Isle of Wight) whilst Poole Harbour is part of the flooded river valley. Here changes in the shape of the coastline have occurred very rapidly in geological terms, with a sand spit developing almost closing off the valley, and creating both the harbour and Little Sea, the lake on the Studland peninsula, in the last few centuries.

In western Dorset the rising sea level had a most unusual effect; a beach was rolled back across Lyme Bay until it met a narrow river valley running south-east. This remarkable situation stabilised in Chesil Beach, a unique feature whose origins and nature are still a matter for study and debate. Elsewhere along the coast, erosion was producing an amazing series of natural features. The virtually round bay of Lulworth Cove, the sea arch and tiny cove at Stair Hole, the more massive arch at Durdle Door, and the sea stacks at Old Harry rocks. These are all active features; erosion is continuing, and the coastline is constantly changing. For example, the rocks at the entrance to Lulworth Cove are very unstable, and the mouth of the cove is gradually widening. A sea stack, Old Harry's Wife, fell at the end of the nineteenth century, whilst Durlston Head, to the south of Swanage, possibly owes its name to a lost sea arch. Durlston is derived from *Thurlston* which, in Old English, means the 'Stone with a Hole"!

Inland the passing of the ice had less dramatic effects. As the permafrost melted, water was able to drain through the chalk and gravels, and rivers settled into new channels in the valleys. Perhaps the most interesting of post-glacial erosion effects are to be found where the tertiary gravels overlie the chalk. Here rain, which is naturally slightly acidic, permeated through the soil (which is also acidic) to dissolve the underlying chalk, creating a doline, a natural crater in the ground. The largest, Culpeppers Dish, is over 30 metres deep. These dolines were formed over a very long period. Rimsmoor Pond, north of Wool, was in existence by 8000 BC, whilst those on Bronkham hill, north of Portesham were probably formed after 2000 BC as they cut and distort a group of Bronze Age round barrows. Much more important, the warming climate allowed trees and other plants to spread north again. Dorset was covered with woodlands, varying according to the soils. This forest was to last until man became a farmer, and cut down the woodlands to create fields.

Soils

To follow the metaphor of the landscape as an animal, if the rocks are the bones then the soils are the flesh. The soils of Dorset vary widely but, as one might expect, they are strongly influenced by the underlying rocks. It is the soils that have had the greatest influence on the agriculture of the county, their fertility, mineral content and drainage properties have been key factors in deciding how the land would be used over the centuries.

The complex geology of west Dorset, a mixture of Liassic limestones and clays together with the greensand, has given rise to a similarly complex mixture of soils. Generally speaking the soils over the Liassic deposits tend to be heavy, with a high clay content whilst those derived from sandstones, grits or corallian limestone are light and tend to dry out easily.

On the chalk three main types of soil occur. Many of the flatter hill-tops and plateaux carry the 'clay-with-flints', a very heavy soil with, as its name suggests, numerous angular

MARSHWOOD VALE: *View of small scale patchwork of fields and hedgerows on undulating terrain, from the foot of Pilsdon Pen, southwards towards the Marshwood Vale.* GR 396008.

flints imbedded in it. Most of the older woodlands on the chalk are on this soil since farmers in the past sensibly used the lighter, more easily worked soils for arable, and managed woodland on the heavier clays. On the slopes of the chalk escarpments are very thin soils, cultivation can easily cut through them and into the underlying bedrock, a condition often seen where such soils are ploughed. Finally in the valleys there are deep layers of alluvium and 'downwash', soil eroded from the upper slopes after early farmers cleared the woodland and first ploughed the land. These are some of the richest soils in the county.

The Isle of Purbeck, south of the chalk ridge, is similar to west Dorset in having a very varied mixture of soils. There can be considerable variation within a single field, from a light sandy soil to a stiff yellow clay. On the Purbeck limestones there are brown clayey loams, which suffer from drought in summer, and are waterlogged in winter. Strangest of all are the soils derived from Kimmeridge clay, grey or black when exposed they will 'rust' and turn brown as their iron content oxidises. They are very sticky and difficult to cultivate.

The soils of eastern Dorset are generally acidic. On the edge of the chalk, the mixture of down-wash from the chalk and the tertiary sands and gravels can produce a rich soil, very suitable for arable farming. Similarly there can be rich alluvium in the river valleys, though this is more usually used for pasture as flooding has always been a possibility. Elsewhere, where clays predominate, the soil is suitable for pasture. However on the lighter sands and gravels the classic heathland 'podsol' is frequently found. This thin grey or black soil, overlying sand is the poorest in the county. It is caused when minerals and nutrients have been washed out of the topsoil by rain water, and are concentrated in the subsoil. Under certain conditions an 'iron pan' can form about a metre down. This is an impervious layer formed of precipitated iron salts, which prevents further drainage and encourages waterlogging. In wet hollows and pools, where sphagnum mosses grow, peat can develop. This often preserves pollen and other traces of plant material, analysis of which gives good evidence of how the vegetation has altered over time.

In north Dorset there are two contrasting types of soil. In the Blackmoor Vale the soils are stiff, heavy and wet and are generally used for pasture. There are lighter soils where down-wash from the chalk is mixed with the clay, at the bottom of the escarpment or in the some river valleys. In contrast the soils on the limestone ridges are light and well drained, indeed drainage is so good that there are often problems from drought in the summer.

Human Influence

To complete the metaphor of the landscape as an animal, whilst rocks and soils provide the bones and flesh, then the skin, the surface features that we see today, are essentially a by-product of human activity. With the possible exception of parts of the coastline there is no part of Dorset which has not been directly affected by human activities over the past six thousand years.

Human beings have lived in Dorset continuously since the end of the last Ice Age. People had lived in Dorset before this date, but there were probably times when Dorset was uninhabited due to climatic reasons. As the ice retreated from northern Europe, and the climate warmed, woodlands spread across the countryside and most of Dorset was probably covered with a mixed woodland. The first inhabitants of these woodlands, the Mesolithic or Middle Stone Age people, were essentially hunter-gatherers and had comparatively little effect on the native woodland. They may have cleared some areas to encourage grazing by game animals but the extent of this in Dorset is unclear at present. It was with the coming of agriculture, about 4500 BC, that man's influence on the landscape became significant.

The first farmers of the Neolithic or New Stone Age, seem to have concentrated on the dryer, and perhaps lighter, woodlands of the chalk. Monuments dating from this period can be found all across Dorset. There are the great long barrows, the causeway camps on Hambledon Hill and Maiden Castle, the circular Henge monuments, probably religious sites, at Knowlton, Maumbury Rings and Mount Pleasant and strangest of all the great Cursus that ran across Cranborne Chase, whose purpose is still a matter of debate. Successors to the Neolithic farmers, those of the Bronze Age, continued the process of clearance. It was they who cut down the woodlands of eastern Dorset. The removal of the trees allowed the soil nutrients to be washed away and created the heathland that we see today. The most obvious traces of the Bronze Age are the numerous burial mounds, round barrows, which dot the Dorset landscape. The farmers of the Bronze Age, and of the Iron Age which succeeded it, have left traces of their fields and field boundaries which can still be seen on the chalk where more recent cultivation has not obliterated them. The Iron Age left other monuments too, in particular the great hill forts, which are such a feature of many Dorset hill tops, especially along the edges of the chalk. By the end of the Iron Age it is probable that most of Dorset had been cleared for cultivation, and those areas which were still woodland were being managed for timber and woodland products such as charcoal. When the Romans arrived in Dorset, in about AD 50, they took over an ordered and managed landscape. The most prominent features of their presence, which can be seen today, are their great roads. Ackling Dyke which crosses Cranborne Chase is considered by many to be one of the most spectacular Roman roads in Britain.

During the Saxon and medieval periods which followed, from the fifth to the fifteenth centuries, much of the landscape that we see today evolved. At times there was probably more of Dorset under the plough than there is today. The lynchet fields which can be found on many of the chalkland slopes show that even these steep terraces were once ploughed, particularly fine examples can be seen on the coastal ridges at Worth Matravers. At this time the rabbit was introduced, the early rabbits were a valuable animal, and were carefully farmed. They seem to have been delicate creatures, who needed carefully constructed homes, they couldn't even dig their own burrows. Traces of these artificial warrens can be found in several places, such as on the top of Pilsdon Pen, where the rampart of the Iron Age hill fort was adapted to form the outer fence of a medieval rabbit farm.

During the medieval period, and later, much of Dorset was legally Forest or Chase. This had little to do with trees but meant that the land was administered under Forest and Chase law, which was designed to preserve deer as a source of meat and, incidentally, sport. The special laws involved restrictions on agricultural practices within the boundaries, but with the compensation of benefits and privileges not applicable to those living outside these areas. As time passed the restrictions, particularly on private landowners whose lands were subject to Forest or Chase law, began to outweigh the benefits, and by the beginning of the seventeenth century Forests and Chases were seen by many in Dorset as unnecessary anachronisms. By the early eighteenth century all the Forests and Chases in Dorset had gone, with one exception, Cranborne Chase which remained, as a medieval chase, until it was finally disfranchised in 1830. It is probable that the survival of the extensive woodlands around Tollard Royal, and elsewhere on Cranborne Chase, was due to the continuance there of a medieval management system which had long since vanished elsewhere in the county.

The products of the woodlands were vital to the rural economy. A managed woodland, and most woodlands were managed, would have been surrounded with a stock-proof barrier. Keeping out grazing animals encouraged coppice and natural regeneration to replenish the cut wood and timber. There were occasional exceptions; at Kingston Lacy in the fourteenth century young oaks were imported from Kent when a new wood was created.

Whilst the majority of Dorset villages have a medieval or Saxon origin, the infertile heathland soils of the Poole Basin had few significant ancient settlements. That land, however, was not unused, it was grazed fairly heavily, and extensively harvested for turf which was, perhaps, the most common fuel in Dorset until the nineteenth century. Enclosure of the heathlands for agriculture began in the seventeenth century, mostly on the slightly better soils beside the rivers. The planting of conifers began in the mid eighteenth century and continued through the nineteenth into the twentieth century when the majority of the coniferous plantations were planted.

From the nineteenth century onwards agriculture has gone through periods of expansion and decline, usually determined by forces outside the farmers' control; wars, foreign imports or government polices which influenced the prices of their products. New technology has also had a direct, or indirect, effect on agriculture. The coming of the railways had a most dramatic effect; with a swift method of transport to London and other major cities, milk production blossomed. By the beginning of this century Bailey Gate station, in the tiny village of Sturminster Marshall, was one of the most important handling depots for milk in England!

The downlands had been mostly unenclosed grassland for many centuries prior to the late seventeenth century when they began to be enclosed, but remained mostly grassland for more intensive sheep rearing. Some areas were converted to arable during the Napoleonic Wars, owing to the high price that corn fetched. This enclosure continued during the nineteenth century aided by the introduction of steam ploughing from the 1860s. In the twentieth century much of the remaining downland came under the plough owing to the need for corn during the Second World War, and subsequently when grants and subsidies made it profitable.

However it is the heathlands which provide the finest example of how these changes have effected the landscape. Before the mid eighteenth century they were of value, supplying turf fuel and grazing. Improvements in livestock led to varieties that produced better meat, but which needed to be well fed and cared for. This meant that the tougher animals which could get a living from the heathland had less value in the market. Then as transport improved coal became readily available, and the sales of turf for fuel dropped. Large estates which owned heathland now planted pines on some of their land, or abandoned other areas. Without the regular grazing and turf cutting, birch, and increasingly pines, spread across the heaths. By the early twentieth century heathland was seen as wasteland, ideal for housing as it was well drained. Indeed much of Bournemouth is built on former heathlands. By the time the true nature of heathland was recognised, that it was an artefact, mostly created during the Bronze Age, and needing constant management to survive, it was almost too late. The two ideas that heathland is 'wasteland', suitable for development, or that it is a 'natural' landscape that need only be left alone to survive, are both still held by some, and are both, perhaps, equally destructive to that landscape.

As well as agriculture, industry too has left its mark on Dorset, although it is not usually thought of as an industrial county. The heathlands have been extensively dug for gravel and ball clay. Bricks and pottery were made in many parts, and indeed still are in a few places. However, the most extensive Dorset industry, and perhaps the most important in landscape terms, has been quarrying. The high quality limestones of Purbeck and Portland have been extensively worked over the centuries. It has been said that there are not quarries on the Isle of Portland but the Isle of Portland is a quarry! Many of these old industrial sites are now looked on as features of our heritage, indeed some are even tourist attractions. The Blue Pool at Furzebrook is one example, the 'Pool' having formed in the hole left behind after digging for ball clay. Another is Brownsea Island, some nineteenth century guidebooks advised tourists against visiting it since there was nothing of scenic interest there apart from a manufactory of drainpipes and lavatory cisterns!

If the majority of the Dorset landscapes have been created incidentally as a result of other activities – agriculture, forestry or industry – there are nevertheless, landscapes in Dorset which have been created deliberately. These are the great parklands and formal gardens established in the seventeenth, eighteenth and nineteenth centuries by rich and influential landowners, covering extensive areas in the county. As a consequence we owe nearly all the large areas of inland water in the county to these formal landscaping activities.

The map of Parks and Historic Designed Landscapes (see opposite) compares the current English Heritage list of Historic Parks and Gardens with the 'parks and ornamental grounds' shown on the 1930 and the modern (1991/3) Ordnance Survey maps. This shows how extensive these planned landscapes, deliberately created and laid over the basic landform, were perceived 65 years ago. Indeed it is frequently possible to find extensive tracts of typical 'parkland' landscape where none is now shown on the Ordnance Survey maps. The extent, therefore, of premeditated interference with the landscape to amend it for human pleasure may be significantly underestimated.

As well as the great Parks, such as Melbury and Wimborne St Giles, there are also deliberately created landscape features, such as avenues of trees by Badbury Rings and

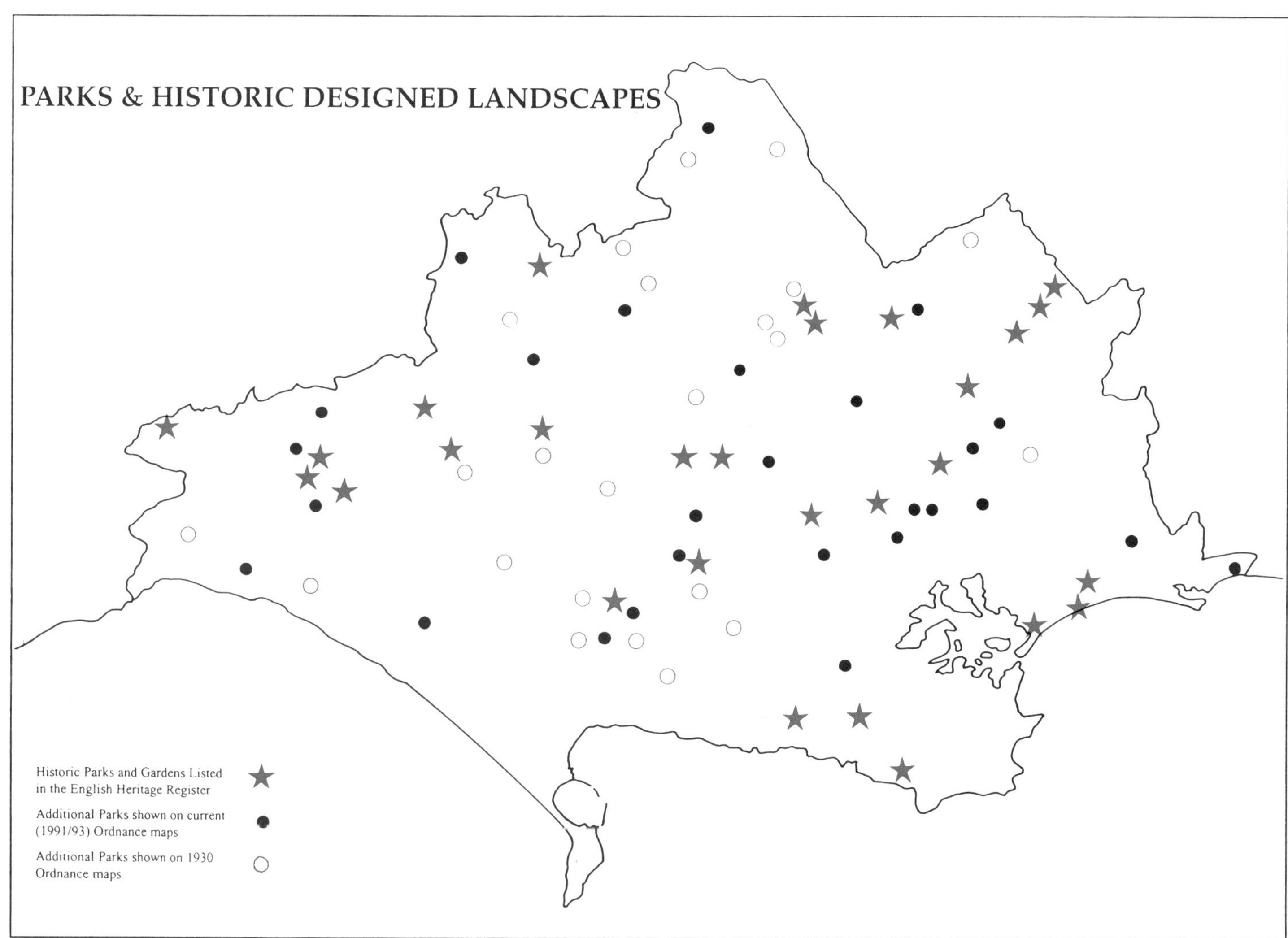

elsewhere on Cranborne Chase, and clumps of trees planted for no other reason than to give an interesting point of reference in the landscape, for example the pines on Colmer's Hill west of Bridport.

Another aspect of deliberately planned landscapes can be found in the estate villages which are scattered throughout the county. In these cases a village was substantially rebuilt by the local landowner, usually in a uniform style and with deliberate planning. One of the earliest, and certainly the most famous, or perhaps it should be infamous, example is at Milton Abbas. Here the ancient town was demolished to make way for a landscaped park, whilst the new village was built nearby, to provide accommodation for estate workers. Whilst Milton Abbas was moved as a result of the aesthetic whim of the landowner, the majority of estate villages were created for far more laudable aims. Early nineteenth century writers commented on the appalling state of many Dorset villages; typhoid and similar diseases were commonplace, and the rebuilding of a village could almost be expected of an enlightened landlord. In some cases a notable architect would be brought in; Iwerne Minster was virtually rebuilt to the designs of Alfred Waterhouse, the architect of the Natural History Museum in London. In the twentieth century Sir Ernest Debenham developed the Bladen Valley estate centred in the Frome valley. For him the architect Macdonald Gill built a remarkable collection of 'Arts and Crafts' houses at Briantspuddle and Milborne St Andrew.

Thus the landscapes that we see today have resulted from both accidental, and deliberate, human activity over the past centuries.

Ecology

Dorset's wildlife is a crucial component of the landscape and its wealth of species and ecosystems stems from a combination of factors. Its location in the British Isles on the warm south coast, with the mild, moist Gulf Stream and Atlantic influence from the west and the more extreme continental influence from the east, gives it a particularly favourable

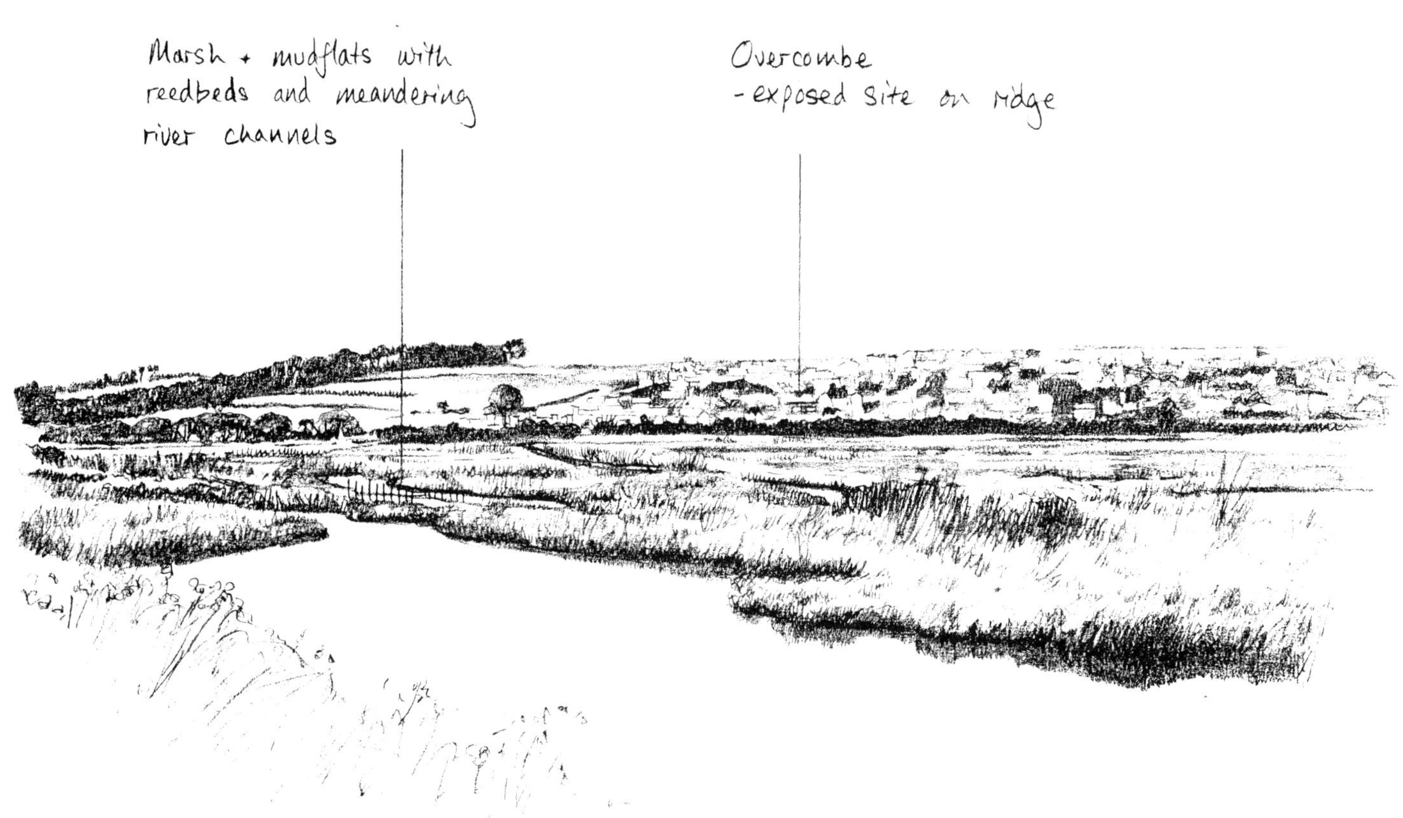

VALLEY PASTURES: *Lodmoor.* GR 687809.

climate. The geology, topography, soils, drainage patterns, and coastal influences, together with millennia of human activity, have together created a remarkable range of ecological habitats, including some of international importance.

This wealth can be illustrated simply by considering the number of animals and plants which are Dorset specialities. There are, for example, comparatively few insects which take their common name from a place, and even fewer who are still only found in that area. Dorset has the Lulworth Skipper which was first identified at Lulworth in 1832 and is still virtually confined to the Dorset Coast, and the Portland Ribbon Wave, whose main British population is on the Island.

The importance of human activity in creating, and maintaining, these habitats cannot be underestimated. Virtually all the terrestrial ones in Dorset owe their existence to direct or indirect human activity. The open landscapes in the county were originally created through clearance of the woodland, and maintained as open landscapes by agricultural practices. Every ancient woodland in Dorset has been managed at some stage in its history, felled, coppiced, pollarded or even, though this is very rare, planted! The continued survival of these habitats depends on the continuation of this management.

Although not a particularly heavily wooded county, large areas of ancient woodland and parkland with ancient trees survive. The oaks of Melbury Park are nationally famous whilst on Cranborne Chase old coppices survive. Where the woodlands are still being managed as coppice the spring flowers can be spectacular; to enter a bluebell wood in the spring is an unforgettable experience, as is a wood rich in ransoms, the wild garlic, where the sense of smell can be even more important than the sense of sight. These woodlands are very important for birds and other animals, and the value placed on them can be judged from the simple fact that Garston Wood on Cranborne Chase is one of the few inland reserves of the Royal Society for the Protection of Birds. Dormice and deer live in these woods as do many spectacular insects. To come across massive stag beetles flying on a summer's evening is truly memorable.

Perhaps the majority of fields in Dorset are still surrounded by hedges. These have been planted over the centuries as a cheap and effective way of enclosing the land. Older hedges tend to have more species than recent ones, but this is not always the case. For many species, birds in particular, hedges are vital for their continued well being, and a well-managed hedge will contain not only hundreds of nest sites, but provide a wealth of food, both animal and vegetable. In woodlands the greatest number and diversity of insects is frequently to be found on the edge, where the wood meets more open country. A hedge is essentially a very thin wood, consisting almost entirely of woodland edge, and can therefore be very rich in insects and other wildlife.

Dorset still contains extensive areas of ancient limestone grassland, first created when Neolithic farmers cleared the downs. Grazing is essential to its existence; where grazing declines, thorn scrub and woodland will spread. The downlands have long been famed for their wide range of flowers and insects. In the spring yellow cowslips are, happily, still common in some places, and in later spring and summer many varieties of orchid can be found. One, the early spider orchid, is virtually restricted to the limestone cliffs of the Dorset coast. In high summer knapweeds and scabious add splashes of purple and blue to the grey-green grassland and provide a rich supply of nectar for feeding butterflies. Indeed the butterflies of the downland are as famed as the wildflowers. They range from the tiny small-blue, smallest of the British butterflies, to the large dark green fritillary which loves to feed on the knapweed. Rarities too can be found here. The spectacular, almost iridescent, adonis blue and shyer, silver spotted skipper are still to be found in the county. As well as these, clouds of commoner butterflies can still be found flying together, rather than just ones or twos as is the case in other parts of the country.

Permanent pasture and old hay meadows still survive in some parts of the county. The colours of the flowers in the spring and early summer can be dazzling. These are probably best appreciated at the Dorset Wildlife Trust reserve at Kingcombe where ancient meadows are managed in the traditional manner. Here you can still shake the yellow hay rattle to see if the grass is ready for cutting. Surprisingly the grasslands of the old water meadows have little botanical interest, however the ditches which fed and drained the meadows frequently support a fascinating range of water plants, and when the meadows flood, as they frequently do in the winter, they provide a safe feeding ground for numerous water fowl, such as mallard, teal and widgeon.

Arguably the most important habitats are the acid, nutrient poor, heathlands of the eastern part of the county. These are remnants of much large areas of heathland which once covered substantial areas of central southern England. Animals and plants are found here which occur in few other parts of the British Isles, such as the sand lizard, smooth snake and one of the rarest heathers, the aptly named Dorset heath. These heathlands are not only one of the scarcest habitats in Britain but also one of the most threatened. Failure to manage heathland properly can lead to a rapid decline in its ecological value, and there is still a lingering public perception of heathland as 'wasteland', not deserving of care.

Along the coast there are many very important habitats. The mudflats and marshes of Poole Harbour, The Fleet, Radipole and Lodmoor support numerous over-wintering birds. The Fleet itself and Chesil are unique areas which are now recognised as being of international importance. To the far west the county ends at Lyme Regis where the crumbling undercliff, the relics of ancient cliff falls (one area, which collapsed in 1839, was a notable tourist attraction at the time!) is now a National Nature Reserve supporting several animals found in few other places in the British Isles such as the bee *Stelis ornatula* and the beetle *Cicindela germanica*.

Reflecting the significance of its wildlife, practically every British book on the subject draws examples from Dorset.

Colour in the Landscape

Colour is a vital element in the landscape, and one which is frequently overlooked. Landscape colours fall into three categories, ephemeral, seasonal and permanent. Ephemeral describes those changes made to landscape colours by the weather and position of the sun. They can have a marked effect on the viewer's appreciation, turning a friendly, welcoming countryside into something threatening within a few minutes. The low angle of sunlight at morning or evening accentuates shadows, raising the profile of ancient field patterns and other earthworks. This constant variation of light and shade, due to our changeable weather, has had immense influence on landscape artists over the years and is one of the delights of travelling in the country. These effects of weather over-lie seasonal and permanent colour changes.

Seasonal changes are both natural, such as the cycle of deciduous woodland, the growth and decay of bracken, the summer flowering of the heathers, and artificial, the growth and harvesting of crops and other effects of the cycle of the agricultural year. The most dramatic seasonal change is that brought about by snow. A snow covered landscape is almost monochrome, white and grey fields, with sharply contrasting hedges and trees in shades of brown. The landscape is simplified, and the structure becomes clearer; minor humps and bumps in the land become more pronounced, whilst boundaries between fields, even simple wire fences, become some of the most striking features in the countryside.

Permanent colours remain unchanged throughout the year, they are the colours of walls and buildings, of water and coniferous woodland. The effects of stone are very marked in some places, on Portland the light grey, almost white stone can be harsh to the eye under bright sun, conversely around Sherborne the warm honey coloured stone is mellow and gentle under exactly the same weather conditions.

As with so many elements of our landscape we can change its colour too. Variations in seasonal colours can be striking, but probably have little permanent effect. Crops such as rape and linseed produce spectacularly coloured fields, but their survival is dependant on grants and subsidies, and it is quite possible that in a few years blue and yellow fields will be little more than a memory. It is change to the permanent colours which should be considered with more care, the introduction of differing coloured stone buildings into an old stone village, or using stone in a brick village are obvious examples. But there are others, about which equal care needs to be taken, for example the construction of a golf course in arable countryside. Over the year arable land will vary from shades of brown to green and gold, but a golf course is always bright green. A development which seems to blend in during May can stand out in August.

At night all colours change, but the night-time countryside isn't a uniform black; here too weather and light, this time from the moon, affects appearance and mood. The countryside at night can be a fascinating place, often disturbing and mysterious, but frequently spectacular. Artificial lighting can have considerable effect on the nocturnal scene, whilst the lights of a distant farm or village can be a welcoming human touch in an alien landscape, a mass of street lights around a road junction can jar and disrupt. For example the Handley Hill illuminated roundabout on the A354, which is situated on a prominent hill top, can be seen for many miles. Locally it has been referred to as the 'UFO landing pad'; a tribute to its 'unearthly' appearance.

Human Perceptions and Cultural Links

Although people have been looking at the Dorset landscape for millennia it is difficult to get any idea of how people regarded the landscape before written accounts become available. The earliest descriptions of the Dorset landscape occur in the sixteenth and early seventeenth centuries. In looking at accounts of the landscape, it has to be appreciated that people view the landscape through eyes coloured by their own preconceptions and interests. To take a simple example, a writer in the early twentieth century who was concerned with afforestation and housing development on areas of the Dorset heathlands was able to describe them as having the visual appearance of rubbish! His only interest in heathland was its removal and replacement with, to him, more beautiful (and more profitable) houses and conifer plantations. These preconceptions have to be taken into account as must other cultural influences. For example, it is virtually impossible for a well-read person to visit Dorset today without thinking of Thomas Hardy, or to enter the otherwise unremarkable village of Tolpuddle and not remember the pioneer trades unionists and their sufferings.

We are fortunate to possess a very early description of the county. In the 1620s, Thomas Gerard wrote a detailed description of Dorset as he saw it. Whilst mostly concerned with the families of the local gentry, it does contain a few, wonderful, descriptions of the landscape of his day.

> *The more Northerne Part, divided from the South almost by a continuall Ridge of high Hills, is somewhat flat, and was in foregoeing Ages wholely Forrests; neither is it yet in this decaying Age of ours altogether destitute of Timber Trees, and Woods; abounding also with verie good Pastures, and Feedeings for Cattell; watered with fine Streames, which take their Courses through rich Meadowes; which Inducements have invited manie of the Gentlemen of these Partes to dwell there: Where neverthelesse in the Winter Season they reape more Profite than Pleasure, for that then this flat Countrie is verie subject to Durt and foule Wayes, from which Inconvenience the South Parte is free, for that consisteth altogether of Hills, ... all overspread with innumerable Flockes of Sheepe, for which it yeelds very good and sound Feedeing, and from which the Countrie hath reaped an unknowen Gaine. Valleys it hath diverse, but not large, in the which, for the most parte, the Townes and Gentlemens Houses are seated, for avoideing those sharpe Blasts which this Southerne Parte is subject to; Cornfields they have plentie, which seldome deceive the Husbandmans Expectation; and adjoyneing to the Rivers good Meadowes, though not in soe great Plentie as the North Parte of the Shire; to which though it bee inferiour for Profite, yet it exceedes it much for Pleasure, being freed from those two generall Enimies of Sports, Durt and Inclosures, and well*

stored with such Game, as their severall Seasons serve for Sports and Recreations.

A rich source of descriptions of the landscape are to be found in the memoirs of visitors. One of the earliest to leave a detailed account of her impressions was Celia Fiennes. The daughter of a parliamentary officer, she travelled widely throughout the British Isles during the late seventeenth century, visiting members of her large and extended family. Fortunately for posterity she recorded her impressions in a series of manuscript volumes. In around 1680 she visited Dorset.

> *At Warrum [Wareham] we passed over a bridge where the sea flowed in and came by the ruines of Corffe Castle... thence you rise a great ascent of hills called the Linch.*
>
> *From this ridge you see all the Island over, which looks very fruitful, good lands, meadows, woods and enclosures; there are many quarys here in these hills of that which they call freestone, from hence they digg it. We went to Sonidge [Swanage] a sea faire place not very big. There I did eat the best lobsters and crabs being boyled in the sea water and scarce cold, very large and sweet.*

If Celia Fiennes was concerned with the pleasures of travelling, and the comforts of the various places she stayed at, the next traveller whose accounts give any detail of the Dorset landscape had a very different motive. Daniel Defoe travelled extensively throughout the British Isles at the beginning of the eighteenth century, looking at the economic basis of the country.

> *The downs round this town [Dorchester] are exceedingly pleasant, and come up on every side, even to the very streets end; and here it was that they told me, that there were 600 thousand sheep fed on the downs, within six miles of the town. This I say, I was told, I do not affirm it to be true; but when I viewed the country round, I confess I could not but incline to believe it.*

As the eighteenth century progressed the concept of tourism began to be developed, and by the end of the century, with the royal patronage that had been granted to Weymouth through the summer visits of George III, Dorset had become one of the earliest destinations. As tourism developed, so did the writing of tourists' guides. Then, as now, they tended not to be great literature! Happily however, one great author did describe the Dorset landscape at the time. Jane Austen visited Lyme Regis on several occasions at the very beginning of the nineteenth century, and included a description of the countryside around Lyme in her novel *Persuasion* which was published posthumously in 1818.

> *Charmouth, with its high grounds and extensive sweeps of country, and still more its sweet retired bay, backed by dark cliffs, where fragments of low rock among the sands make it the happiest spot for watching the flow of the tide, for sitting in unwearied contemplation; – the woody varieties of the cheerful village of Up Lyme, and, above all, Pinny, with its green chasms between romantic rocks, where the scattered forest trees and orchards of luxuriant growth declare that many a generation must have passed away since the first partial falling of the cliff prepared the ground for such a state. This scene so wonderful and lovely is exhibited, and may more than equal any of the resembling scenes on the far famed Isle of Wight*

The countryside around Lyme Regis must have made a very strong impression on Jane Austen as she rarely included any description of the landscape in her novels. She was much more interested with relationships between people and, on the occasions when she did describe the natural world she was prone to make unfortunate mistakes (in *Emma* an orchard is described as being in blossom in July!)

The nineteenth century produced two Dorset authors whose work has dominated the subsequent artistic and cultural view of the county; William Barnes and Thomas Hardy. Barnes included numerous descriptions of the Dorset countryside in his poetry, which was mostly written in the Dorset dialect.

The Zwellen downs, wi' chalky tracks,
A-climmen up their zunny backs,
Do hide green meads an' zedgy brooks,
An' clumps o' trees wi' glossy rooks,
(The White Road up Athirt the Hill).

His work provided inspiration for others. Ralph Vaughan Williams, for example, set many of his poems to music and *Linden Lea*, one of these settings, is perhaps one of the most famous English songs.

Thomas Hardy, who very much admired the work of William Barnes, was not only the greatest author Dorset ever produced, but was also particularly skilled on describing the countryside. His accounts of the Wessex landscape have rarely been equalled and never surpassed. The following passage from *Tess of the d'Urbervilles* describes perfectly the junction of the chalk landscapes and the north Dorset landscapes, where the chalk uplands overlook the Blackmoor Vale.

The traveller from the coast, who, after plodding northward for a score of miles of calcareous downs and cornlands, suddenly reaches the verge of one of these escarpments, is surprised and delighted to behold, extended like a map beneath him, a country differing absolutely from that which he has passed through. Behind him the hills are open, the sun blazes down upon fields so large as to give an unenclosed character to the landscape, the lanes are white, the hedges low, the atmosphere colourless. Here, in the valley,

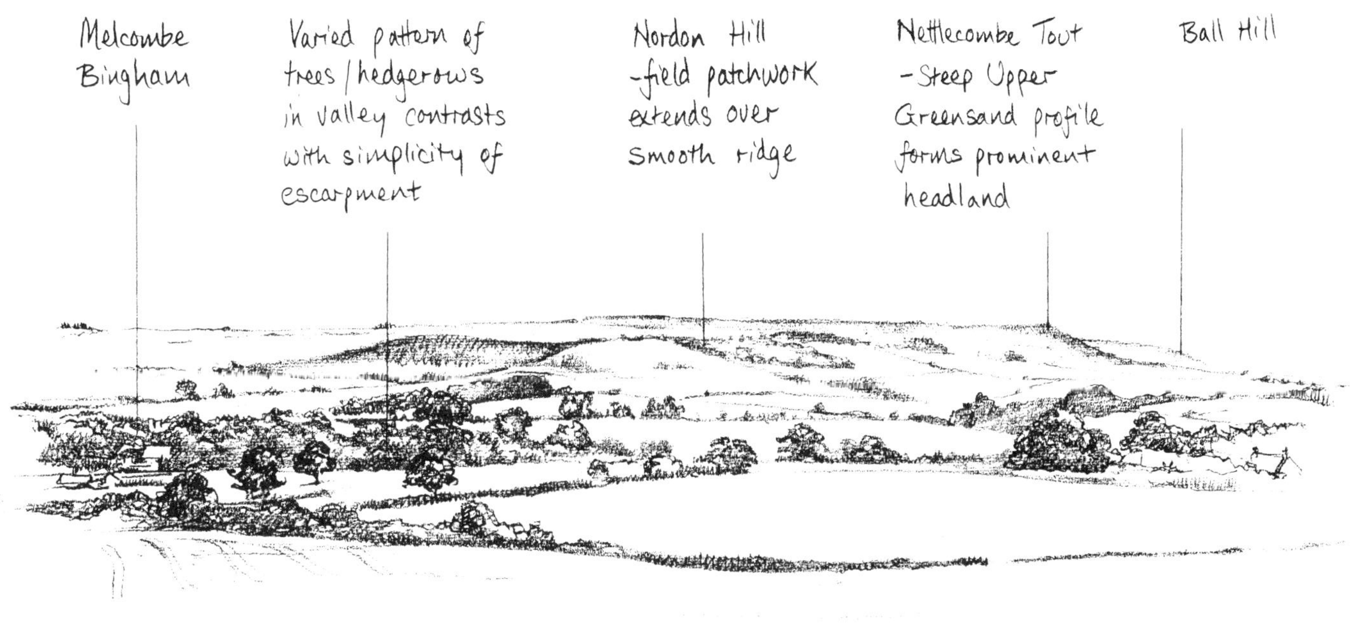

CHALK ESCARPMENT: *From Ansty Cross looking towards Nordon Hill across the indented bay in the north escarpment.* GR 775033.

the world seems to be constructed upon a smaller and more delicate scale; the fields are mere paddocks, so reduced that from this height their hedgerows appear a network of dark green threads overspreading the paler green of the grass. Arable lands are few and limited; with but slight exceptions the prospect is a broad rich mass of grass and trees, mantling minor hills and dales within the major. Such is the Vale of Blackmoor.

No twentieth-century author has yet reached the heights of Thomas Hardy's work, although undoubtedly the Powys Brothers came close. Like Jane Austen, their work is more concerned with relationships between characters than the landscape itself, although they frequently do use the landscape as metaphors within their writings. The contemporary novelist John Fowles has also made great use of the Dorset landscape in his novels, and many people's view of Lyme Regis will always be associated with the sad tale of *The French Lieutenant's Woman*. The film version is probably better known than the original book, and here again we can see how well some aspects of the Dorset landscape have survived. Contemporary film makers regularly find suitable locations in the county for the production of major historical films.

Despite this the visual arts have been less well represented within the county, perhaps because there has never been a Dorset painter to match the stature of Hardy in the literary scene. However the growth of tourism during the eighteenth and nineteenth centuries, coupled with enthusiastic prose concerning the beauties of Dorset, attracted numerous landscape artists. J.M.W. Turner came specifically for the scenery. In 1811 he painted a series of water-colours on, or close to, the coast of such features as Corfe Castle and Lulworth Cove. These were later engraved and published as part of a series, *Picturesque Views of the Southern Coast of England* (1818-26). John Constable honeymooned in Dorset, staying at Osmington, a visit which resulted in his painting of Weymouth Bay, but produced no other major works. James McNeill Whistler visited Dorset at the end of the century, and his stay at Lyme Regis in 1895 not only resulted in several paintings and an important collection of lithographs, but helped him come through an artistic crisis brought on by his wife's serious illness (she died in 1896).

One nineteenth century Dorset artist did achieve eminence, not so much for his paintings as for his teaching ability. Francis (Fra) Newbery came from Bridport, and, in 1885, was appointed headmaster of the Glasgow School of Art, where his most famous pupil was the artist, designer and architect Charles Rennie Mackintosh. In later life Newbery returned to Dorset and presented Bridport with a series of historic and allegorical paintings, in one of the latter was the figure of 'The Spirit of Bridport' which now adorns signs throughout the town. Possibly following Newbery's advice Rennie Mackintosh came to Dorset in 1895 to sketch buildings and architectural features, later he was to live for a time in Worth Matravers painting wonderfully idiosyncratic landscapes. A few years after Mackintosh's first visit, another artist, more usually associated with the north of England, visited Dorset. Beatrix Potter made several drawings of Lyme Regis, which was one of the sources of inspiration for the port of Stymouth in *The Tale of Little Pig Robinson*.

At the beginning of the twentieth century Augustus John stayed for a time near Poole, where he produced brightly coloured paintings of undulating heathland. He also used the Blue Pool as the background for his frieze 'Lyric Fantasy'. A few years later the multi-talented Roger Fry visited Poole, but he was less concerned with the Dorset landscape than with the encouragement given to his ceramic work by the Poole Potteries. In more recent years Dame Elizabeth Frink lived and worked in the county. Her statues can be found in several places in Dorchester. Today numerous potters, artists and other craftspeople add to the cultural diversity of Dorset, and it is certain that the landscapes of Dorset, which have provided numerous artists, great and small, with a wealth of inspiration over the centuries, will continue to do so far into the future.

Place Names in the Landscape

The place names of a county reflect, and add to, its character. Different parts of the country have different types of place name. A name from Dorset may be similar to one from Hampshire or Somerset, but will differ from those of East Anglia or Cumberland. Probably the best way to appreciate this is to try and invent a place name. It will soon become apparent that some names will 'feel' right and others will not. Another way is to read a novel written by an American set in England. The vast majority of American writers have little idea of English place names and their invented names invariably 'feel' wrong. It is hardly surprising that the best inventor of local place names was Thomas Hardy.

These variations reflect the differing ways in which England has been settled and occupied over the past two thousand years. As soon as people moved into an area, places began to acquire names. At first it would have been sufficient to talk of 'the wood' or 'the river', and in Hampshire the Isle of Wight is still known as 'the Island'. However as soon as there were several woods, or rivers or valleys to distinguish, then place names would be created. Many place names include words which describe landscape features, and may reflect how important, or obvious these were when the name was coined.

Common landscape features to be found in Dorset place names include; *dun* a hill top, found in *Eggardon* and *Pilsdon*, or *tun* a homestead or village, as in the various Wootons, a name which means a *tun* by a wood. Rivers and river crossings were also important landscape features, hence the numerous *ford* place names. An uncommon water place name is to be found in *Ashmore*, the pond or *mere* where ash trees grew; another tree gave its name to *Hazelbury Bryan*, the *bury* part of the name is derived from *bearu* a grove. The *bury* in *Badbury* on the other hand is derived from *burg*, a fortified place. Despite problems such as this, place name interpretation can give a fascinating glimpse into how the landscape was perceived in the past.

Place names are still being created and changed. Recent alterations (within the last century or so) have given rise to some curious anomalies. For example there are several groups of villages which take their names from the rivers or streams on which they stand. On Cranborne Chase there are the *Gussage's* and the *Tarrant's*, also in eastern Dorset there are a group of *Winterborne's*. There is a second group of *Winterborne's* to the south and west of Dorchester, although here some are spelt *Winterbourne* (Abbas, Steepleton and Farringdon). The change in spelling appears to be fairly recent as on the Ordnance Survey map of 1930 all the villages were spelt *Winterborne*. Changes of village names along a river are particularly obvious on the *Piddle*. Originally there were a number of villages which had '*Piddle*' as part of their name. However during the nineteenth century, apparently for reasons of 'delicacy' most of these names were changed to '*Puddle*', thus we now have *Tolpuddle, Affpuddle, Puddletown* and others. Even minor names were changed, such as *Little Puddle Bottom*, a coombe which runs down to *Piddlehinton*; which with *Piddletrenthide* are the only villages which retain the original river name. This 'delicacy' concerning place names did not die out with the Victorians, as it is not many years since the hamlet of *Shitterton* near Bere Regis had its name changed to *Sitterton* for precisely the same reason that *Piddle* became *Puddle*. More recently there has been a move to return to *Shitterton* on the grounds of antiquity.

There are other cases where the spelling of place names has changed without any obvious reason. For example *Hazelbury Bryan* was *Haselbury Bryan* on the 1930 map, and *Spetisbury* was *Spettisbury*. In the latter case the modern Ordnance Survey has confounded matters by calling the hill fort above the village of *Spetisbury*, *Spettisbury Rings*. Another case where there is no apparent reason for change is *Littlebredy*. In 1930 it was written *Little Bredy* (a form still commonly used), now the Ordnance Survey spell it as one word, but still call the neighbouring village *Long Bredy*!

Changes in spelling are still occurring. For example local people will tell you that *Blackmoor* Vale should be spelt

Blackmore. There seems little reason for the change and here we have kept to the 'official' spelling and used *Blackmoor*, though it is quite likely that in fifty years time everybody will be spelling the name with an e!

Place names are still being created as new developments occur. Here there is an opportunity for the maintenance of local distinctiveness. Just as an 'anywhere' design for housing is damaging to the local character, so is an 'anywhere' name. Road names should reflect the locality, and in Dorset there have been some very imaginative examples in recent years. At Trickett's Cross near Ferndown names such as *Corbin Avenue*, *Lockyers Drive* and *Dugdell Close* commemorate the commoners who were responsible for the partial enclosure of Parley Common in the seventeenth century; whilst at Chickerell the names *Glennie Close*, *Trenchard Way* and *Elziver Close* recall characters in the historical novel *Moonfleet* by J. Meade Faulkner which is set in that locality.

LANDSCAPE CHANGE, ASSESSMENT AND MANAGEMENT

Change in the Landscape

We have seen that the character of Dorset's landscape has been shaped by many centuries of human occupation, and evolving patterns of land use superimposed on powerfully expressed landforms. Much of the county is rural and the visual structure of the landscape is determined by the scale of its heathlands, grasslands and villages, and the patchwork of fields, woodlands and hedgerows. In particular, parts of west Dorset, the chalk escarpments and Purbeck retain an historic field pattern, influenced by the early configuration of woodland clearance, cultivation and settlement, while the extensive arable fields of the chalk uplands illustrate the effects of agricultural change in the early twentieth century. At times, man's intervention has given rise to rapid change; in other periods, landscape development has been almost imperceptible. Clearly the landscape is dynamic and living, even though some aspects reflect a cycle of ageing, dying, rejuvenation or simply a lack of management. Towards the end of the twentieth century, the Dorset landscape is again experiencing strong forces for change.

The analysis of the different landscape character areas, and the specific qualities and key characteristics which determine their visual character, help to predict which landscape areas will be most vulnerable to pressures for change, and whether change can be accommodated without degrading the particular combination of landscape features which create a sense of place. Change in itself is not necessarily harmful but its consequences do need to be understood and where appropriate, carefully directed. The overall aim should be to maintain or enrich the quality of Dorset's landscapes and the characteristic features which give each landscape character area its identity; and give Dorset as a whole its harmony and special sense of place.

AGRICULTURE

The single biggest force influencing the Dorset landscape now arises from changes in the financial incentives for different types of farming and the ability of farmers to earn a living from the land. The future appearance of the rural landscape is, therefore, linked to European and national agricultural policy changes and developments in the agricultural economy, including grant regimes aimed at landscape conservation. The conversion of downlands and pastures to arable fields, the enlargement of fields and removal of hedgerows, and scrub encroachment due to lack of management, demonstrate the scale of changes in both the visual character of the landscape and its ecological value. Set-aside, to reduce production, has created apparently redundant strips and fields, whilst farm diversification poses its own changes as farmers seek alternative incomes. Golf courses, the re-use of redundant farm buildings for holiday accommodation, Pick-Your-Own schemes and livery services for horses and ponies are examples of possible developments.

WOODLANDS

Dorset is not a heavily wooded county, only 9.5% is woodland and of this total, 83% is devoted to commercial forestry, a large proportion of which is coniferous and was planted between 1920 and 1950. However under the Dorset Forests and Heathlands Project (1991), strategic areas of conifer plantations have been converted back to heathland to secure the future of this important habitat which supports many rare species. Many of the smaller and ancient woods are vulnerable to change or decay resulting from lack of management, yet the numerous small copses, clumps, linear belts and isolated trees make an important contribution to the visual character of the landscape, especially in north and west Dorset. Furthermore, labour intensive coppicing has been dwindling for many decades. In the 1970s Dutch Elm Disease exposed previously enclosed landscapes, whilst the storms of 1987 and 1990, which were particularly severe in south-east Dorset, had devastating effects across the county but also opened up views which had not been seen for generations.

HEATHLANDS

The heathlands were created by the clearance of woodland in the Bronze Age which led to the leaching of soil nutrients. They now depend on active management to maintain the low fertility of the soil and prevent the widespread invasion of scrub species and pines. Traditionally seen as waste land, some 85% have been converted to farmland, forestry or built upon since the first reasonably accurate maps were drawn of them in 1759. In addition they have been used for ball clay extraction and there are several modern mines, some open-cast, on the Purbeck heaths. The heathlands are also the site for most of Dorset's oil wells. The remaining heaths are of European significance for their wildlife.

PARKLANDS

Dorset's many parkland landscapes make a valuable contribution to the quality and character of the landscape, not least because of their historic interest but also because they include many of the larger broad-leaved woodlands, a comparatively rare county resource. The map (page 23) shows how many parks have disappeared in the past half century though, in many cases, elements of the parkland landscape survive in the present countryside. The principal mechanism for management of the remaining parks is the Heritage Grant Scheme, intended to alleviate the high costs involved in sustaining these designed landscapes. More recently Countryside Stewardship has included Historic Parkland Restoration within its scope. Diversification represents one possible threat to the unity of parkland landscapes. Shooting remains an important activity on many estates, and is a key to both habitat protection and the conservation of woodlands.

THE COAST

Dorset's spectacular, varied coastline is relatively undeveloped but is the focus for most of the county's tourism. Much has Heritage Coast status so there are strategies for its management and conservation, as well as strict planning controls. There are, nevertheless, considerable problems in reconciling landscape, conservation, recreation and sea defence issues. For example some cliffs in west Dorset, which are unstable due to their geology and coastal erosion, are an important habitat for several rare species. Long established tourist facilities and caravan parks are often intrusive features, especially on isolated exposed coastal sites. The emerging Dorset Coastal Strategy and Poole Harbour Management Plan, together with the management plans for the Heritage Coasts, promote an integrated approach to coastal management.

MINISTRY OF DEFENCE

The Ministry of Defence has been a significant landowner in Dorset since the early part of the century and still controls an extensive area, including the coastline and the heathlands inland between West Lulworth and Kimmeridge Bay, Bovington, Barnsfield Heath, Blandford Camp, and Portland Harbour. This land has been protected from civilian development and includes areas with valuable ecological habitats and an unspoilt, distinctive visual character. In general the MOD has a responsible attitude to the care of its land, although landscape quality is inevitably compromised by localised pressures and training activity.

COUNTRYSIDE MANAGEMENT ACTION

The most important schemes affecting the Dorset landscape are Countryside Stewardship and Environmentally Sensitive Areas (ESA's) (initiated by the Countryside Commission and the Ministry of Agriculture respectively). Both schemes encourage significant incremental beneficial changes in landscape character by way of annual payments for 10 years. The Countryside Stewardship scheme targets particular landscapes in the region and aims to demonstrate that conservation and public enjoyment of the countryside can be combined with commercial land management. The extensive South Wessex Downs ESA aims to conserve and enhance the characteristic chalk downland landscape and habitats, to protect features of historic interest, encourage the conversion of arable fields to downland, and secure the future management of the open chalk grasslands by traditional agricultural methods. The Avon Valley ESA aims to conserve and enhance the water meadows of the River Avon. The schemes also accommodate historic landscapes. In addition the Woodland Grant Scheme specifically targets the problems of woodland decay. MAFF's Farm Woodland Scheme encourages new woodland on farms and the Hedgerow Incentive Scheme encourages the management and restoration of hedgerows on a ten year time-scale. The Local Authorities provide advice and practical assistance for countryside management throughout Dorset, the local centre for the British Trust for Conservation Volunteers co-ordinates voluntary tasks, and Rural Action contributes a support network and grants.

DEVELOPMENT PRESSURES

The county's Structure Plan highlights the need for policies to protect the countryside and promote environmental conservation. It states that future development will be concentrated in existing towns, rather than the countryside. However the inherent contribution of many of Dorset's towns and villages to landscape character is acknowledged by also including some measures for protecting towns with particularly important landscape settings. The Green Belt around the Bournemouth-Poole conurbation recognises the significance of urban fringe landscapes and the containment of necessary development. Regional Guidance (RPG10), backed by the South West Regional Planning Conference's own environment report, supports the conservation of the environmental quality and character of South West together with the careful planning and integration of development into the landscape.

INFRASTRUCTURE

Proposals for new roads and services are a major force for change with significant implications for landscape character. A sound understanding of the county's landscapes is particularly relevant in guiding the processes of route selection and design with a view to conserving the key features which contribute to the intrinsic character of the landscape. Small narrow lanes, often sunken between high hedgebanks, unlit and unkerbed, are important features of many parts of the Dorset countryside. Highway maintenance and improvement works, if really necessary, need great sensitivity to ensure that this kind of important visual character is conserved. Developments which could have particularly significant visual and aesthetic impacts include radio masts, pylon lines, and wind turbines.

MINERAL EXTRACTION AND WASTE DISPOSAL

Dorset has a wide range of mineral resources and a long history of mineral extraction, which has left areas such as the Isle of Portland and the Purbeck limestone plateau peppered with active and disused quarries. Mineral extraction still continues and can have a significant visual impact on the landscape. Oil and ball clay are of national importance and Purbeck and Portland limestones are valuable building materials. Aggregates, including plateau and valley gravels and sands, are of local and regional value. Reclamation afterwards is now a requirement, and most land is restored to its original use, but there may be opportunities for the creation of new landscape features or the improvement of landscape quality. Similarly with an ongoing need for waste disposal sites throughout the county, all proposals should be subject to careful examination to ensure that they have no serious environmental impact and should be designed to create a landform and vegetation cover which integrates smoothly with the landscape character of its surroundings.

RECREATION AND TOURISM

Tourism is an increasingly important aspect of Dorset's economy. It is closely linked to landscape quality because the landscapes themselves are important attractions and visitor pressures can rebound on these landscapes. In addition, the needs of the local population add to the pressures exerted by visitors. The general trends indicate that resorts must increasingly capitalise on their landscape setting, so the relationships between the visual character, the particular identity of an area and the well-being of the local economy are likely to be of great importance. The coastline is Dorset's most significant tourist destination but it is here that visitor pressure has the greatest impact, as much of the coast is characterised by small-scale, secluded, fragile landscapes, easily overwhelmed by the buildings, large caravan sites, car parks, noise, litter, traffic and the problems of erosion often associated with tourism. A focus on 'Green Tourism', however, should encourage greater awareness of conservation issues by operators and visitors, and stimulate projects which sustain the local environment and culture.

Assessing Landscapes

USES OF LANDSCAPE ASSESSMENTS

Structured descriptions and assessments of landscapes are obviously a sound basis for identifying management strategies and activities to sustain those landscapes. They are also valuable for preparing evaluations, either for the designation of areas for special status or for the impacts of change or developments. In addition they can provide the basis for site or area management plans. However, at a time when quality of life and respect for the environment are taking an ever increasing profile, they have a significant role in strategic and local planning.

Landscape assessment can, therefore, help us to understand how and why landscapes are important, promote an appreciation of landscape issues, conserve valued landscapes, guide and direct landscape change, and accommodate successfully new development within the landscape.

PREPARING A LANDSCAPE ASSESSMENT

Landscape assessment is a structured process whereby individual landscape units are described and analysed to determine their key characteristics and to map their distribution. Although it is tempting to base the landscape character areas on geology and landform considerable emphasis has to be given to the vegetation and land cover, the land uses, the health and age of the elements comprising the landscape as well as cultural, historic and aesthetic aspects. Using an ordered approach means that one suitably trained surveyor will produce a very similar assessment to another, even though they may differ in amalgamating some smaller areas or dividing larger ones into different units. The public response to the Landscape Character Map produced by Landscape Design Associates leads us to believe that it is a valid and extremely useful basis for more detailed work and, at the same time, it gives a clear picture of Dorset in relation to the regional overview of the environment of the south-west.

This landscape assessment quite simply combined field work with information gathered from consultations and desk studies. A structured, consistent method was used to record and collate the information, to analyse landscape character, and provide a critical assessment of the essential features of the Dorset landscape. This involved an initial familiarisation tour to identify the main landscape features of the county, followed by a period of consultation and desk study, and then the more detailed field survey during the summer of 1992.

LANDSCAPE DESIGN ASSOCIATES
DORSET COUNTY LANDSCAPE ASSESSMENT
FIELD RECORD SHEETS

Viewpoint: Grid Ref:

Direction of view:

Date: Time:

Weather:

DESCRIPTION

Landform

context (specific names)
geology
topography
hydrology/coast

Landscape Components and Structure

Land use – agricultural type/moor/woods/trees etc.

Pattern and scale – the grain of the landscape (man-imposed/natural)

Vegetation – hedgerows/trees/woodlands: type, distribution and character

Hydrological/coastal features - ponds/lakes/marsh/cliff/dunes

Landmarks – memorable features

Road network characteristics – including tracks/paths

Other cultural features – walls/avenues/rides/green lanes/hill forts

Other built elements e.g. pylons/mineral workings

ANALYSIS AND CRITICAL ASSESSMENT

Depending on the particular landscape, emphasis will be placed on those criteria which are most significant in forming landscape character:

Harmony/Unity – the way that elements are organised to form coherent/memorable patterns and views

Enclosure

Diversity – degree of variation within a larger landscape area

Rhythm – repetition of similar elements

Texture – degree of management

Colour

SUBJECTIVE RESPONSE

A considered response to the impact of the landscape on human emotions, taking in factors such as:

- exposure to weather elements and visual expanse
- intimacy and security
- invigorating/inspiring/challenging/boring?
- pleasant/unpleasant
- closeness to nature
- feeling for human history

CHANGE

- indications of change
- threats/improvements
- vulnerability/susceptibility to change (from a visual point of view)

RARITY

- In relation to Dorset/Nationally

Note: Full details of survey methods can be found in the Countryside Commission's publication *Landscape Assessment, New Guidance* CCP 423 (1993).

Desk studies focused on analysing historical, geological, geomorphological, ecological, archaeological, artistic and literary information to appreciate the physical, historical and cultural influences responsible for shaping the Dorset landscape and the perceptions of it. Aerial photographs were analysed for the overall pattern and scale of a landscape. This work provided an initial guide to the likely landscape areas for more accurate investigation by field survey.

The field survey involved a structured visual analysis from a variety of viewpoints in which the extent of the landscape character types was assessed. Annotated overlays on 1:50,000 scale O.S maps were used to record the boundaries between areas with different landscape characteristics. Viewsheds, landmarks, strong visual edges, and the transitions between different landscape areas were all noted. At a range of vantage points, the distribution, form and alignment of landscape components, together with an analysis of how they are organised to form specific patterns and compositions, were set down on field record sheets. This recording format provided an opportunity to combine in a systematic manner, factual, visual evidence with a creative description and a more subjective response. Photographs and sketches were made to record typical and atypical examples of landscape character and particular landmarks which contribute to the specific identity of an area.

Combining the map work, aerial photographs, research and site surveys the landscape character areas were mapped at 1:50,000 scale (which was eventually reduced to 1:100,000 for simplicity and ease of handling) and the descriptions of each area were written.

In building on some aspects of the consultants' work and relating it to other projects, we are conscious that different individuals may see other landscape character areas, or subdivisions of existing ones. Invariably those who know a locality well are likely to feel that it is distinct from adjacent areas. That may well be true; one of the useful attributes of landscape assessments is that broad scale landscape character areas can be sub-divided into local units. Indeed, with increasing detail such assessments have considerable practical value for landscape management and planning purposes. These assessments nest inside one another rather like Russian dolls. This publication focuses on the county scale and does, therefore, provide much greater detail than will be found in national or regional landscape assessments and appraisals. The character areas will, however, almost certainly be capable of sub-division two or three times, as has already been demonstrated by East Dorset District Council's survey of their part of the Cranborne Chase AONB, or the landscape description carried out by West Dorset District Council for the Brit Valley Joint Management Project.

Landscape assessments can, therefore, be of great assistance in many aspects of countryside planning and management. Initially they help us to understand how and why landscapes are important, and promote an appreciation of landscape issues. They then help guide and direct landscape management, conservation, change, and the successful integration of development within the landscape.

The Purposes of Landscape Management Guidance

The landscapes of southern England have evolved as a by-product of the interaction between geology, landform, natural forces and man's activities. With very powerful machinery and the uniformity that comes with cost effectiveness, man now has the ability to change these landscapes quickly and dramatically. Most of this change reduces local distinctiveness, increases blandness, reduces character and increases 'sameness'. On the other hand, after decades concentrating on production, national and international attitudes and policies towards agriculture are now encouraging agricultural practices which have direct beneficial impacts on the countryside. There is also an ever increasing public awareness of the need to manage landscapes to sustain their interests and ensure their continuing health. Landscape management is now, for significant parts of the countryside, no longer a by-product of other activities but a process in its own right.

Landscape management can be at a strategic level in, for example, a structure plan, or an area-wide landscape or individual forestry strategy. It can also be quite detailed, such as the management prescriptions for Environmentally Sensitive Areas or site and park management plans.

A forum of land managers, and other people closely involved in the conservation and management of Dorset landscapes, was convened during the production of the Landscape Assessment and the Character Map. Their views were sought on the most productive ways to carry the work forward. The discussion concentrated on sustaining the range of identified landscapes, their key characteristics, and their sense of place, rather than seeking wholesale changes to return them to some imprecise, idealised state of, say, 60 or 100 years ago. This conservation approach does, however, take account of recent changes, future pressures, and can accommodate special projects restoring or re-creating particular landscapes. Nevertheless, because of the variety that exists within each character area, the different levels of resources available, and the personal objectives of individual land managers, it was felt that rigid rules or precise prescriptions for landscape management would be inappropriate. There was a clear preference for the provision, from an informed and professional viewpoint, of **landscape management guidance.** Such guidance could then be adopted and adapted to a particular locality or situation.

The emphasis, therefore, in this book is towards **management guidelines to sustain the landscapes of the county.** We identify the main features of the landscape character areas and indicate the management topics that should be given consideration. We deliberately avoid setting out hard and fast, specific, or particular prescriptions for management or maintenance tasks in any individual locality. The intention is to provide **guidelines** at a county scale that identify the key landscape issues to be tackled, plus some ways of doing that, whilst leaving the responsibility for the detail of a particular locality to the local land manager or local community to work out. We are particular conscious that in some situations a considerable amount of hard manual labour may be required although in others machinery may be able to provide a satisfactory and quicker result.

THE LANDSCAPES OF DORSET

Introduction

On the southern coast of England, Dorset is generally considered to be one of the South Western counties with Devon, Cornwall and Somerset. The county also shares, via the chalk downs, many attributes with Wiltshire. However the Poole Basin, east of the great mass of chalk, has much greater ties with Hampshire than it does with Devon or Cornwall, and often it has more in common with Hampshire than with the rest of Dorset!

Dorset covers 2652.74 km² (1024.23 square miles), and most of it is rural. The main urban conurbation of Bournemouth and Poole in the south-east covers only 111 km², or just over 4%. However over 44% of the population is concentrated here. Of a total Dorset population of 647,245, the conurba-

Very gently rolling arable field mosaic extends to valley side-slopes
Fields become smaller and tree cover increases towards valley floor
Valley cross-section is a shallow indentation rather than a steep trough
Narrow strip of pasture with hedgerow trees and farmbuildings within valley

CHALK VALLEYS: *The Cheselbourne Valley from Puddletown Down.* GR 761978.

tion's population is 282,228* . The other large towns in the county, with populations over 9000, are Weymouth (49,450), Christchurch (40,330), Ferndown (16,650), Dorchester (15,070), Wimborne Minster (13,630) and Verwood (10,290).

The landscape assessment recognised, at a county scale, twenty-three landscape character areas which, in turn, could be grouped into six major landscape zones.

- WEST DORSET LANDSCAPES
- CHALK LANDSCAPES
- SOUTH DORSET LANDSCAPES
- ISLE OF PURBECK LANDSCAPES
- EAST DORSET AND POOLE BASIN LANDSCAPES
- NORTH DORSET LANDSCAPES

Smaller scale landscapes on steeply undulating terrain are noted within four of the character areas. The landscape assessment map also shows important visual edges in the rural parts as well as a zone of urban influence around the Poole/Bournemouth conurbation.

An overview of each major zone introduces the descriptions of the individual character areas. These follow a consistent pattern covering;

- landform and context
- landscape components and structure
- settlement pattern and development
- human response

Each area assessment concludes with a 'summary of key landscape characteristics' followed by 'guidance notes' for the management of that particular landscape.

* *Population figures taken from 1991 census returns.*

WEST DORSET LANDSCAPES

272km² 10.24%

The West Dorset Landscapes are a complex group extending westwards from the chalklands to the Dorset border with East Devon and Somerset. They are, however, particularly scenic and varied, in places rolling and often with smaller scale steeply undulating landscapes superimposed. Frequently the resistant Upper Greensand is dominant forming a series of high ridges and rounded hills which have distinctive, steep upper slope profiles and flat-topped summits. In the centre is the wider bowl-shaped depression of the Marshwood Vale formed on marls of the Lower Lias, whilst to the south the rolling landscape meets the sea where a variety of low tumbled cliffs rise to Golden Cap (191m), the highest point on the coast of south-west Britain. The differing colours of the cliffs add to this diversity, and the

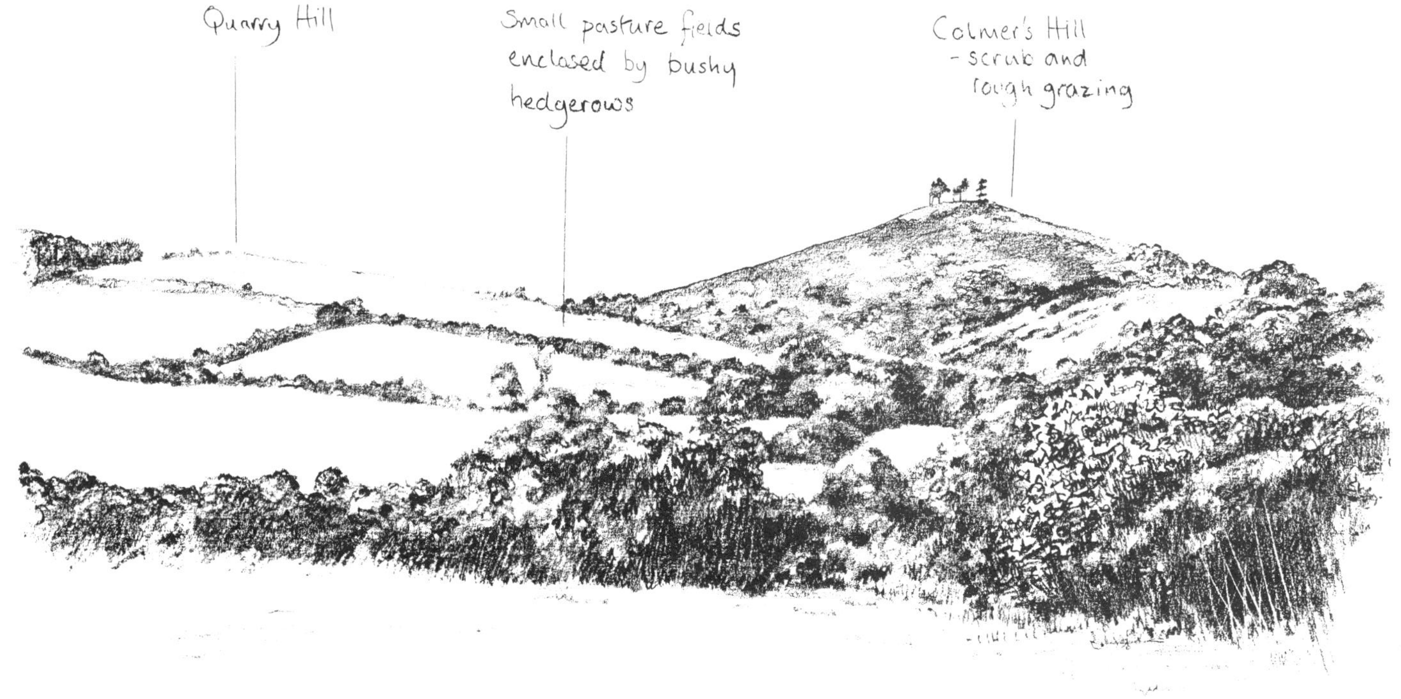

WEST DORSET FARMLAND: *Colmer's HIll.* GR 441929.

coastline has justly been awarded Heritage Coast status. Whilst most of the coast has a wild and exhilarating feeling, tempting you to walk further and further along the coast path, at Black Ven, between Lyme Regis and Charmouth, the opposite can be the case. Here, at the site of the largest mud flow in Europe, the dark, oppressive cliffs produce a feeling of insecurity, which is not just psychological as the unstable ground is physically very dangerous!

The variable, undulating farmland scenery continues across the borders into Somerset, East Devon, and the greensand of the Blackdown Hills. South-east of Beaminster the hummocky hills become progressively more conical and more clustered together in the Powerstock area where they are sufficiently distinctive to form a separate landscape area.

A wide range of wildlife habitats, relatively undisturbed and rich in species, exist within the West Dorset Landscapes. The most important ecological sites are the unimproved grasslands, ancient woodlands, hedgerows and hedge-banks, wet flushes and bogs, the heathland habitats on the greensand summits, and the coastal cliffs.

Whitchurch Canonicorum.

The landscape has long been settled, and it is impossible to say with certainty how old many of the field systems are; indeed some could be of Iron Age date or even earlier. Lynchet fields on many of the steeper hillsides provide evidence for early medieval arable farming, but from the later medieval period onwards the agriculture has been predominately pasture based; indeed the Marshwood Vale is still famous for its cheeses. In contrast, around Bridport and Beaminster flax and hemp were extensively grown. Beaminster produced sail-cloth whilst Bridport was famous for rope and nets. The well known Dorset euphemism 'stabbed with a Bridport dagger', meaning hanged, shows how closely linked Bridport and rope were in the popular mind. Through the area settlement is scattered, small villages and farms occur at frequent intervals along the twisting roads, the colour of the local building stones (of several different varieties) add warmth and harmony to the landscape.

Apart from minor anomalies caused by the Boundary Commission, virtually all the West Dorset Landscapes lie within the Dorset Area of Outstanding Natural Beauty and three main landscape character areas can be recognised:

- **WEST DORSET FARMLAND**
- **MARSHWOOD VALE**
- **POWERSTOCK HILLS**

West Dorset Farmland

The West Dorset Farmland landscape includes the greensand ridges and clay vales to the west of the chalklands. The area has a diverse topographic structure, with broad, rolling hills, and a closer scale of steep greensand ridges and deeply incised valleys superimposed on parts of the wider scene. In particular, the distinctive profiles of these ridges are characterful landmarks which give this landscape a strong, expressive identity.

Most of north-west Dorset and the Brit Valley has a broadly rolling landform, characterised by views to the more elevated greensand ridges. However, the far north-west corner has a slightly different character; the elevated land here is a broad plateau with long views to the north over the wide valley of the River Axe (which forms the border with Somerset). Here, the Upper Greensand ridges form long, slightly curving hills with a broad north-south alignment.

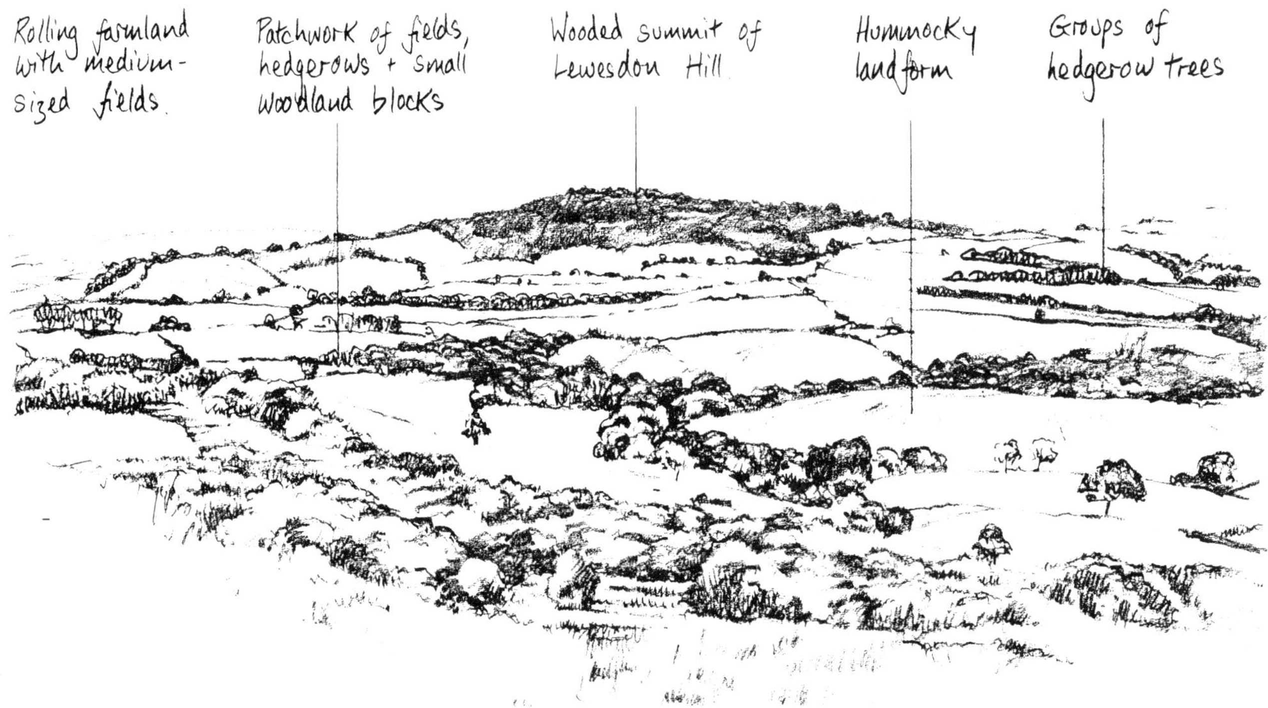

WEST DORSET FARMLAND: *Looking east/south east from Pilsdon Pen towards Lewesdon Hill.* GR 414013.

The principal hills are Pilsdon Pen, Blackdown Hill and Blagdon Hill.

Pilsdon Pen is also part of the substantial encircling ridge which divides this broader north-western landscape from the wide bowl of the Marshwood Vale. Several of these hill tops are crowned with easily recognisable Iron Age hill forts. A group of deeply incised valleys lie in the western sweep of this greensand ridge formed by Lambert's Castle and Coney's Castle. The deep gullies at the heads of these valley systems are a feature of the area and the largest of these, Fishpond Bottom, has a particularly steep valley head, with a striking rounded form. Many of the summits support heathland vegetation, heather, gorse, bracken and acidic grassland of considerable ecological interest. These were graphically described by Dorothy Wordsworth in 1795. She was staying with her brother William, at Racedown, just west of Pilsdon Pen, and she wrote in her journal;

> *We have hills, which seen from a distance almost take on the character of mountains, some cultivated nearly to their summits, others in their wild state, covered with furze and broom.*

To the south of the Marshwood Vale, a greensand ridge has been eroded to form a cluster of hills, each with a distinctive summit. These hills form a sequence of dramatic headlands along the west Dorset coast, enclosing coastal valleys and framing long views out to sea. This coast is particularly secluded, with small valleys separated by prominent headlands, such as Golden Cap and Thorncombe Beacon. However, owing to the presence of impermeable layers of Lower Liassic clays, the cliffs between Charmouth and Lyme Regis have suffered many landslips giving them an uneven landform where substantial parts have slumped away, leaving dramatic concave slopes, treacherous mudflows, and steep undercliffs.

Further east, many of the hills in the Bridport and Netherbury area have a symmetrical, conical profile. One is a prominent landmark; Colmer's Hill stands out because it has a group of Scots pines on its pointed summit, planted to create a landscape feature.

This whole landscape character area is predominantly agricultural, structured by a patchwork of fields and hedgerows. The scale of the farmland is determined by variations in the landform. In areas with a broad, rolling landform, arable fields predominate, but there is often a mixture of cultivation and pasture. The fields are medium-sized, and the strong, regular patchwork becomes larger wherever the slopes are relatively shallow. Here, the landscape structure tends to mask changes in topography and emphasises the extensive scale of the agricultural pattern. However in the areas with a steeply undulating landform, only pasture farming is viable. A fine-grained pattern of small and medium sized fields exists here, with irregular shapes, fully enclosed by straight, dense hedgerows. Hedgerow trees – principally oak, ash and beech – occur sporadically and are quite sparse in some of the more elevated areas. Wherever they are found, they are an important visual influence, giving the landscape a more secluded, domestic character. There are occasional mature Scots pines in the hedgerows of the north-west plateau area which add visual focus and interest.

Woodlands in the broad, rolling hills occur in large dense blocks, rather than patches or copses. The trees are largely deciduous, with beech and oak being the most common species. They have strong, geometric outlines which stand out clearly against the field patchwork and contribute to the variety of the mosaic. On the steep slopes woodlands typically have organic shapes and link with the broad ribbons of hedgerow trees and copses. In addition, there are ancient beech avenues along the ridgetops surrounding the valley system. However, woodlands are visually most prominent when they occur on the elevated greensand ridges; examples are the wooded summits of Lewesdon Hill and Langdon Hill. All these woodlands add to the intimacy and enclosure of the landscape, but also sometimes form distinctive local landmarks in their own right. One striking example is on Conegar Hill, where a small, dense block of woodland on the north side of the hill stands out very clearly against the open, broad rounded ridgetop.

Many of the fields have wet flushes and even small bogs. They are often apparently unmanaged, hummocky grazing land with a rich, varied visual texture. The organic pattern of woodlands, copses and hedgerow belts is most extensive on the steepest slopes such as the head of a valley. Frequently the lanes are very narrow and flanked by high hedgebanks, and all these roads and hedgerows are twisting and irregular in shape.

There are numerous scattered farmsteads throughout which form a visual focus in many views. Some may be quite exposed where hedgerow trees are sparse. Within the steep valleys, the larger villages are always on the valley floors – often at the wider point where several valleys coalesce, such as at Wootton Fitzpaine. Many of the clustered villages and hamlets are found at the junctions of the dense network of narrow lanes.

The numerous topographical landmarks give the West Dorset Farmland landscape a lively, expressive character. There are many contrasts; the steep valleys are deeply enclosed and very intimate, the rolling hills have a more expansive scale, and the greensand ridges are exposed and windswept. The arable fields on the broader landform have a functional, managed appearance, with a regular consistent

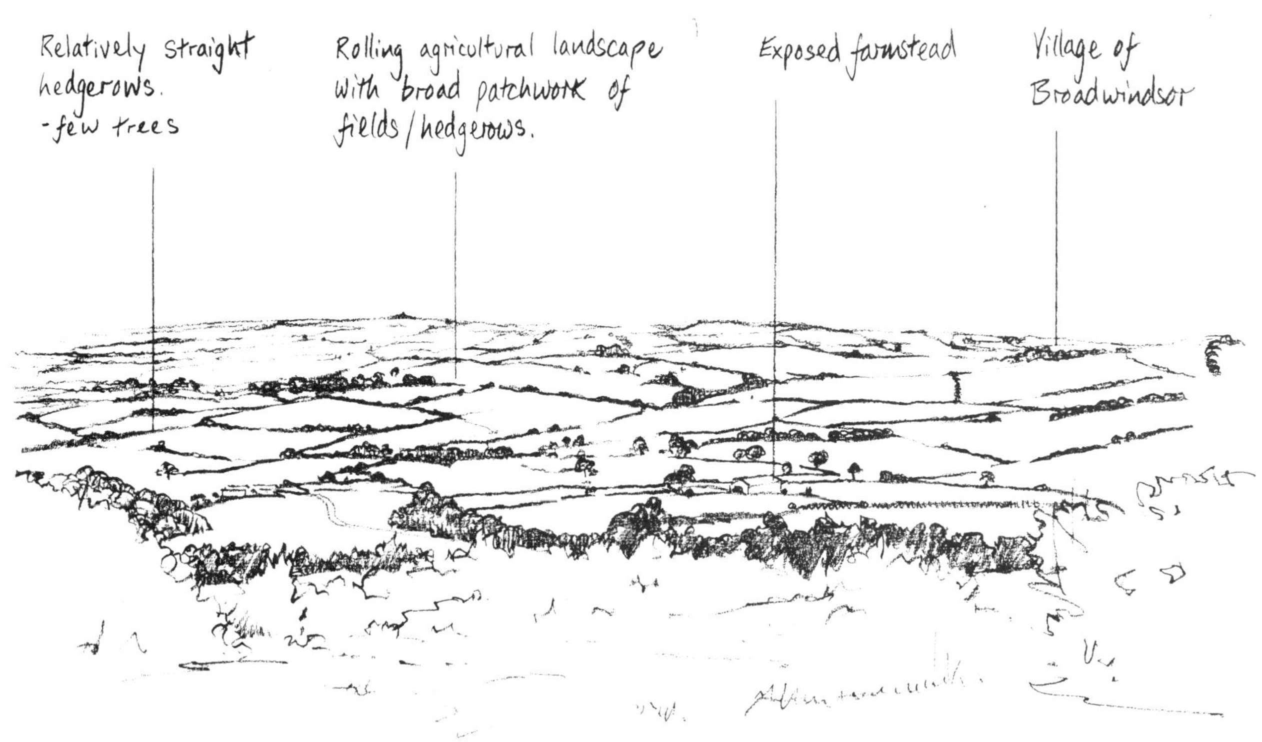

WEST DORSET FARMLAND: *Looking east/north east from Pilsdon Pen over rolling farmland with broad patchwork of hedgerows and fields.* GR 414013.

rhythm. By contrast, the steep valleys have a richly textured, diverse landscape, with a dense, organic pattern of fields and woodlands. Nothing in this landscape is straight or predictable. The West Dorset Farmland landscape is deeply rural and unspoilt, especially in less managed, undulating areas, where time seems to have stood still.

THE KEY CHARACTERISTIC FEATURES OF THE WEST DORSET FARMLAND ARE:–

- Diverse topography, with broad, rolling hills, steep greensand ridges and some deeply incised valleys.
- Rolling patchwork of fields and hedgerows which becomes more irregular and small in scale on steeply undulating terrain.
- Distinctive, steep greensand summits are important topographical landmarks.
- Greensand summits have a heathy character, with acidic grassland, heather, bracken and gorse.
- Broad-leaved woodlands are interspersed within the farmland patchwork.
- Narrow, winding lanes, often with high hedgebanks.
- Numerous scattered villages, with a clustered form.
- Dramatic coast with secluded beaches, landslips, and naturally eroding sea cliffs.

MANAGEMENT GUIDANCE

i There are large and small scale sub-areas within the West Dorset Farmland landscape area which make an important contribution to the character of the West Dorset Landscapes. Management strategies and action should, therefore, identify, reflect and emphasise these sub-areas and variations of scale.

ii The elevated Upper Greensand ridges are important topographical landmarks. It is important to retain these open summits, particularly those with a strong and interesting landform such as Pilsdon Pen, and those on which there are archaeological features or tracts of unimproved acidic grassland and heather, which need management to reduce or contain scrub invasion. However, the prominent woodlands on other summits, such as Lewesdon Hill and Langdon Hill, should be conserved. The strengthening of character, identity and contrast through retaining open areas, or by sensitive planting schemes needs careful consideration from different viewpoints. Individual planting decisions need to be taken with the benefit of appropriate professional design advice.

iii The visual structure of this landscape is determined by the scale of its patchwork of fields and hedgerows. Management should focus on hedge laying, regular trimming, and the enhancement of the hedgerow network.

iv Where hedgerows have been removed or replaced with fencing, replanting is necessary to increase the strength of the hedgerow network, defining the lane and field boundaries. New planting should be designed to strengthen the existing visual structure of the farmland patchwork.

v Emphasis should be placed on the protection and conservation of existing woodlands, in particular the remnants of ancient woodland, to ensure their long term visual and ecological contribution to the landscape is maintained.

vi Woodland management should focus on an increasing dominance of broadleaved species, replacing conifers in plantations.

vii The diverse flora associated with the steep hedgebanks should be protected and maintained by appropriate mowing regimes. The partial shade and diverse qualities given by tree and shrub species on the hedgebanks should be retained by sensitive trimming, coppicing or laying to create visual richness and suitable light and shade conditions for the hedgebank flora. Detailed ecological appraisals will be needed in the most valuable sites.

viii The farmsteads tend to be exposed in areas where arable fields are predominant and would benefit from associated tree planting.

ix In areas characterised by small-scale, irregular field patchworks, it would be visually and ecologically beneficial to maintain traditional pasture grazing.

x It is particularly important to retain the secluded character of the more undeveloped valleys and coastline which are notable for their unspoilt qualities. For example, landscape improvement works are necessary to help integrate and screen some existing tourism developments, and new proposals should be rigorously assessed in relation to their ability to be integrated into the landscape.

xi Selective management works are needed to minimise the physical and visual impact of erosion pressures along the coastal footpath.

Marshwood Vale

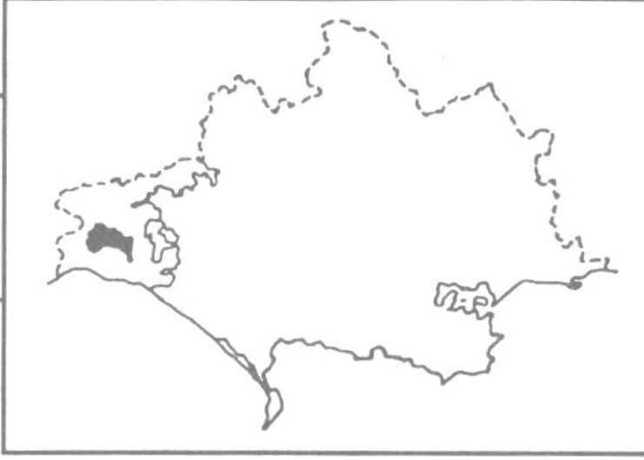

The Marshwood Vale is a wide oval bowl-shaped depression, some $4^{1}/_{2}$ miles by $2^{1}/_{2}$ miles, in the centre of the West Dorset Landscapes. It is enclosed by a series of high ridges and hills of Upper Greensand which surround the Vale to the north, west and south and by lower rolling farm land to the east. It is drained by a dense network of tributaries which lead to the Rivers Char and Simene. The Char Valley flows south-westwards, cutting through the steep, undulating coastal landscape while the River Simene drains the shallower, rolling terrain as it flows along the eastern margin of the Vale where its valley side forms a distinct north-south ridge defining the boundary.

Intrusive line of pylons.

Marshwood Vale - Scattered hedgerow oaks, individually spaced.

Edge of Vale clearly defined by Greensand ridges.

MARSHWOOD VALE: *View to Marshwood Vale from higher land 2 miles NW of Bridport.* GR 392962.

There is a difference in character between the richer, more densely treed and lower lying Vale to the west on the marls of the Lower Lias and the somewhat blander landscape of the Vale to the east. Within the Vale, most of the fields are devoted to pasture farming. They are generally medium-sized and combine with dense, neatly maintained hedgerows to form a regular, fully enclosed patchwork. The fields in the western Vale are slightly smaller and have more irregular shapes than those further to the east. Some of the hedgerows are associated with steep hedgebanks. Again, there is subtle east-west contrast with those in the west being more prominent and dramatic.

The most striking visual feature of the internal landscape of the Vale is the pattern of mature hedgerow oaks. These oaks occur with consistent regularity and are widely spaced so that each tree has been able to develop to its full, broad profile. Many are stag-headed, indicating the age and vulnerability of this important ecological and visual component. However, their maturity makes these oaks all the more striking and dramatic; without them – there are areas where they are sparse or absent – this would be a bland and relatively uniform agricultural landscape, largely gaining its character from the surrounding hills. This blandness is most evident where there is least enclosure. The density of the hedgerow oaks increases generally towards the west but they also tend to be concentrated along the lanes, with internal field boundary hedges being more open. The hedgerows are particularly rich and varied in species including hazel, ash, field maple, and blackthorn as well as the oaks. There are few woodlands in the immediate area and they are an occasional feature on the slopes of the hills enclosing the Vale. The main concentrations of trees occur in narrow wooded ribbons which follow the stream corridors.

The Vale is also an ancient landscape, the chief features of which were noted by Thomas Gerard in the 1620s;

> *Behind these Hills lieth a little Territorie called Mershwood Vale, rich and well stored with Woods, by meanes wherof it affordeth convenient Dwellings.*

There are, however, no major villages in the Vale, only scattered hamlets and farmsteads – although these occur so frequently in some areas that they almost coalesce. Larger villages occur on the higher land bordering the Vale and the church tower at Whitchurch Canonicorum is an important local landmark.

The 'birds-eye' panoramic views over the Vale from the surrounding hills reveal its overall, homogeneous pattern. The dominant theme is one of small-scale features repeated over a large area. The many isolated trees and lack of major woods or settlements give this lowland a distinctive speckled texture which contrasts with the undulating patchwork of hedge and woodland which surrounds it. A major 400 kv pylon line traverses the centre of the Vale on an east-west alignment. It is particularly intrusive in views within the Vale landscape to the south and west. However, it is almost invisible from some distant viewpoints against the backdrop of the field patchwork, but becomes evident as it ascends the western ridge to the south of Lambert's Castle.

The Vale is a serene, placid landscape which forms an idyllic foreground for views across west Dorset. The sequence of individually distinctive summits encircling the area provides a backdrop for all views from within this lowland, as well as landmarks for orientation. The sunken, narrow lanes force a relaxed pace so the landscape of the Vale seems infinite. The eastern margins are relatively bland and slightly scruffy but further west it becomes deeper, more enclosed and secretive. Here the Char Valley is so tranquil that any car feels like an intrusion.

THE KEY CHARACTERISTIC FEATURES OF THE MARSHWOOD VALE ARE:–

- Broad oval bowl-shaped clay vale, enclosed by distinctive Upper Greensand ridges.
- Predominantly pasture, with a medium-sized, enclosed field patchwork.

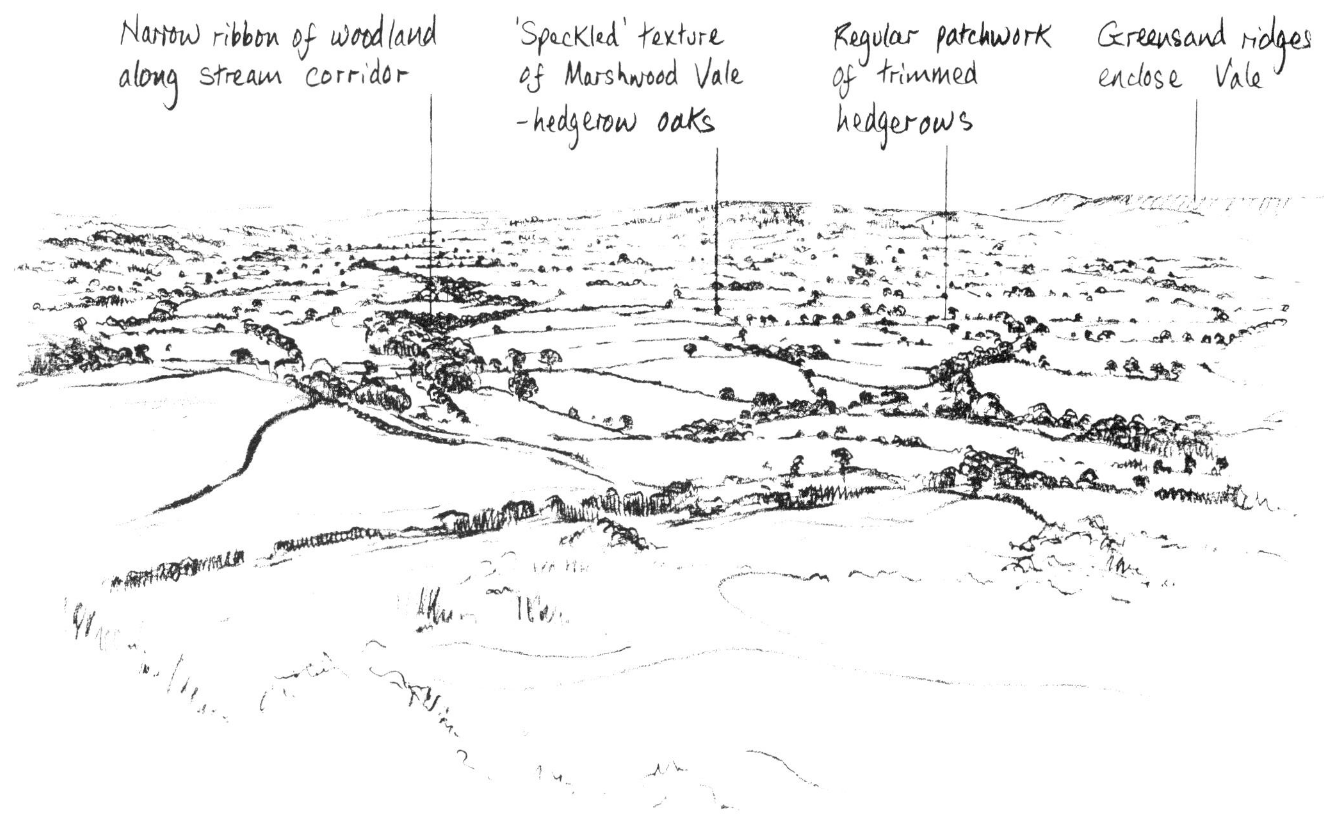

MARSHWOOD VALE: *Looking south from Pilsdon Pen over Marshwood vale.* GR 414013.

- Homogeneous patterns of hedgerows and individually spaced, but ageing, hedgerow oak trees create a rich, speckled texture when viewed from the surrounding hills.
- The hedgerows create an enclosed, secluded atmosphere within the Vale.
- Narrow ribbons of trees follow winding stream corridors, but hardly any woods.
- Field boundaries are straight except where influenced by stream corridors.
- Scattered, isolated farmsteads, connected by a winding network of narrow lanes with steep hedgebanks, but no sizeable villages.

MANAGEMENT GUIDANCE

i The homogeneity of the Vale is the key to its character – even one inappropriate development could destroy the unity of the scene as perceived from the many surrounding high vantage points.

ii Hedgerow removal should cease. Opportunities should be sought to restore mixed species hedgerows where loss is apparent, as hedgerows contribute to the enclosed, secretive character of the Vale.

iii Because of the unique contribution of hedgerow oaks, planting of this species throughout the Vale should be encouraged at spacings of 30-70 metres along the hedgerows.

iv The fine, neatly trimmed, species-rich hedgerows, including locally flower-rich hedgebanks in the lower-lying western part of the Vale, should be protected and carefully managed to ensure their important contribution to the Vale's character is maintained.

v The form and scale of changes in domestic and agricultural buildings should be critically assessed to ensure their appropriateness and integration within the landscape.

vi Corridors of mixed native tree and shrub species could be encouraged along the many stream corridors, occasionally forming continuous belts of trees in association with the field pattern, without disrupting the characteristic dominance of the hedgerow oaks.

vii Tree planting, with native species, would help to integrate the hamlets and farmsteads better in the landscape particularly by copses and denser hedgerow tree masses on their margins.

Powerstock Hills

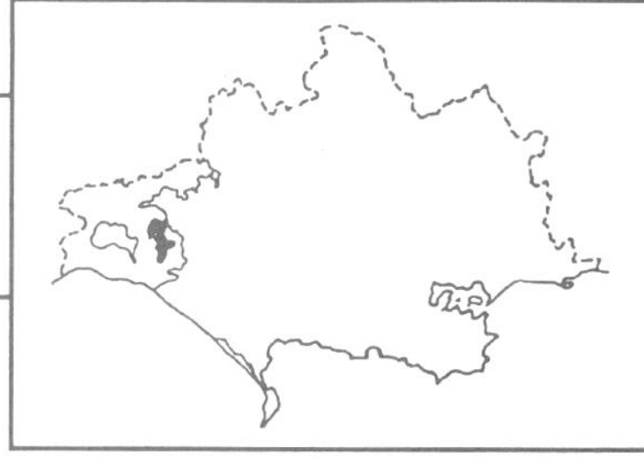

The Powerstock Hills form a miniature landscape of small hills and steep valleys between Beaminster and Eggardon Hill. The area is underlain by Bridport Sand, with some outcrops of limestone. Separated by distinctive clusters of small conical hills the very steep, sharply incised valleys gradually become more elongated to the east as they connect to the ridges alongside the chalk/greensand escarpment. To the west, the line of conical hills stands out clearly against the broad rolling arable fields of the Brit Valley. There is also a gradual transition from north to south. The northern hills, around Melplash, have a more open character and the conical landform has more visual influence here since there are fewer trees to disguise its profile.

Steep slopes ensure that this landscape is devoted to pasture, rough grazing and woodland. It is the varying combinations of these different land uses which give the area its diverse character. Sheep grazing on rough, open grassland tends to occur on the hilltops with woodland and pasture on the valley sides. There are, however, many variations and each hillock has a distinctive, quirky character with its own particular combination of trees, hedgerows and fields. The hillocks are all of a similar size and scale so the landscape has a consistent overall rhythm.

The hedgerows are discontinuous around many of the fields and there is an irregular patchwork of fields and woodland which tends to break down towards the hilltops. Hedgerow trees, copses and blocks of woodland occur randomly throughout this landscape, often on the summit of hillocks. When trees stand alone, or are clustered in small groups, they are very distinctive and add great character to the scene; the scale of the landscape is so close that such trees are often silhouetted on the skyline. The blocks of woodland are generally small and irregular in shape. The commonest trees are beech and ash but there are also lime, sycamore and oak. The occasional Scots pine provides a strong accent in the hedgerows, especially on the higher valleys to the east where the hedges become sparse and contain much bracken.

There is no single overriding landmark in the area, but views are typically short and the hills have such distinctive characters that each is an individual focus. There are few opportunities for views out from the tightly confined hill system except on the abrupt western boundary or, more spectacularly, from the margins of the chalk escarpment to the west.

Connected by a labyrinthine network of lanes there are numerous settlements scattered throughout the hills and the villages of West Milton, Loders and Powerstock are found alongside the streams in the valley floors. The yellow stone buildings and walls, steep landform, and high hedgebanks along the narrow lanes, all contribute to a strong and comforting sense of enclosure. When the hedgebanks are bordered by mature beech trees the lanes become deep, green tunnels, for example on the northern side of Loders. The streams are more often associated with bogs and marshy areas than flat, lush meadows. Although a dominant line of pylons straddles the whole valley system the views are typically short, so it is only intrusive in a limited area. From more distant viewpoints the pylons tend to blend in with the surroundings and are masked by the complex landscape system.

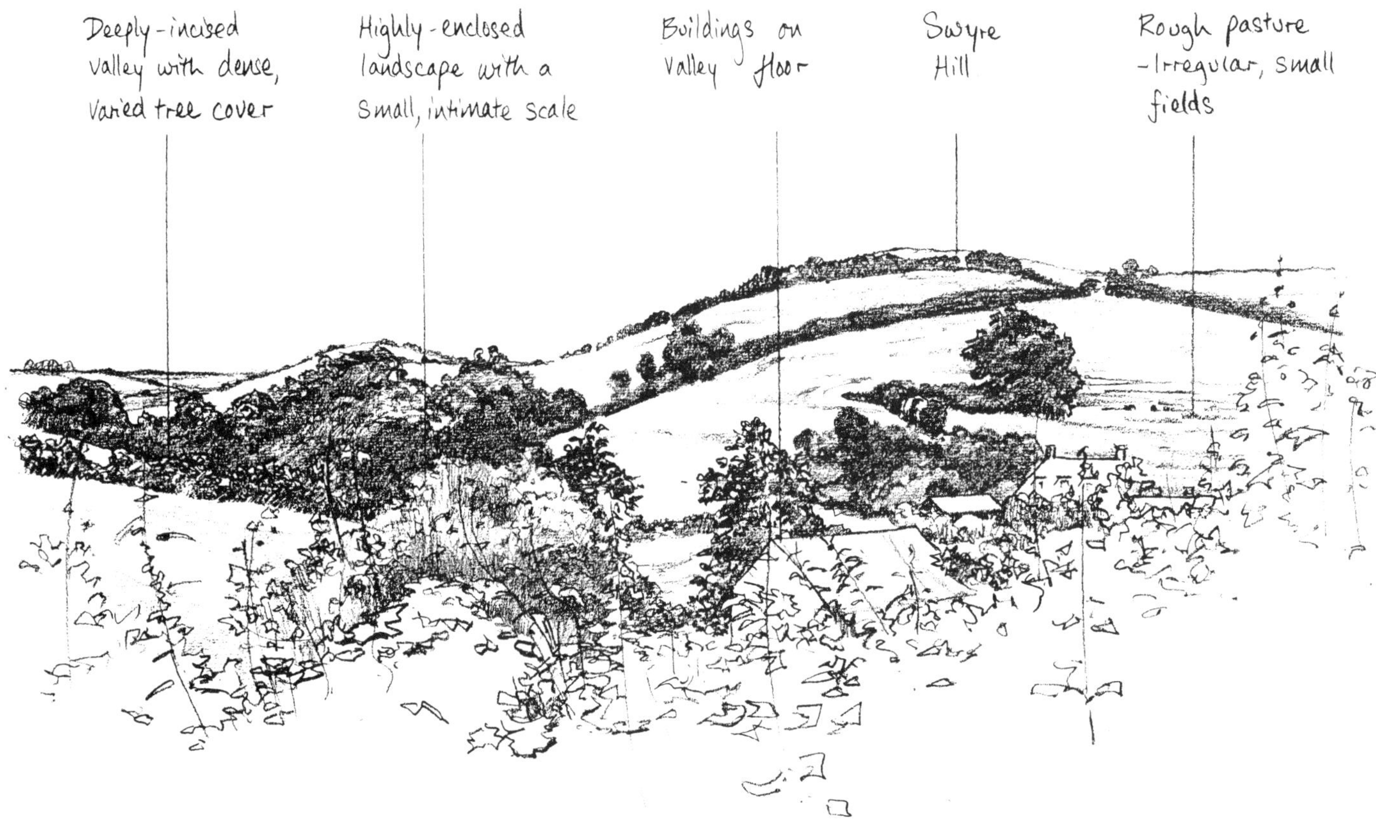

POWERSTOCK HILLS: *Swyre Hill from West Milton.* GR 508962.

This landscape is enclosed and so intimate that it feels like a microcosm, remote from the outside world. Furthermore, the hills seem chaotic, crowded, and so tumbled together that the valley systems often feel disorientating and the distinctive hillocks are each a quirky landmark, giving the landscape a slightly bizarre, whimsical character.

THE KEY CHARACTERISTIC FEATURES OF THE POWERSTOCK HILLS ARE:–

- Highly enclosed landscape on a small, intimate scale.
- Narrow, twisting lanes and deep hedgebanks.
- Numerous small, conical hills divided by a deeply incised, branching network of valleys.
- Small fields, with irregular shapes.
- Varied tree cover with dense wooded valleys and more open hilltops.
- Scattered settlements and main villages alongside rivers in the valleys.
- Local stone giving a distinctive yellow/orange colour to the settlements.

i The small-scale diversity, varying from densely wooded valleys, open hilltops and wooded summits, is a key aspect of landscape quality and character in this area. It is important that landscape management and improvement works are designed on a small, intimate scale, should not weaken the contrasting identity of individual hills and valleys, and should focus on the maintenance of this diversity and enclosure.

ii The lanes are a significant contribution to the character of the area and every effort should be made to retain and sustain their form and structure.

iii The important hedgebanks should be managed to retain their distinctive character through appropriate protection measures, regular management, selective coppicing, and possibly sensitive additional planting.

iv Hedgerows should be conserved and enriched with new planting of appropriate native species.

v Where stone walls are a feature they should be repaired, and in places rebuilt, using local stone.

vi Existing woodlands should be actively managed, using native species already present in the area for any replanting.

vii This is an area where traditional building styles and materials in the villages and hamlets make a particular contribution to local distinctiveness, so special attention should be given to retaining these styles and materials. In particular the use of local stone, with its distinctive colour, is far more appropriate than other alien 'natural' stones.

CHALK LANDSCAPES

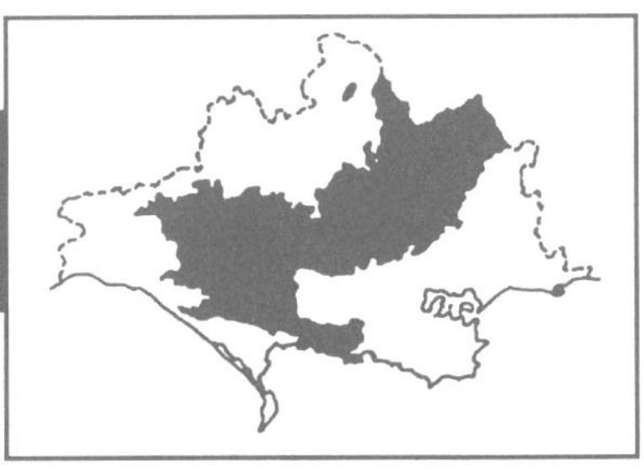

970km² 36.53%

The Dorset chalklands stretch in a broad belt across the county from the extensive chalklands of Wiltshire in the north-east to Beaminster in the west. To the south they form the northern edge of the Weymouth lowlands, meeting the coastline at Chaldon Down. The Dorset chalk has a broad, inverted saucer-shaped profile with a gentle dip-slope towards the Frome Valley/Poole Basin and escarpments bordering the Blackmoor Vale to the north, the Powerstock Hills in West Dorset and the Bride Valley/Weymouth Lowlands to the south. The chalk escarpments form dramatic visual edges dropping sharply away to allow panoramic views out over the adjacent landscapes together with a backdrop and horizon for views from within them.

The Dorset chalklands are drained by the river systems of the Frome, the Piddle and the Stour. The valleys generally have a north-south alignment and subdivide the chalk uplands, influencing patterns of movement and settlement.

The chalk uplands probably once supported oak-hazel woodlands but this was gradually cleared for agriculture by Neolithic and Bronze Age farmers eventually to form extensive open grasslands. The pattern of land division finally established in Saxon times, though possibly older, is repeated consistently in all the chalk valleys. Continuous hedgelines indicate the land units which were associated with a small settlement and typically formed a long, narrow strip running across the valley, including land on steep slopes as well as the valley floor. As populations gradually increased, the separate settlements expanded until they amalgamated to form more continuous linear villages along the valleys, leaving the chalk uplands for extensive grazing.

The sheltered valleys were ploughed for crops and the water meadows on the valley floor were intensively managed for grazing and hay production. These meadows were flooded twice a year using a system of hatches and dams, with ditches to spread the water evenly. In early spring the water covered the fields for 2 to 3 weeks to keep the frost at bay to ensure that early grass was available to feed the ewes and lambs before they went up on to the downs. The process was repeated in early summer to provide a field of hay. Dairy cows were then grazed for the rest of the annual cycle. The remains of the grid-like patterns of the ditches and sluices are still a characteristic feature of many valleys today.

From the seventeenth century onwards the enclosure movement progressively parcelled up much chalk upland for more efficient sheep grazing. Many of these enclosures resulted in the establishment of new, outlying farmsteads and by the nineteenth century the chalk downlands were renowned as high quality grazing. During the Second World War the existing pattern of chalkland farming was disrupted by the introduction of compulsory Cultivation Orders, under which large areas of downland were ploughed and brought into arable cultivation. The chalk upland landscape rapidly became the mosaic of arable fields which has persisted to the present day, albeit at a larger scale as farmers pursue economic efficiency rather than landscape quality.

Chalk grassland is a rare semi-natural habitat, important for its diverse flora and associated insect life. The habitat is maintained by continuous grazing but agricultural changes, leading to the expansion of subsidised arable farming at the

CHALK LANDSCAPES: *The Cerne Valley from Dickley Hill. GR 653004.*

expense of traditional sheep grazing, have resulted in a dramatic reduction in this important habitat. The subtle colours and textures of downland brought about by their ecological make up contrasts with the even greens of sown leys or fertilised fields. Most chalk grasslands are now confined to steep valley sides and escarpments which have proved too difficult to plough, but even here their survival is threatened by scrub encroachment due to the decline of extensive grazing systems. The coastal chalk grasslands around Lulworth Cove on the south coast are particularly rich, but are threatened by recreational pressures and erosion.

The Chalk Landscapes can be divided into three main landscape character areas:

- **CHALK UPLANDS**
- **CHALK ESCARPMENTS**
- **CHALK VALLEYS**

Grims Dyke

Chalk Uplands

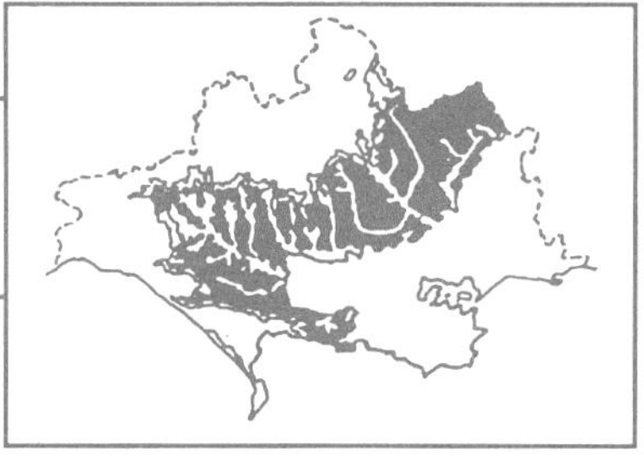

The Chalk Uplands form the most extensive and homogeneous landscape character type in Dorset.

This scenery is characterised by a very broad rolling landform, with gently curving convex profiles. The only abrupt breaks in slope occur where the landform is sculpted into sweeping branching coombes on the upper margins of the valley systems and towards the escarpment. Elsewhere the landform is more gentle and homogenous. The Chalk Uplands meet the coast at Chaldon Down, a particularly broad, elevated ridge which is truncated abruptly at the coast and deeply incised by a branching valley system to the north. The Purbeck Chalk Ridge, an outlier of the main area of chalk is treated separately as part of the Purbeck Landscape. To the east of Chaldon Down, Hambury Tout and Bindon Hill are prominent steep, narrow chalk ridges running parallel to the coast and providing a striking contrast to the lowlands inland. Lulworth Cove, a well-known exposure of the chalk, lies to the south of Bindon Hill.

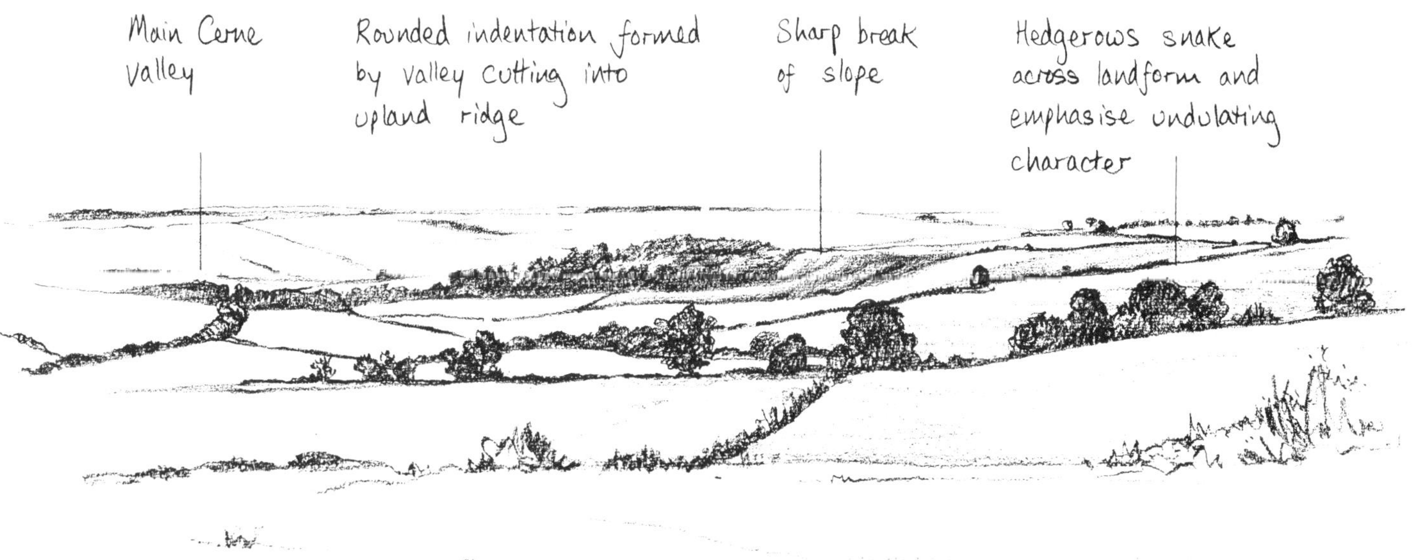

CHALK UPLANDS: *Undulating upland Chalk scenery on the ridgetop above Cerne Valley.* GR 617002.

The highest point on the south Dorset chalklands is Black Down (237 metres) where an isolated area of Tertiary gravels outcrops above the Upper Chalk. With a steep conical profile and heathy soils it contrasts with the surrounding rolling chalklands. Hardy's Monument, a tall stone pillar stands on the summit of Black Down, ensuring that this hill is a prominent landmark for the south Dorset chalklands. This elevated heathland habitat extends eastwards along the ridge that effectively separates the coastal Weymouth Lowlands from inland Dorset.

From the valley of the river Stour the chalk runs north east to the Hampshire and Wiltshire borders. This is a very open landscape with fewer hedges than the rest of the Chalk Uplands, but with the most extensive woodlands. In these east Dorset chalklands the transition between the Chalk Upland and the Chalk Valley landscapes is very subtle and not easy to appreciate. There are few prominent landmarks, although the village of Ashmore at 217 metres has the honour to be the highest village in Dorset, and is one of the few villages to lie on these uplands.

Chalk Uplands usually have few trees but there are tracts of woodland, much of which is old coppice, where the chalk bedrock is covered by superficial deposits, such as clay-with-flints or Reading Beds. The woodlands are mostly deciduous; many were once managed as coppices, and a few still are! The fields tend to be large, and of a similar size, with straight functional edges so the landscape seems ruled into neat, regular compartments. The fields are predominantly arable, with many variations in colour and texture due to the variety of crops and seasonal cycles. They are divided by sparse, narrow hedgerows, or wire fences, forming a network of thin dark lines which criss-cross and emphasise the landform. The few hedgerow trees tend to be concentrated in small clumps or shelter belts around farmsteads and stand out clearly in an otherwise open landscape. The hedgerows are mostly in poor condition and become

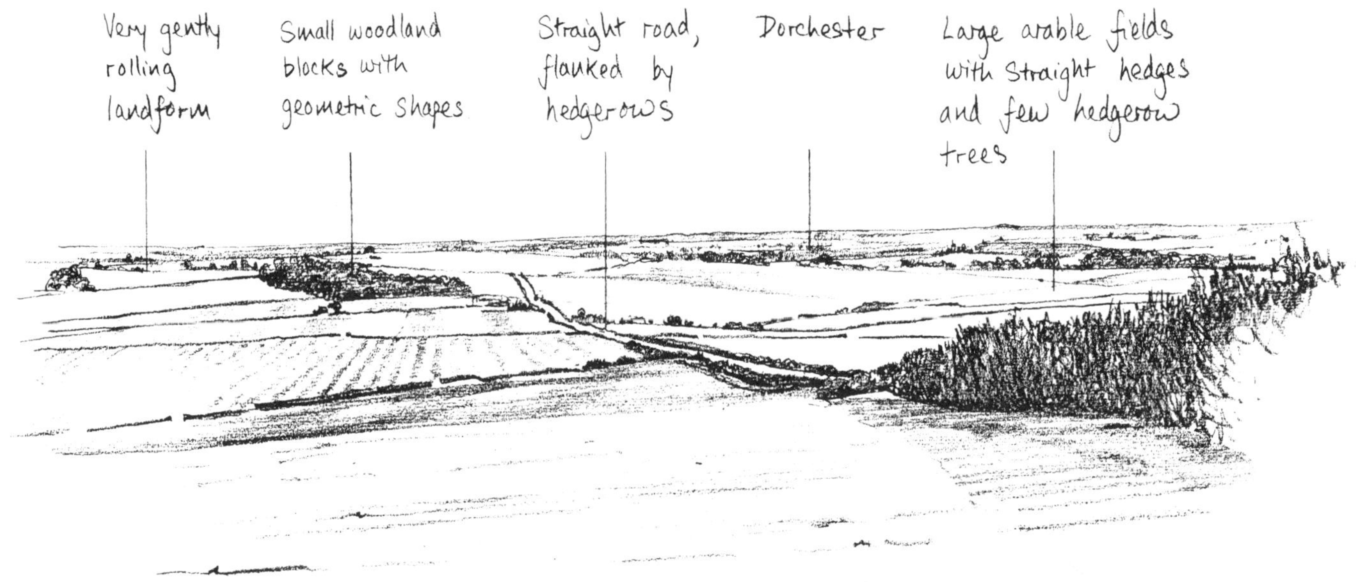

CHALK UPLANDS: *The ridgetop road descending Charlton Higher Down towards Dorchester.* GR 685953.

intermittent on the more elevated slopes. They do not fully enclose all the fields and frequently wire fences are the effective barriers. Tracts of woodland are particularly important landscape features on the chalklands to the east of the Stour Valley.. Most of these woods are deciduous and some are classified as semi-natural ancient woodlands, remnants of the ancient hunting ground of Cranborne Chase which covered this area until 1830. Isolated small fragments of semi-natural chalk grassland remain on steep embankments and beside trackways.

Numerous ancient settlement sites, long barrows and burial mounds from the Neolithic and Bronze Ages provide evidence that the chalk uplands have historically been well-settled, but since medieval times villages have mostly been confined to the sheltered valleys. They are connected by a regular network of roads which extends across the upland divides. Isolated farmsteads on exposed chalk upland sites date from later phases of enclosure from the seventeenth century onwards. Most of the roads in the Chalk Upland landscape follow a fairly straight alignment since there were few topographic barriers to cause diversions and some, such as the A37, originated as Roman roads.

This is an expansive landscape of panoramic views across extensive, relatively homogenous chalklands. The Chalk Uplands is a very exposed, moody landscape, dominated by the sky and weather conditions so it feels very close to nature, despite the agricultural mosaic. The landscape is most spectacular following a rainstorm when there is crystal clear visibility and the clouds cast dynamic shadows, interchanging with reflective patches of light. The extensive, gently rolling terrain produces a landscape with a strong sense of depth and many rippling, layered horizons. On a misty day the landform tends to blur and the woodland blocks stand out prominently on the skyline, whilst in the height of summer the dry, white dust can make the landscape seem grey and flat.

THE KEY CHARACTERISTIC FEATURES OF THE CHALK UPLANDS ARE:-

- Broad, rolling landform with gently curving convex profiles.
- Expansive scale.
- Homogenous landscape, with an open character; landmarks are visible over long distances.
- Large patchwork of arable fields defined by straight, thin hedges or wire fences.
- Isolated, blocks of woodland with sharp geometric edges.
- Woodland usually deciduous, frequently old hazel coppice.
- Sparsely populated with a widely-spaced network of straight roads.
- Numerous archaeological sites such as barrows and ancient field systems

MANAGEMENT GUIDANCE

i All areas of existing downland should be conserved, protected from sprays and fertilisers, with a programme of grazing management.

ii The verges of roads and track should be managed to retain a species rich short grassland.

iii Archaeological sites should be actively protected, in particular the ancient field systems.

iv Parts of the Chalk Uplands would benefit greatly from conversion of arable fields to permanent grassland, in particular those areas close to surviving chalk grassland. Conversion should be followed by a suitable grazing regime.

v Existing woodlands, which tend to be on hillside slopes, should be actively managed and possibly extended to form new outlines, reflecting the flowing contours.

vi Many of the older woodlands are old hazel coppice which would benefit from a regular coppicing regime.

vii Any new building should be low and, if possible, placed within a fold of the landscape, to avoid an intrusive vertical element in a rolling horizontal landform.

viii Hedgerows and hedgerow trees are only locally important and, in such situations, should be conserved and replaced, but should not disrupt important open vistas and areas of distinctive, sweeping landform. Unless part of an historic landscape feature any individual trees should be irregularly spaced.

ix Local areas of heathland, on acid soils, should be managed to conserve their particular habitat characteristics.

Chalk Escarpment

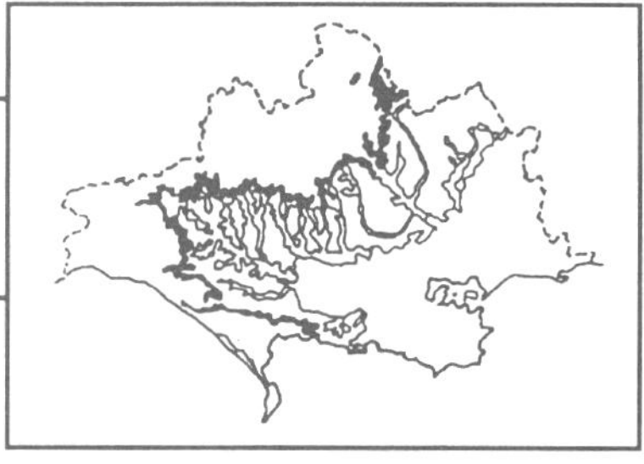

The wide range of geological influences and patterns of erosion on the outer margins of the chalk combine to form escarpment scenery of unusual variety and beauty. The escarpment slopes form prominent visual edges with a bold, dominant scale. They are a platform for long panoramas as well as a backdrop, and often a landmark, in views from afar. The strong contrasts of relief and patterns of land use along the escarpment produce evocative and dramatic scenery which is a powerful influence on the character and legibility of Dorset's landscapes.

There are marked variations in landscape character and landform along the escarpment slopes according to their geographical and geological context. The following description of landscape character is therefore divided into three sections relating to the northern, western and southern aspects of the chalk escarpment.

Iron Age hill forts are strung along the top of the chalk escarpment; Hod and Hambledon Hills are the most impressive sites on the northern escarpment, Eggardon Hill on the

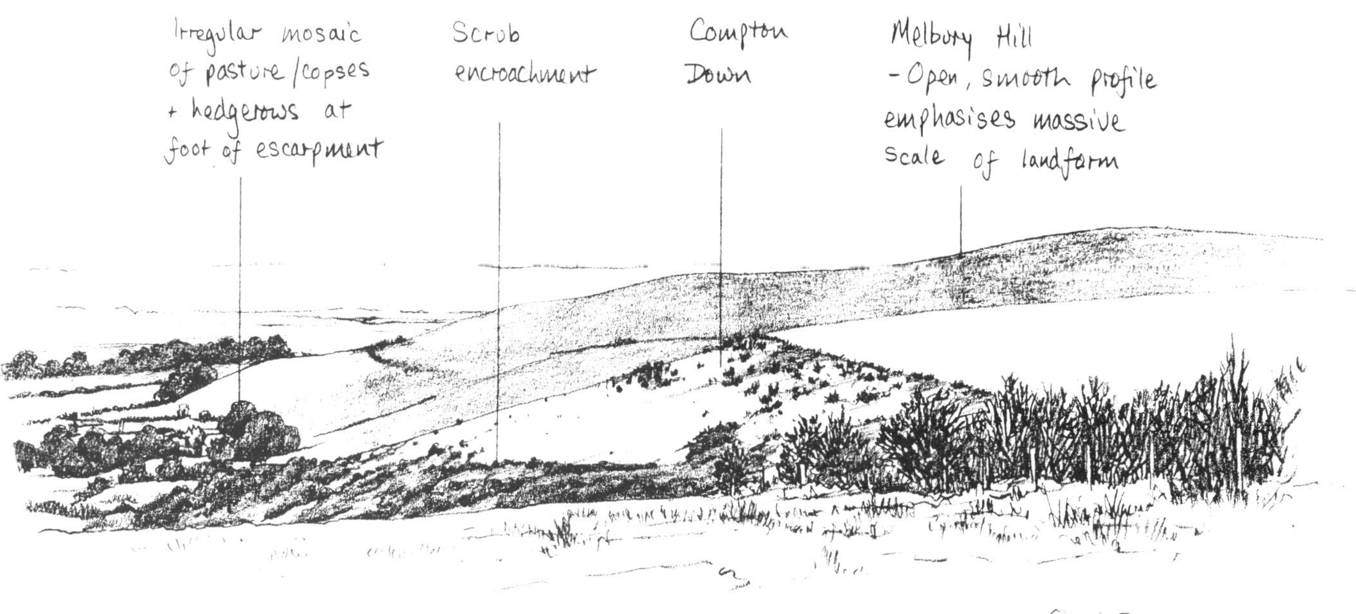

CHALK ESCARPMENT: *North east escarpment: Melbury Hill and Compton Down from Fontmell Down.* GR 886188.

western escarpment, and Chilcombe and Chalbury on the southern escarpment. As well as these massive sites there are many lesser hill forts looking out over the lower land to the north, west or south.

Northern Chalk Escarpment

The Northern Escarpment is a series of hills and ridges which vary from the grand monolithic mounds of the north east to the smooth gentle ridge of Nordon Hill at Higher Melcombe and the steep slopes of Ibberton.

The highest and most dramatic summits occur where the chalk escarpment meets the Wiltshire border near Shaftesbury, rising to 262 metres on Charlton Down. This escarpment typically has very sharp breaks at the top and bottom of the slopes. Sometimes the arable fields on the flatter uplands extend right up to the scarp slopes so the boundaries are very clearly defined. The chalk ridges are deeply incised and consist of a series of headlands jutting out into the Blackmoor Vale, divided by deep coombe valleys. The hills and ridges along the north escarpment have distinctive profiles and patterns of tree cover so each is inevitably a landmark from the Vale. The large scale and rough texture of the escarpment ridge contrasts with the highly patterned landscape of the Vale below. Further west the escarpment is more wooded so sharp breaks in slope are generally well camouflaged. The chalk ridge also becomes progressively lower towards the west, where it has often been subject to subsidence and slumping along the spring-line. Even where the ridge is less dramatic, it always has a strong enclosing presence and forms a backdrop to the neighbouring lowland landscapes.

The lower, slumped slopes to the west often have dense woodlands with irregular, organic edges which blend easily with the lowland landscapes beyond. Melbury Park, a large estate on the lower slopes to the east of Corscombe, is heavily wooded. The blocks of coniferous woodland, with geometric edges, occur more frequently on the steeper slopes to the east of Ibberton Hill. They are a striking contrast to the patchy, irregular tree cover of the Vale and can provide a powerful expression of the structuring presence of the scarp slopes. Open grasslands, often including fragmented areas of semi-natural chalk grassland, are more typical of the steep, elevated, north-east escarpment towards Shaftesbury. They have an uneven texture and grey-green colour, interspersed with patches of scrub, forming irregular mosaic patterns on the hillside.

There are numerous villages tucked in sheltered bays in the escarpment ridge, or at the foot of the slopes. Few buildings are sited on the steep slopes, but some farmsteads are scattered on the higher land of the softer escarpment landscapes further west. The villages have protected sites and are always close to the springs and streams which rise at the bottom of the slopes. They are connected by a dense network of narrow, twisting lanes which is crossed in places by more direct routes through the chalk valleys. The narrow lanes, twisting up the escarpment slopes, have high hedgebanks and often become tunnels through dense woodland before emerging on the ridgetops.

The analogy of a coastline seems appropriate in describing the headlands, bays and outliers of the edge of the Northern Escarpment and the views from the highest summits are as exhilarating and liberating as those from cliff tops. However, they are also more fascinating and intriguing since the landscape below is such a complex maze. Landforms with strongly contrasting characters are juxtaposed within a limited area along the Northern Escarpment, creating an evocative, powerful and inspiring landscape.

Western Chalk Escarpment

The Western Escarpment is a curving, steep elevated ridge at Beaminster Down but becomes lower to the south, where it is eroded by the wide branching valleys of the chalklands to the east. These slopes have been subject to subsidence and have a hummocky, uneven form which is camouflaged by dense woodlands. From Eggardon to Askerswell it is, again, steep and heavily indented.

CHALK ESCARPMENT: *South Chalk escarpment at Sutton Poyntz.* GR 695844.

The scattered valley woodlands of the River Hooke link with the more extensive deciduous woodlands blanketing the slopes of the Western Escarpment. These escarpment woodlands gradually form the rich organic network of copses, hedgerows and pastures of the West Dorset farmland. To the south of Eggardon Hill, the Western Escarpment is a more open steep, rugged ridge with grass and patches of scrub on the upper slopes. A sparse network of hedgerows divides the lower slopes into irregular fields and there is a very gradual transition to the more ordered patchwork of farmland on the valley floor.

Small villages, with a clustered form, tend to occur at the foot of the escarpment, and narrow lanes form a network connecting these villages with those in the chalk valleys above. The major line of pylons which ascends the escarpment at the head of the Loders Valley is very intrusive as there are no trees to disguise it.

The views along the Western Escarpment from Eggardon Hill are spectacular and quite special since it is unusual to find such extensive areas of deciduous woodland in Dorset. The landscape of West Dorset is a particularly expressive landscape and the panorama from the West Escarpment edge is at a similar elevation to the Greensand Summits so these views have more depth than those from the Northern Escarpment, with many high ridges which form a series of horizons fading into the distance.

Southern Chalk Escarpment

The edges of the Southern Escarpment have a more uniform character than those to the north and west. It is a high, cliff-like ridge, separating the fairly flat, open chalk uplands from the expansive, regular mosaic of the fields in the Bride valley and the Weymouth lowlands below. In contrast to the more indented ridges to the north and west, the Southern Escarpment follows a fairly straight east-west alignment so views tend to be directed out over the lowlands to the south rather than along the escarpment itself. The only exceptions to this occur where the escarpment curves around at the head of the Bride Valley and in the Osmington area.

The escarpment slopes are mostly open grassland with a rugged, exposed character. The steepest areas have some patches of scrub and an intermittent network of straggling hedgerows extends part way up the slopes from the lowland patchwork below, accentuating their height and cliff-like appearance. The patches of scrub, predominantly gorse, often emphasise the scale and rounded curves of the land-form. At West Bexington and Abbotsbury the escarpment comes very close to the coast and has a particularly rugged character with very little vegetation other than stunted gorse bushes and tussocky grass. The rough, textured slope displays much evidence of soil creep with numerous thin narrow ridges following the contours, emphasising the drama of the steep slopes. At the head of the Bride Valley and in the Osmington area, the escarpment landscape has a smaller scale and more secluded, verdant, character. These areas have a more varied, complex landscape structure, with a dense cover of trees and an irregular patchwork of small fields. The views from the Southern Escarpment out over the Weymouth lowlands are dominated by the unique configuration of Chesil Beach and the Isle of Portland.

The Southern Escarpment has a massive, exposed solid character, with hardly any woodlands to provide a focus or a distraction. It is therefore a particularly sharp visual edge, forming a consistent backdrop for views from the lowlands to the south. The escarpment is most atmospheric along the ridgetop edge, away from the main roads. From here there is a strong relationship between the exposed chalklands and the sea beyond, and the landscape seems primitive, minimalistic, and carved dramatically by powerful natural forces.

THE KEY CHARACTERISTIC FEATURES OF THE CHALK ESCARPMENT ARE:–

- Steep, distinctive chalk margin and interface between landscape types, affording panoramic views over the surrounding countryside.
- Powerful edge forms a dramatic backdrop to adjacent lowland landscape.
- Marked variations in landscape character and land-form between northern, western and southern scarp slopes.
- Open grassland and blocks of woodland often form broad distinctive patterns.
- The woodlands are highly visible landmarks.
- Smaller-scale patchwork of fields and hedgerows often gives way to larger fields or open downland some way up the escarpment slopes.
- Settlements concentrated at the foot of escarp-ment slopes.
- Prehistoric hill forts crown many escarpment slopes.

MANAGEMENT GUIDANCE

i The particular pattern formed by the combination of woodland, fields and hedgerows on any part of the escarpment is unique, and emphasis should be placed on maintaining, and in places enhancing, this strong spatial diversity. The visual structure of the escarpment landscapes should be assessed from the surrounding lowlands to ensure that particularly fine relationships between the escarpment and its adjacent landscape are maintained. The landscapes of the escarpment often include bold contrasts, but there are also more subtle transitions; this variety, which is most apparent along the escarpments to the north and west of the chalklands, should be maintained. The Southern Escarpment of the chalk has a more consistent, open character.

ii The steep slopes of the escarpments have extensive chalk grassland sites, and these should be protected from scrub encroachment, erosion and woodland planting. An active management programme of traditional grazing and strategic scrub clearance could maintain and extend the existing, fragmented chalk grassland sites and potentially link them to create dramatic, open and ecologically rich escarpment landscapes.

iii Existing woodlands should be conserved as some of them are ancient woodlands which are biologically diverse and significant for nature conservation. The current balance between coniferous and deciduous woodland should be changed over time, in favour of more native, broadleaved woods.

iv The form of some of the existing, geometric, blocks of woodland is often distracting, and management and planting could create a softer, more organic edge.

v Many of the older woodlands are old hazel coppice which would benefit from a regular coppicing regime.

vi Where ancient hedgerows exist they should be maintained for their biological diversity and historical pattern. On the Southern Escarpment the old stone walls should be maintained.

vii Because the escarpment forms a backdrop to many views the control of insensitive development, and intrusive features such as pylon lines, is particularly important to maintain and enhance the dramatic landforms.

viii The individual character of the lanes and their verges should be sustained.

Chalk Valleys

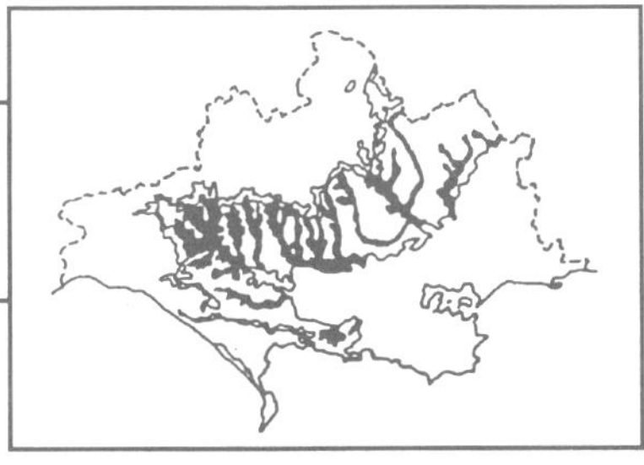

The chalk uplands are dissected by the river systems of the Frome, the Piddle and the Stour, which flow south and eastwards across the chalk from the escarpment towards Poole and Christchurch harbours. In all the river valleys water quality is good, which has led to the establishment of watercress beds and fish farm. Traces can still be seen of old water meadow systems in many of the valleys. Each river has produced valleys with a characteristic landform and there are clear variations in landscape character from one chalk valley to the next. It is for this reason that the valley systems of the Frome, the Piddle and the Stour are described separately. Nevertheless brick and flint buildings, reflecting the availability of materials, are a consistent and typical feature of all the areas.

Frome Valley System

The Frome and its northern tributaries, the Hooke, Sydling Water, and the Cerne, form a branching network of valleys extending to the western and northern chalk escarpments. The two southern tributaries, the South Winterborne River and the Chaldon River are less extensive and more isolated. The South Winterborne flows eastwards across the chalklands to join the River Frome to the east of Dorchester and the Chaldon River dissects the north side of Chaldon Down, the southern limit of the Dorset chalklands.

The geological structure of the chalk becomes more diverse towards its western limits, with extensive outcrops of Upper Greensand within the valleys, this is especially evident in the branching valleys of the Upper Frome and Hooke rivers, which have an undulating landform and many surface streams. The upper section of these valleys are generally wide with indented, gentle side-slopes.

The Sydling Water and Cerne valley systems lie further east, where Upper Chalk is a stronger geological influence. These valleys have deep, trough-shaped cross-sections, with steep side-slopes and a wide, flat valley floor. The valley sides are indented, with smooth, rounded hollows and many steep coombes. An abrupt break in slope indicates the division between the valley landscape and that of the chalk uplands emphasised by a change in land use from arable fields to rough scrub and grassland. These two valleys are quite close together and have carved the chalk ridge separating them so that only a narrow, branching upland divide remains. The landforms seem crisply sculpted and deliberately carved, especially when the sharp breaks of slope are in strong sunlight. These valleys become narrower and more enclosed towards the south and they typically have a very constricted, narrow cross-section at the confluence with the principal channel of the River Frome. In these narrower sections, the river often flows within a deep channel, forming a narrow valley within the main valley and leaving flat terraces on either side of the river corridor.

Different patterns of land use within the valleys generally emphasise and define its landform. This is particularly noticeable in the deep valleys of the River Cerne and Sydling Water where there is open grassland and scrub on the steep slopes of the coombes, arable fields on the side slopes and a combination of arable and pasture fields on the flat valley floor. Long hedgerows often occur at the division between the grazed slopes and the arable fields within the

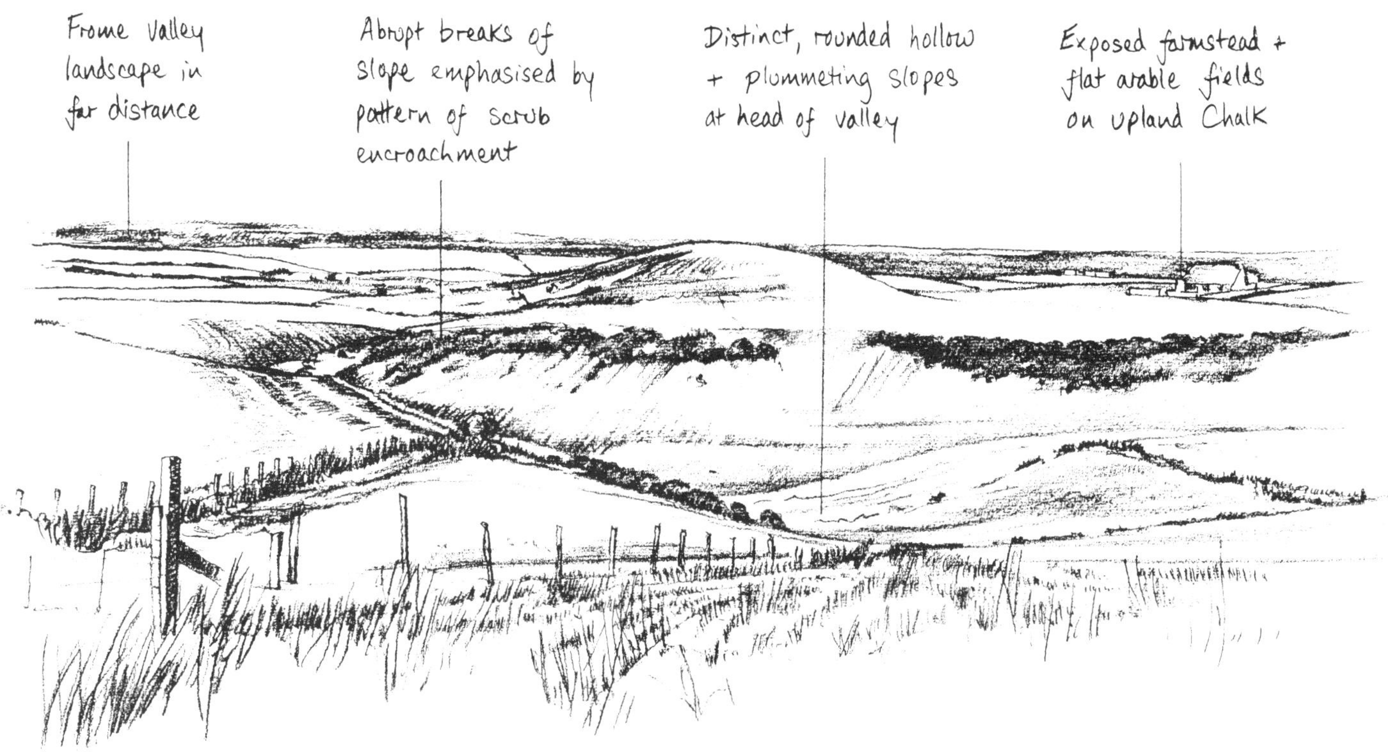

CHALK VALLEYS: *The Head of the Chaldon Valley System from Chaldon Down.* GR 772816.

valley, following the contours and emphasising the landform. The fields usually have straight hedgerows, containing many hedgerow trees on the valley floor but relatively few on the side slopes. There are often blocks of old coppice woodland on the valley slopes. When these have strong, definitive edges they stand out clearly against the surrounding pale fields and become local landmarks along the valley sides. They are usually deciduous, with many areas of relic hazel coppice.

With the exception of the western valleys of the River Hooke and the Upper Frome, these chalk valleys have a simple settlement pattern with villages beside the chalk streams on the valley floor, linked by a single, long road, following the alignment of the valley. Villages within narrow sections of the valley, such as Sydling St Nicholas and Godmanstone, usually have a linear form, while those in a more spacious setting have a clustered form. The village of Cerne Abbas is an example. This village is associated with a famous landmark – the Cerne Abbas Giant a figure carved into the chalk on the side of the valley just north of the village.

The western valleys have a more scattered settlement pattern, with a branching network of lanes. Most of the villages have a clustered form and there are numerous hamlets and small farmsteads. In all these valleys, there are more copses and hedgerow trees in the vicinity of the villages and farmsteads. There is a strong sense of enclosure

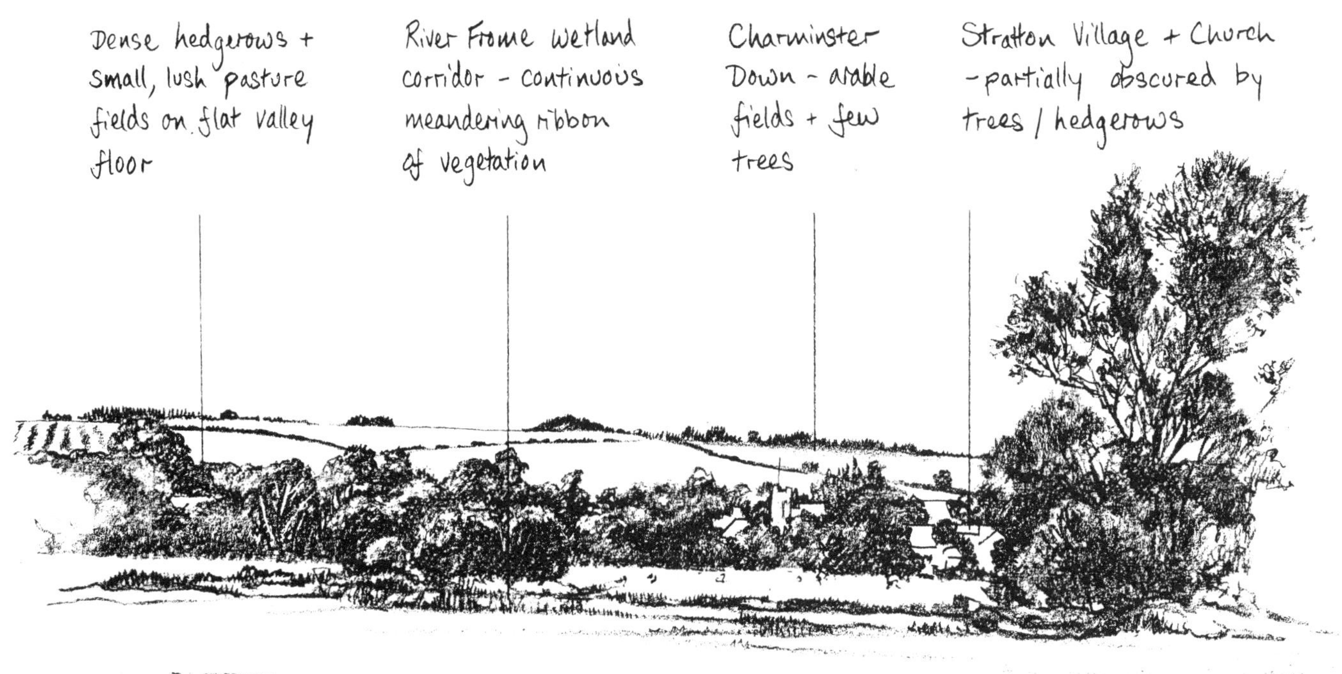

CHALK VALLEYS: *The Frome Valley at Stratton.* GR 649934.

and refuge in the deepest valleys, such as that of the River Cerne, even at points where the valley is relatively broad. This feeling is heightened by the contrast between the valley landscape and that of the more exposed chalk uplands which surround it and by the fact that some of these valleys are invisible from a distance. The western valleys have a more verdant, secluded, intimate landscape which has a continuity with the surrounding woodlands on the western chalk escarpment and the chalk uplands. The landscape of these valleys has a relatively small scale, while the deeper valleys to the east have a more dominant, powerful landscape.

Piddle Valley System

The River Piddle flows across the middle of the Dorset chalklands, from the northern escarpment at Buckland Newton to Puddletown, where it turns and flows south-eastwards towards Poole Harbour. The main tributaries are the Milborne, the Cheselbourne and the Devil's Brook (in the Dewlish Valley).

Each of these valleys has a gentle, v-shaped, cross-section which becomes progressively narrower and steeper towards the escarpment to the north. They are generally deeper and more sharply defined than those associated with the River Stour to the east. They have a branching structure, with many dry valleys joining the main system at right angles. These are usually quite short and end in rounded coombes. They typically have pastures on the valley floor and small arable fields on the side slopes so there is some continuity in land use between the surrounding chalk uplands and the valley. Sometimes only the denser tree cover and a strip of lush pasture indicates the presence of a valley, especially along its lower reaches where the narrow valley landscape seems to slip between the broad ridges of arable fields. In general the valleys associated with the River Piddle are fairly open, with few large blocks of woodland, although these occur more frequently on the steeper slopes near to the escarpment. The obvious exception is the northern part of the Milborne Valley, on the Milton Abbey Estate. Here the break of slope between the valley and upland landscapes is defined by dense woodlands which extend around the head of each coombe, emphasising the dramatic landform and creating a fine landscape composition. The small estate of Dewlish House, just below the village of Dewlish, also has tracts of woodland on the slopes of Park Hill, providing a sense of enclosure in this relatively steep section. The woodlands are predominantly beech, but they also contain some oak.

There are few isolated trees on the upper slopes, but the fields on the valley floor are sheltered by belts of hedgerow trees. Groups of trees also cluster around the many villages and farms and often indicate the location of the stream corridor winding within the pasture fields.

These valleys are all well settled and villages tend to have a linear form, in parallel with the road and river on the valley floor. Larger, clustered villages such as Puddletown, occur in the wider, shallow valley on the margins of the chalk. The relatively shallow topography on this part of the chalk means that there is a dense network of roads linking villages across the upland chalk divides as well as along the valleys.

All the chalk valleys associated with the River Piddle have an unobtrusive scale and a secluded character. The verdant pastures and clustered trees are confined to a narrow strip of land which has long been a focus for settlement. The surrounding open arable fields make these narrow valleys seem especially important as hospitable destinations in an otherwise exposed landscape.

Stour Valley System

The Stour flows from the Blackmoor Vale in North Dorset to Christchurch Harbour, cutting through the chalk at Shillingstone to Sturminster Marshall. This is the broadest of the Dorset chalk valleys, with gentle side slopes. The river meanders on a wide, almost flat valley floor. The principal tributaries are the Winterborne to the west, and the Tarrant, Allen and Crane to the east. Their valleys are gently winding and typically have shallow profiles, although there are some abrupt steep slopes within short sections of the valley. 'The Cliff' in the Tarrant Valley is one such example, where the Tarrant has eroded a relatively elevated upland divide just to the south of the village of Tarrant Monkton.

There is typically a gentle transition between the landscape of the chalk uplands and that of these eastern chalk valleys, as a patchwork of arable fields extends across the boundary between the two different landscape types, becoming slightly smaller in scale within the valley. The valley floor is usually entirely devoted to pastures on either side of the meandering river channel. The river is often flanked by groups of trees, but sometimes has an open character, with pastures extending right up to the riverbanks. Where they occur dark blocks of woodland are prominent landscape features and show up clearly in a rather gentle landscape, characterised by subtle colours. The most extensive blocks of woodland are associated with the designed parkland landscapes at Moor Crichel in the Allen Valley, Tarrant Gunville in the Tarrant Valley and Bryanston in the Stour Valley.

The ruins of Knowlton Church are an enigmatic landmark on the slopes of the Allen Valley. The village with which it was associated finally disappeared in the eighteenth century. There remain numerous small villages within the valleys, sited on the outer margins of the river floodplain. They usually have a straggling linear form or are clustered at the entrance to the estates. Narrow, twisting roads link the villages along the valley floor but there are also often straight roads directly across the valleys – the slopes are so slight that they are no impediment to communication.

The Stour Valley is busy and well-settled, constantly humming with the noise of traffic. Its smaller tributary valleys seem more isolated and remote. They have a tranquil, secluded atmosphere. The pastures and villages along the valley floor have a domestic scale and provide a contrast to the neater, more functional surrounding patchwork of arable fields. There is a strong sense of depth since long views up and down the valleys are characterised by a series of overlapping horizons, emphasised by belts of trees which measure the scale and form of the valley.

THE KEY CHARACTERISTIC FEATURES OF THE CHALK VALLEYS ARE:–

- Valley systems share a strong central line with short side branches, frequently dry, and display a wide variety of profiles.
- Landform contrasts are often emphasised by agricultural patterns, with arable cultivation on gentle slopes, rough grazing on steep valley sides and pasture on the flat valley floors.
- Smaller scale patchwork of fields and hedgerows than on the upland chalk.
- Traces of old watermeadow systems in various stages of decay.
- Valleys have more trees than chalk uplands, with patches of woodland and winding ribbons of trees along the stream corridor.
- Settlements, often built of flint and brick, are concentrated on valley floors.
- Communications follow main valleys.
- Secluded, sheltered character.

MANAGEMENT GUIDANCE

i The remaining areas of chalk grassland on the valley sides are increasingly subject to scrub encroachment. These should be conserved through scrub clearance and management through grazing. The prevention of scrub encroachment should be concentrated on those areas where chalk grasslands are of ecological importance and where the composition and unity of an especially fine chalkland scene would be enhanced.

ii The valleys are generally characterised by attractive winding streams. The streams are typically fringed by copses, narrow belts of trees and scattered trees, often willows. It is important that management is directed towards the conservation of these features, particularly as many trees are suffering from old age and natural regeneration is being prevented by the proximity of arable farming to the stream edges. Consideration should be given to the pollarding of willows to revitalise them.

iii The establishment of broader stream-side corridors should be sought, with a rich assemblage of habitats, including grassland, woodland and the regeneration of water meadows.

iv The coombes and heads of the valley have a predominantly southerly aspect and are particularly important in ecological as well as landscape terms, frequently running up to the escarpment and giving an all encompassing feel to the landscape. Management should be aimed at sustaining these characteristics.

v Where woodlands occur in the valleys, they are particularly important in creating diversity of character and their protection and management is therefore significant. Hazel coppice has significant amenity and wildlife interest and reversing the decline in regular management should be a priority.

vi The care and protection of water quality should be an important aspect in all management plans and activities.

vii Some chalk streams suffer from decreased flows. Water management strategies should ensure that the visual and ecological contributions these streams make to the landscape are not lost.

Plate 1

1. Beaminster. The town nestles in a fold in the landscape, around it small woodlands and heavily wooded hedgerows mix easily within the medium sized, mostly pasture, fields.

2. Looking west across the West Dorset farmland and Marshwood Vale. The high ridge between the Vale and the sea is crowned with an isolated clump of woodland, lower down the hedgerow trees stand out amongst the grass fields of the Vale.

Plate 2

Plate 3

3. Looking east from Golden Cap. The mixture of pasture and arable fields runs straight up to the coast, which has eroded back over the years.

4. Looking down a dry coombe into the Cerne valley. Note the streamside vegetation, the change from arable fields to unimproved grassland up the valley side, and the ancient monument on the steeper valley slopes.

Plate 4

Plate 5

5. Dry valley cut into the escarpment at Fontmell Down. Note the improved grassland in the valley bottom, the scrub on the left hand slope and the woodland on the right hand slope.

6. Chalk upland east of Nether Cerne. Large fields with thin hedgerows, and geometrically shaped woodland.

Plate 6

Plate 7

7. The Bride Valley looking towards The Knoll. A mixture of field sizes with well wooded hedgerows.

8. Looking from Abbotsbury Castle towards Portland. Note the rough grassland and scrub running up to St Catherine's Chapel, with old cultivation terraces on the hill slope. The Chesil Beach separates the open sea from the narrow waters of The Fleet. Portland presents its typical wedge-shaped outline.

Plate 8

Plate 9

9. Chapman's Pool. Tumbled limestone cliffs in the foreground contrasting with the softer shales on the western side of the bay.

10. Looking along the Purbeck Chalk Ridge towards Corfe Castle. Notice how the unimproved slopes of the Chalk Ridge merge into the arable and pasture fields of Corfe Valley. The colour of the village of Corfe is derived from the local stone.

Plate 10

Plate 11

11. Looking across Godlingston Heath towards Poole Harbour. A mixture of scrub and rough woodland merging into heathland in the middle distance, and in the far distance the Poole/Bournemouth conurbation.

12. East Dorset Heathland. A typical mixture of open heathland merging into improved farmland with conifer plantations in the distance.

Plate 12

Plate 13

13. Frome Valley. The flat valley floor is used primarily for pasture and beyond, on the rising valley sides, arable fields and woodland.

14. The Avon. A wide river set in a broad flood plain with meadow and pasture on either side with dense streamside vegetation.

Plate 14

Plate 15

15. Traditionally managed hay meadow at Kingcombe. The wide range of flowers gives areas of colour within a generally green landscape.

16. Heathland/scrub mosaic. A typical mixture of heathland and developing pine scrub which is found in many parts of Eastern Dorset.

Plate 16

17. View from Bulbarrow, looking across the North Scarp Hills towards the Blackmoor Vale. A generally green countryside due to the predominance of pasture farming with numerous hedgerow trees dominating the landscape.

Plate 17

Plate 18

18. Managed hazel coppice. Young growth from the newly cut coppice stools in the foreground, with the standard timber trees in the background.

19. Fallow deer at Stock Gaylard. A formally designed parkland landscape.

Plate 19

Plate 20

20. Ashmore. Note the differing use of traditional materials in the buildings around the pond, local stone and thatch, and more recent brick, flint and tile.

21. Drystone wall at Durlston. A typical boundary in those parts of the County where stone is common.

Plate 21

Plate 22

22. Corfe Valley from Whiteway Hill. The modern post and rail fencing manages to fit within the landscape.

23. Metal fence at Stock Gaylard. A superficially inappropriate material which does not intrude due to the lightness of construction and its use within the context of a formal landscaped park.

Plate 23

viii Surviving features of the old water meadow system are worthy of preservation, and consideration should be given to restoring water meadows to working order.

ix The hedgerows and field patterns should be maintained, hedges should be managed and replanted as necessary.

x The character of the villages should be sustained through village appraisals and the use of traditional materials and designs.

SOUTH DORSET LANDSCAPES

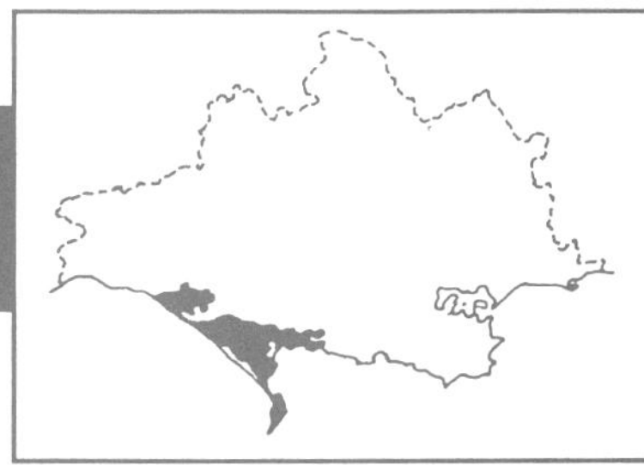

122km² 4.6%

This section covers the South Dorset coast between the villages of Burton Bradstock and Osmington Mills including the lowlands north of Weymouth and the Bride Valley. The southern chalk escarpment forms an open, cliff-like ridge, enclosing this area from the north. A second lower escarpment, that of the Portland Limestone, occurs just south of the chalk escarpment and forms the complex, broken relief of the Osmington area.

Further south, the limestone escarpment is more spectacular where it rears up to form the wedge-shaped, rocky slab of the Isle of Portland, with a summit of almost 140 metres. This is a peninsula rather than a true island since it is connected to the mainland by the long slender shingle ridge of Chesil Beach.

The lowlands between the chalk escarpment and the coast consist of a series of broad, gentle hog-back limestone ridges which alternate with lowland clay vales to form a minor ridge and valley relief.

The valley of the River Bride has a slightly different context and a more varied set of influences. It represents a transition between the West Dorset farmland character type and that of the Weymouth lowlands.

The coastal grassland landscape area occurs where the slopes of the chalk and limestone ridges are directly exposed to the sea. These grasslands extend from the mouth of the River Bride at Burton Freshwater to the western end of The Fleet at Abbotsbury.

St Catherine's Hill, Abbotsbury.

The South Dorset landscapes can be sub-divided into three landscape character areas:

- **SOUTH DORSET LOWLANDS**
- **COASTAL GRASSLANDS**
- **ISLE OF PORTLAND AND CHESIL BEACH**

South Dorset Lowlands

The South Dorset Lowlands are divided into two sub-areas, the Weymouth lowlands and the valley of the River Bride, which are separated by an outlier of the chalk. The Weymouth lowlands lie between the shores of The Fleet and the southern chalk escarpment. The Bride valley is also bordered to the north by the southern chalk escarpment, but lies further west. There is a gradual transition to the West Dorset farmland landscape towards the western end of the valley.

Weymouth Lowlands

The lowlands between Weymouth and the chalk escarpment are divided evenly into a series of limestone hog-back

Rough, hummocky grazing land on steep escarpment slopes

Broad patchwork of fields extends up over the long ridges.

Chesters Hill

Linton Hill

SOUTH DORSET LOWLANDS: *From the south Chalk escarpment at Abbotsbury Plain looking south towards Linton HIll. GR 586857.*

SOUTH DORSET LOWLANDS: *From Green Hill looking towards Bowleaze cove and the Isle of Portland.* GR 695844.

ridges, separated by broad clay vales. The ridges and valleys are always of similar proportions and follow an east-west alignment so this lowland landscape is effectively divided into a sequence of alternate strips until it meets the indented, low coastline behind The Fleet. This lowland area feels quite protected from the influence of strong coastal winds and waves, partially because of the high chalk escarpment, but also because Chesil Beach is an effective buffer which bears the full brunt of coastal battering. The inner coastline bordering The Fleet therefore resembles the margins of a lake with the mosaic of fields and hedgerows extending right down to the water's edge. Further east the landscape becomes more complex and varied with a smaller scale and more undulating terrain. In the Osmington area the indented Portland Limestone escarpment outcrops below that of the chalk to give a beautiful undulating coastal landscape of woodlands, small fields and villages, enclosed by the curving arm of the high chalk escarpment. There are spectacular views to the Isle of Portland, framed by the coastal hills.

The broad ridge and valley landscape of the Weymouth lowlands is characterised by large fields, with straight hedgerows, forming a broad patchwork which extends right over the ridges so the landscape seems continuous and the height of the ridges is effectively diminished. This patchwork breaks down at the foot of the southern Chalk Escarpment where steep slopes with rough, hummocky grass and stunted gorse bushes contrast abruptly with the agricultural landscape below. There is mixed farming throughout the lowlands but with a predominance of arable fields on the shallower slopes within the valleys. The steeper valleys near Osmington are predominantly pasture, with grazing, woodland and some scrub on the upper slopes. The fields and woodlands have organic shapes and the hedgerow trees form loose ribbons which interconnect with the patches of woodland. The fields are generally hummocky in character, with rough texture. Many are used as horse pasture.

The Weymouth Lowlands have a subtle, homogeneous character with very few abrupt transitions. The urban areas and the busy Weymouth – Dorchester corridor are inevitably intrusive since this is not a landscape which can absorb such activity easily. The landscape seems very spacious, and has little enclosure, except along the foot of the chalk escarpment. The Osmington area has a more wooded, secluded atmosphere and provides an important contrast in an area where there are typically broader-scale landscape patterns.

Bride Valley

The River Bride flows within a broad fairly shallow valley with an asymmetrical profile. It is flanked by the chalk escarpment to the north and a lower limestone ridge to the south. There are several prominent landmarks such as The Knoll, a greensand outcrop with a distinctive small block of trees on its summit, and Abbotsbury Castle on part of the coastal ridge which is linked to the chalk escarpment further to the east. These summits are an indication that this valley represents a transitional landscape between the West Dorset farmland and the broader, blander Weymouth lowlands to the east. The lower reaches of the valley have the irregular, undulating landform and pastures of the West Dorset farmland landscape type and the greensand outcrop of Shipton Hill is a prominent summit overlooking the valley. This landform gradually smoothes out as the valley becomes more fully enclosed by the chalk escarpment and the Bride Valley has a more varied landform than that of the Weymouth lowlands.

Within the Bride Valley there are some surprisingly large fields enclosed by hedgerows, but stone walls are also important features in some places. There is mixed farming with a predominance of arable land on the inland slopes of the coastal ridge and steep grazing on the chalk escarpment. This valley has a denser cover of trees than those in the lowlands north of Weymouth, and there are many blocks of woodland which stand out clearly against the mosaic of fields. Hedgerow trees tend to occur in dense belts, leaving extensive areas which appear very open. In general, tree cover increases towards the river and around the small villages on the valley floor. They form strong, legible lines in the landscape.

Individual woodlands, gnarled, single hedgerow oaks and the church towers in the villages of Litton Cheney and Puncknowle are important local landmarks within the valley. There is a particularly diverse range of trees including horse chestnut, lime, oak, ash, sycamore and a great deal of beech. Glimpsed views to the sea are possible when there is a side valley, as at Swyre, and towards the mouth of the river. Most villages and roads are within the valleys rather than on the ridges.

The Bride Valley has a balanced, harmonious landscape with few major intrusive features and a series of gentle transitions which give it a subtle diversity. The landforms are so even that the occasional high point, such as The Knoll, is clearly legible. This is a landscape of wide panoramic views and there is very little sense of enclosure since the valley is so broad that the chalk escarpment tends to provide a backdrop rather than enclosure. It is a tranquil, gentle landscape which seems consistent and logical with strong landforms that structure rather than dominate the lowland.

THE KEY CHARACTERISTIC FEATURES OF THE SOUTH DORSET LOWLANDS ARE:–

- Broad ridge and valley landscape which follows an east-west alignment.
- Enclosed to the north by the southern Chalk Escarpment
- Horizon formed by the smooth profiles of the broad, hog-back ridges.
- Patchwork of geometric fields widens out to form larger fields on the open ridgetops.
- Mixture of boundary types, hedges, walls and fences.
- Smaller-scale, undulating relief occurs where valleys cut back to the chalk escarpment near Osmington and Littlebredy.
- Mixed farming, but higher proportion of arable fields on shallower slopes.
- Villages on valley floor and at foot of the chalk escarpment.

MANAGEMENT GUIDANCE

Weymouth Lowlands

i Existing woodlands over the area should be conserved and managed.

ii Further woodland planting should be concentrated on the fringes of Weymouth to diffuse views of the urban area, screen tourist developments and soften the impact of existing power lines.

iii The scale of the landscape should be maintained by maintaining the existing field sizes.

iv Where hedgerows are an important feature in defining the patchwork of fields these should be conserved and supplemented with new planting, particularly on the lower slopes.

v Where stone walls are a feature they should be repaired, and in places rebuilt, using local stone.

vi The slopes of the low hills bordering The Fleet would benefit from the conversion of existing arable fields to pasture land, with occasional copses. Because this area is important in ecological terms, a special management study would be justified.

The Bride Valley

i The Bride Valley is more wooded than the Weymouth Lowlands. Any new broad-leaved woodland plantings should reinforce existing blocks of woodland to create bold masses, primarily concentrated on the side slopes of the valley, following field patterns and leaving the tops of the ridges clear to allow views of their undulating profile.

ii There should be no large woodland planting towards the head of the valley where there is a transition to a more open downland character.

iii The valley bottom could be enriched with streamside planting and the extension of grassland on the lower slopes.

iv Along the edges of villages, which form such special visual features along the valley, particular care needs to be taken to ensure trees frame fine views and provide visual balance and diversity without excessive screening.

v Where hedgerows are an important feature in defining the patchwork of fields these should be conserved and supplemented with new planting, particularly on the lower slopes.

Coastal Grasslands

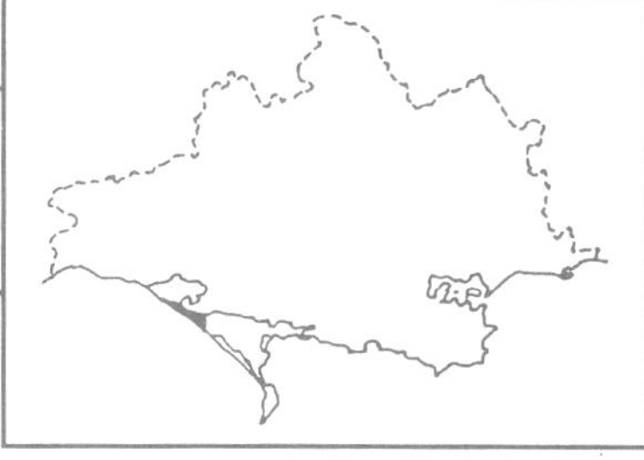

This coarse grassland is found on the exposed south-west facing slopes of the ridge separating the Bride Valley from the sea and on the lower slopes of the chalk escarpment where it meets the coast near Abbotsbury. It is a landscape which tends to occur in small patches whenever grassland is fully exposed to the full force of coastal elements, but it is only identified as a landscape character area in its own right when it is backed by a ridge which effectively divides it from the landscape inland. Typically there is an uneven slope from a shingle beach to the steep, south facing ridge behind.

COASTAL GRASSLANDS: *The coastal grassland and beach near West Bexington – looking east along Chesil Beach.* GR 504886.

The coastal strip is rough grazing land. There is a transition from long coarse grass, with clumps of bramble and gorse, to shorter grass with patches of scrub on the steeper ridge behind the beach. Wire fences occasionally supplement the thin, gappy and windblown hedgerows. Between Burton Bradstock and West Bexington the land immediately behind the beach is wet and marshy, with several substantial reed-beds. Further reed-beds surround Abbotsbury Swannery, at the head of The Fleet. There are few trees and no landforms blocking the panoramic views along the coast, so the curve of Chesil Beach and the headlands of West Dorset and the Isle of Portland are clearly visible. This landscape is very empty with little permanent settlement. However there are several car parks with associated signs and fences giving an untidy, almost urban impression.

The erosive force of the elements is very evident and evokes a strong sense of exposure while, at the same time, creating feelings of insecurity and vulnerability.

THE KEY CHARACTERISTIC FEATURES OF THE COASTAL GRASSLANDS ARE:–

- Exposed, open, windswept grassland, with no trees and stunted, scrubby hedgerows.
- Backed by steep ridges to the north, and long views out to sea.
- Gradual transition from patches of scrub and long, coarse grass on the uneven terrain behind the beach, to shorter turf on the steeper slopes inland.
- Reed-beds on the landward side of the beach.
- Sparsely populated, some seasonal tourist facilities.

MANAGEMENT GUIDANCE

i The pastures behind the beach are generally unkempt and of poor agricultural quality. Grazing is essential to keep scrub, principally gorse and bramble, at bay so that the potential for long, sweeping views along the coastline is maintained.

ii There is much scope for improvements to car parks, signage and fencing. Structures should be designed in a simple style, in keeping with the exposed coastal environment.

iii On the inland ridges exposed to the sea existing patches of scrub should be kept in check by a programme of traditional grazing, although this scrub encroachment seems to be less of a threat than on the chalk grassland away from the coast.

iv Reed-beds should be managed both for nature conservation and to provide a traditional thatching material.

Isle of Portland and Chesil Beach

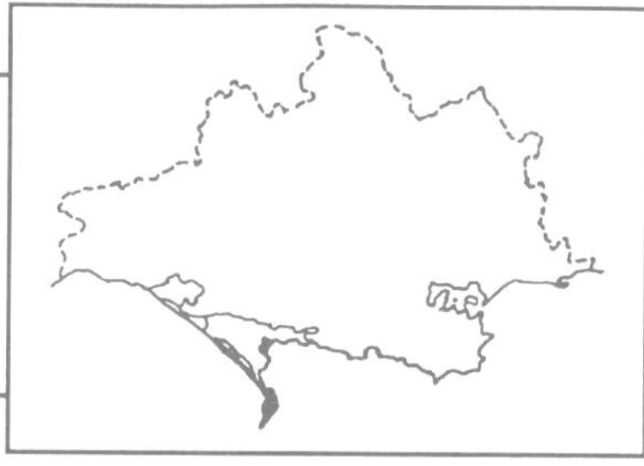

The Isle of Portland is a slanting outcrop of limestone which forms a dramatic peninsula of rock jutting into the English Channel at the end of Chesil Beach. The highest point is at the northern end (140 metres) where there are steep, rugged cliffs with immense rocks piled up against them. The cliffs become progressively lower towards the southern point where the land is only a few feet above the sea. There are long panoramic views out to sea and back towards the Dorset coastline. The topography of much of the peninsula is very rugged and deeply scarred with quarries and extensive spoil heaps spread across the surface. Although much of the land seems derelict, some of the quarry areas are just dormant whilst others are listed as Sites of Special Scientific Interest. With predominantly stone buildings, stone walls, and large chunks of stone used to mark tracks, road edges, and car parks, Portland stone has been the unifying feature across the Island for centuries. In 1880 Thomas Hardy noted that:

> *Slabs of stone [were] the common materials for walls, roof, floor, pig-sty, stable-manger, door-scraper and garden-stile.*

The stone is a light grey colour, whitish in places, so it stands out very clearly and is the most dominant feature of this exposed landscape. There are very few trees so the skyline is very open.

The small fields are enclosed by stone walls and the rough bramble hedges which have grown over them. These stone walls are a feature of the island and, away from the roads, tend to be very poor condition, often obscured by mound of bramble, and are frequently supplemented with rough wire fences. Further south towards Portland Bill, the network of walls almost disappears and there are a few, extensive pastures, previously grazed by Portland sheep, whilst the fields on Portland Bill are one of the few open field systems still working in Britain. A rare and important historical feature.

The lack of trees and ubiquitous stone walls were graphically described by Thomas Gerard in 1625, though happily the inhabitants of the island are now supplied with a better sources of fuel!

> *On the toppe you may see the whole Island lieing verrie flatte, in compasse about seven Miles; the Grounde verie good for Corne, and indifferent Pasture; but soe destitute of Woode and Fuell, that the Inhabitants are glad to burne their Cowe Dung, beeing first dried against Stone Walls, with which their Groundes are enclosed alltogether.*

The cliffs, undercliffs and abandoned coastal quarries on the Isle of Portland are extremely rich in wildflowers, lichens and invertebrates, including several very rare species such as the Portland Spurge and the cretaceous form of the Silver Studded Blue butterfly. There is very little original unimproved limestone grassland but long abandoned quarry spoil heaps maintain a very rich turf of typical limestone grasses and wildflowers.

The scenery of the Isle of Portland is remarkable for its context rather than its beauty and has a ruggedly distinctive, untidy, character. The cliffs are very dramatic and there is an exhilarating feeling of being on the edge of the country.

ISLE OF PORTLAND: *Looking south towards Portland Bill from Southwell.* GR 694705.

Portland is a memorable place and a powerful contrast to the rest of Dorset. The landscape can feel quite desolate even though it is so well settled and there is general disorder and a characteristic lack of rhythm, especially around the urban areas and quarries.

The buildings have a stark, exposed character, even in the villages of Weston, Easton and Southwell densely clustered together towards the middle of the island, whilst isolated buildings, such as St George's church, are truly dramatic landscape elements. At the northern end of the island the massive Verne Citadel dominates the scene, giving a stark reminder of Portland's penal past. Even though the navy has now left, Portland has many traces of its military history, from its medieval and Tudor castles, through the Victorian defences, to the remains of the Second World War 'Mulberry' harbour.

The landscape is windswept and exposed to the natural elements. The sea and sky become progressively more dominant towards Portland Bill where the buildings seem huddled and vulnerable on the final ledge before the slab of Portland Bill slips into the sea. This is not a landscape where scars can be masked so there is a strong sense of history and continuity with the industrial past.

The popular view from Portland Heights is dominated by Chesil Beach, a massive ridge of pebbles, 15 metres high and between 150 and 200 hundred metres wide, which runs roughly parallel to the coast for eight miles until it joins the coastline at Abbotsbury, then continues along the coast to West Bay. The very regular, almost artificial, appearance of an obviously natural feature, makes it one of the most unusual landscapes of the Dorset Coast, emphasised when walking along it by the curious grading in pebble sizes, small at the north-western end, large at the south-eastern. Between it and the mainland lies The Fleet, a unique brackish water lagoon of high scientific value. It is tidal and has many estuarine characteristics. Important populations of swans, terns, widgeon and other birds colonise the area around Chesil Beach, especially the sheltered water near Abbotsbury where there is a long-established swannery. It is a particularly unusual and important site for marine plants, such as *Zostera*, especially in the sub littoral zones. The shingle bar is noted for its special lichens, mosses and flowering plants.

THE KEY CHARACTERISTIC FEATURES OF PORTLAND ARE:–

- Dramatic, wedge-shaped peninsula of limestone rock, with prominent cliffs on all sides.
- Unique coastal landmark with long, panoramic views out to sea and back to the rest of the Dorset coast.
- The local pale grey Portland Limestone is a dominant visual influence, on natural exposures, quarry faces, field walls and buildings.
- Exposed rocky landscape, heavily pitted with quarries.
- Considerable evidence of past stone working and military activities.
- Small fields, divided by stone walls.
- Minimal tree cover and only a few scrubby bramble hedges.
- A sensitive skyline, easily disrupted by buildings, signs, overhead wires and industrial artefacts.

THE KEY CHARACTERISTIC FEATURES OF CHESIL BEACH ARE:–

- Long shingle beach with water on both sides.
- Feelings of exposure, grandeur, and permanence mixed with instability as the shore changes with the tides and the shifting shingle moves beneath the feet.
- Wild, natural feeling with little signs of human activity.
- Unusual feeling of natural uniformity, on both the grand scale of the long, almost straight, beach and the smaller scale, the pebbles being naturally graded so that they are all the same size at any one place.

MANAGEMENT GUIDANCE

Portland

i The limestone is such a strong influence, along with the side effects of quarrying, that caring for the visual character of Portland should recognise its rugged and rough texture which, together with its massive scale, conspire against any great neatness and tidiness.

ii Stone walls are an important component of Portland's visual character and should be maintained and repaired, using local stone. Encroaching bramble should be kept in check so that the stark visual quality of the stone wall boundaries is retained.

iii The existing ancient field patterns should be preserved.

iv The industrial heritage should be recognised, and the urge to 'tidy up' old sites should be resisted until a detailed study of the particular area has been made.

v Protect areas of unimproved limestone pasture and cliff-top from intensive farming practices.

vi The older quarries have nature conservation value as well as a characteristic weathered, rugged quality, which need sensitive consideration and handling in any proposed reclamation schemes.

vii Design of buildings and details should echo the rocky character of the area. 'Anywhere' designs are particularly inappropriate.

viii Owing to the maritime exposure trees are not a characteristic feature of Portland, so low, native, salt and wind tolerant shrubs would be more appropriate than new tree planting.

Chesil Beach

i The unique uncluttered appearance, dramatic natural structure, and wild character of the Beach should be respected.

ii Additional buildings and parking areas would be inappropriate and existing facilities should be managed to integrate them better into the landscape.

iii Where there are potential conflicts between the conservation of the wildlife and special qualities of the Beach, and recreational uses, the balance should be in favour of conservation.

iv Where there are public access points to the Beach, management plans, such as that for Ferrybridge, are an appropriate way to resolve potential conflicts.

ISLE OF PURBECK LANDSCAPES

77km² 2.9%

Here the Isle of Purbeck is defined as the south-east of Dorset between the coast and the northern edge of the chalk ridge which extends west to east from Rings Hill to Ballard Down. The lowland heathlands around Poole Harbour are described within the section on the East Dorset and Poole Basin Landscapes. Correctly speaking, the Isle of Purbeck is a peninsula rather than an island, but this title is an apt description for such a distinctive corner of Dorset. There is an extraordinary geological variety within a relatively small area, with each formation having a characteristic landscape associated with it. A dramatic wall of chalk, that was once continuous with the Isle of Wight, divides the heathlands to the north from the Isle of Purbeck. The chalk stacks of Old Harry Rocks are the resistant remnants of this lost coastline, breached and drowned as a result of a rise in sea-level in post-glacial times, with deep bays at Studland and Swanage on either side.

The Corfe valley, sandwiched between the chalk ridge and the elevated limestone plateau to the south, is formed in the soft clays and sands. In the south-east the limestone plateau dips steadily until it breaks off sharply to form rugged coastal cliffs, incised by deep valleys. Further west it narrows to a thin ridge, an inland cliff, enclosing the undulating clay lowlands and indented coastline towards Kimmeridge.

The diverse and valuable geological resources here have resulted in a long history of extractive industry. Purbeck 'marble' is a polishable, fossily limestone which has been quarried on the plateau since Roman times. In the Middle Ages it was principally used for tombs, fonts and effigies, until it was largely replaced by alabaster in the fifteenth century. The outskirts of Swanage were the most intensively worked Purbeck stone quarries operating from 1700 to 1905, using shafts which reached 120 feet down. These spread west towards Langton Matravers. Small quarries operating today have reverted to open-cast methods. Cliff quarries, at Winspit and Seacombe, no longer operate. Shale, clay, alum and most recently oil have all been extracted from the local rocks and there is evidence that the Romans manufactured salt at the ancient industrial centre of Kimmeridge Bay. 'Kimmeridge Coal', a thin black shale in the Kimmeridge Clay, was quarried and carved into jewellery and other decorative items from the late Bronze Age to the Roman period. The 'nodding donkey', lifting oil to the surface on the coast at Broad Bench, is the only indication of modern extractive industry on this coastline. The chalk ridge itself has been quarried since Victorian times, when pits were dug along the foot of the slope, especially on the south side between Corfe and Godlingston. The chalk was used for fertiliser, the manufacture of cement and the processing of ball clay. A brickworks was established in the seventeenth century at Ulwell, to the north of Swanage, using clays from the Wealden Beds, which still produces specialist bricks.

The Isle of Purbeck Landscapes can be divided into four main landscape character areas which relate closely to its geological structure:

- PURBECK CHALK RIDGE
- CORFE VALLEY
- PURBECK LIMESTONE PLATEAU
- WEST PURBECK COAST

Purbeck Chalk Ridge

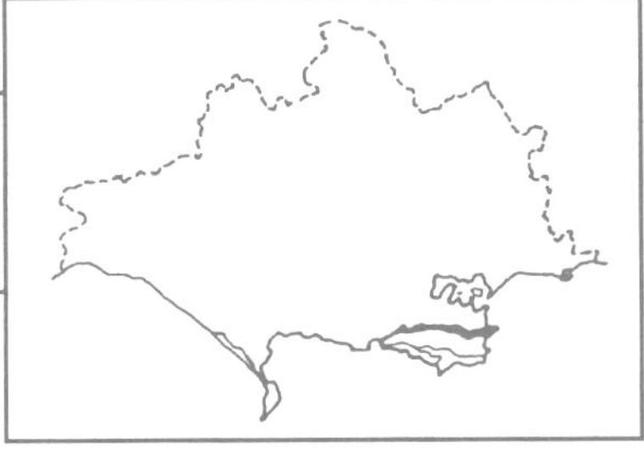

The underlying chalk strata slope at an acute angle, creating a steep, prominent ridge, which arches eastwards from Rings Hill, forming an elevated spine across the Isle of Purbeck, separating the secluded Corfe valley landscape from the heathlands to the north. The top is relatively flat and the landform has the typical smooth, convex curves of a chalk upland. This dramatic barrier, broken only by the minor Ulwell valley and the deep, narrow valley of the River Corfe, flowing north towards Poole Harbour, is guarded by the ruin of Corfe Castle at what was once an important strategic gateway to the Isle.

The clear silhouette, un-camouflaged by trees, has a bold dominant scale and becomes higher, more massive, yet indented towards Godlingston Hill. At the eastern end of Ballard Down the grassland ridge breaks abruptly into a striking white coastal cliff face on the north side of Swanage Bay. The western part of the ridge becomes narrower and more undulating. Ridgeway Hill and Creech Barrow, a steep conical summit on the north side, are prominent features. Here an outcrop of greensand is indicated by a large patch of heather and bracken.

The ridgetops are a mixture of arable, ley, and open chalk grassland, with extensive patches of scrub on the slopes. This scrub becomes more dominant towards the east and is especially prominent on Brenscombe Hill. The north slopes of Ballard Down, at the east end of the ridge, have a more gently sloping profile and a patchwork of arable fields extends almost to the ridgetop. Elsewhere the steep slopes on the north side are densely wooded. Many are semi-natural ancient beech and oak woodlands, of historic and ecological importance. At the foot of the ridge, a narrow band of productive farmland separates the chalk from the heathlands to the north. On the south side, the small-scale patchwork of fields and small woodlands in the Corfe Valley extends up the lower slopes of the ridge and gradually becomes more fragmented to leave grassland and scrub on the steepest slopes. The upper limit of the farmland patchwork often forms a strong, undulating line emphasising the height of the ridge.

Although there are numerous ancient archaeological sites, dating from the Neolithic, Bronze and Iron Ages, with a dense concentration of barrows on Nine Barrow Down, there are no villages on the ridge itself. Clusters of buildings occur in a straggling line along the foot of the steep slopes and those on the northern flanks are hidden within dense woodlands. There is, however, one unusual building on the ridge. Grange Arch or Bond's Folly is an 'eye-catcher' built to provide a point of interest to a viewer at Creech Grange. The deep Cocknowle chalk quarry, within a narrow crevice between Knowle Hill and Stonehill Down, forms an unexpected dramatic scar, hidden from view from the outer margins of the ridge.

The Purbeck Chalk Ridge is a powerful windswept landscape which feels untamed and exhilarating. The ridgetop is exposed to the elements and offers spectacular panoramic views across Dorset. There is a strong sense of continuity with the evolution of the landscape and man's influence on it. The ridge preserves a primeval, monolithic character which is a powerful contrast to the small-scale farmland patchwork below. This is a defiant, awe-inspiring landscape

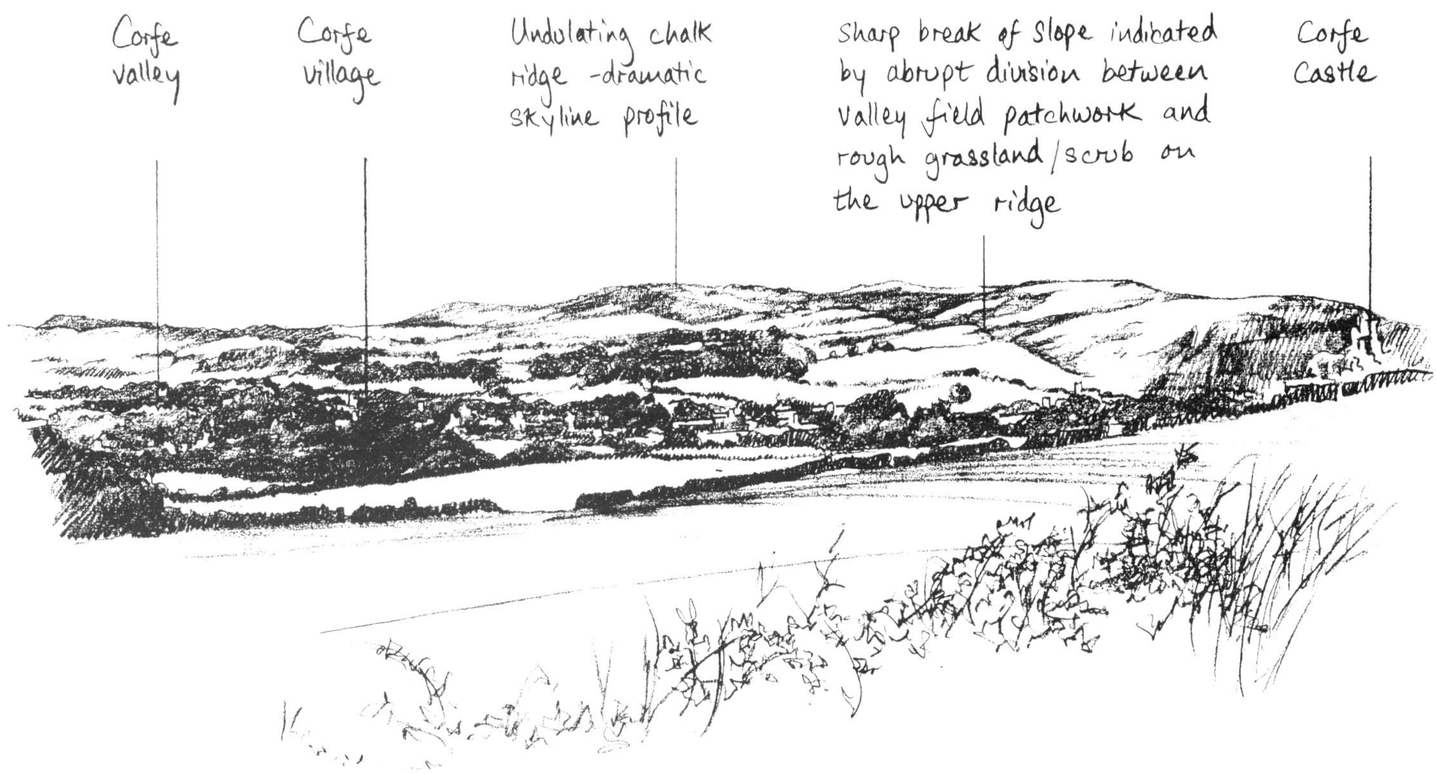

PURBECK CHALK RIDGE: *Looking west along the Purbeck chalk ridge from East Hill.* GR 974818.

and it is easy to understand why ancient societies may have considered the summits to be sacred.

THE KEY CHARACTERISTIC FEATURES OF THE PURBECK CHALK RIDGE ARE:–

- Steep, narrow chalk ridge, separating the Corfe valley from the heathlands to the north.
- A strong visual barrier, broken only at the central gap, emphasised by the landmark of Corfe Castle.
- Exposed landscape, with a bold, dominant scale
- Ridgetops consist of open arable and grassland, with extensive patches of scrub on the slopes.
- Patchwork of fields extends up lower slopes on south side of ridge but breaks down on steeper slopes with an abrupt transition to open grassland.
- Northern slopes clothed with areas of Ancient Woodland.
- No settlements on the top or steep slopes but small farmsteads at the foot of the ridge.

MANAGEMENT GUIDANCE

i The distinctive, undulating profile of the ridge is an important visual characteristic with important ecological associations which should be actively conserved by maintaining and restoring open species-rich grassland along the ridgetops and slopes.

ii Some of the most extensive remaining areas of chalk grassland occur on the Purbeck Chalk Ridge and management regimes should be targeted to control the scrub encroachment which is a significant threat to this ecologically important habitat. In some areas, scrub encroachment is so far advanced that cutting and burning may be necessary before a programme of traditional grazing can be an effective control.

iii Restoration of downland, taking advantage of schemes like Countryside Stewardship, should be encouraged.

iv The extensive broadleaved woodlands on the north side of the ridge are a visually prominent backdrop for views from the lowlands of the Poole Basin, so their overall shape and character are significant. Continuous, extensive areas of woodland are visually more appropriate than smaller patches, which might form a distracting pattern. Any new woodlands should echo the existing broadscale and be carefully designed to connect and reflect their bold character. The form of the upper woodland edge is particularly important and the tree line should be kept below the horizon to avoid conflicting with the ridge profile.

v Those semi-natural ancient woodlands with a high biological diversity are particularly significant for nature conservation and should have priority for sensitive and appropriate management.

vi The combination of steep slopes and pressures for tourism make footpaths on the chalk ridge subject to erosion. Path maintenance, signing and re-routing are important management strategies since such erosion rapidly becomes a prominent white scar and represents another threat to the chalk grassland habitat.

vii The narrow lanes of the chalk ridge have a particular visual character which require local, detailed, individual consideration.

Corfe Valley

The valley of the Corfe River tapers towards the west and is hidden between a steep band of chalk to the north and a more gentle slope up to the coastal limestone ridge to the south. The influence of the sea is felt at Tyneham in the west and Swanage to the east. It has a broad, sweeping profile. The valley floor is never flat, reflecting the compressed geology and generally becomes more undulating at the base of the chalk ridge. Between Corfe and Ulwell, the landscape is particularly contorted and undulating, with tiny farmsteads hidden in shallow hollows and winding narrow lanes which seem sunken into the hillside. The southern limestone ridges have a more consistent slope, with the prominent summits of Swyre Head, Tyneham Cap and Worbarrow Tout forming a sequence of skyline landmarks.

The Corfe Valley has a varied pattern of predominantly pasture fields, enclosed by hedgerows, with dense belts of hedgerow trees. There are large copses and small mixed woodlands on the slopes of the limestone ridges. The hedges here are fairly straight and tend to run at right angles to the contours, but on the more gentle slopes of the valley floor the fields form a more irregular patchwork. The fields become larger on the slopes of the limestone ridges, but the network of hedgerows extends right up to the horizon line, emphasising the sweeping profile of the valley. Further east, stone walls tend to replace the hedgerows on the higher slopes. The undulating margins of the valley give it a strong rhythmic quality. The fields lap up the side of the high chalk ridge forming a strong curving edge between pasture and rough grazing, which mirrors the profile of the ridgetop above. Corfe Common is a low dome of unimproved acidic grassland to the south of the village where the uneven and hummocky terrain, with patches of bramble, gorse and rough grazing, contains groups of ancient burial mounds.

The pattern of small, irregular fields is of historic significance, settlements in the vicinity of Tyneham, for instance, were typically very small and associated with long, narrow strips running across the valley to include land on steep slopes as well as the valley floor. Strip fields and lynchets, often superimposed on an Iron Age field pattern, cover over 200 acres within the valley, and the deep tracks linking the various settlements indicate that it was once much more densely populated than it is today. Now small farmsteads and villages built of rough limestone are scattered throughout the valley, connected by a web of winding, narrow lanes. These routes become clear lines in the landscape as they ascend the ridges which enclose the valley, but lower down are obscured within the maze of fields, woodlands and hedgerows. There is a concentration of settlements running along the foot of the chalk ridge, culminating in the seaside resort of Swanage. Some of the villages are picturesque and the church towers at Steeple, Church Knowle and Kingston are local landmarks, whilst occasional stands of Scots pines are strong visual accents.

The contrast between the exposed, dramatic ridges of the surrounding hills and the domestic patchwork of farmland and picturesque villages gives the Corfe Valley a special charm and seclusion. The undulating small-scale landscape along the foot of the northern hills retains its secretive intimacy and to the west of Corfe the valley is very peaceful, unspoilt and deeply rural. The western part, beyond the village of Steeple, is controlled by the military. The fields

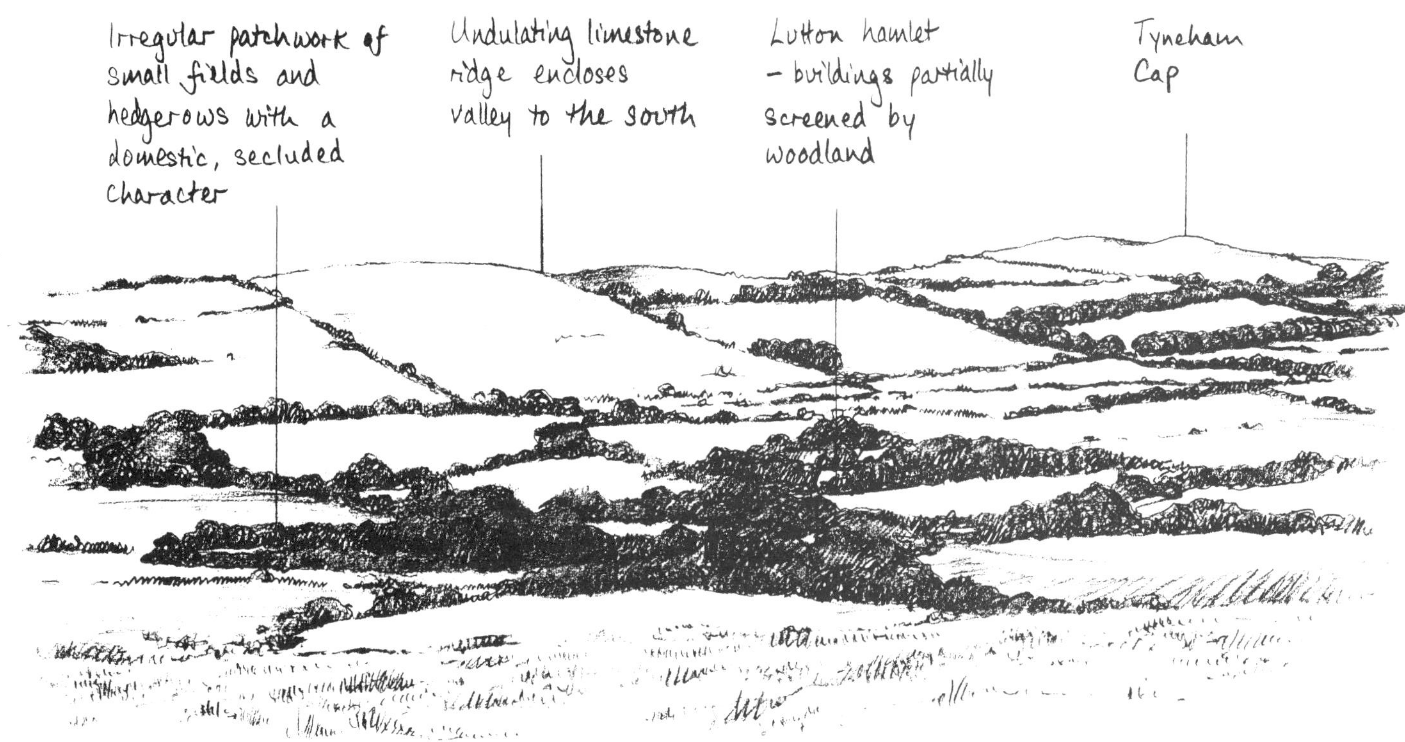

CORFE VALLEY: *The Corfe Valley from West Creech Hill.* GR 904817.

here have a remote and slightly derelict atmosphere. However the atmosphere further east changes with the urban influence of Swanage and the profusion of garages, camp sites and signposts.

THE KEY CHARACTERISTIC FEATURES OF THE CORFE VALLEY ARE:–

- A 'v' shaped secluded valley to the west of Corfe Castle, strongly influenced by the steep chalk ridge to the north and by the margins of the Purbeck limestone plateau to the south.
- Sweeping, asymmetrical profile, with a rippling valley floor, to the east of Corfe Castle.
- Views to the sea at both the western and eastern margins of the valley are framed by the dramatic profiles of its enclosing ridge.
- Irregular patchwork of small fields, contained by substantial hedgerows, which interconnect many scattered small woodlands.
- A largely pastoral landscape, despite some arable activity.
- Stone walls take over from hedgerows on the southern slopes.
- Large isolated area of acidic grassland to the south of Corfe village.
- Numerous small villages and farmsteads scattered across the valley. Church towers are prominent local landmarks.

- An urban 'feel' to the eastern section around Swanage.

MANAGEMENT GUIDANCE

i The attractive harmonious character of the Corfe Valley landscape depends on maintaining a careful balance between the scattered woodlands, hedgerows, and open fields. The patchwork of fields should predominate, with organically-shaped woodlands managed and designed to interconnect with the existing network of hedgerows.

ii The hedgerows are very important in defining the characteristic, irregular patchwork of fields. Many have persisted for centuries and also have a high ecological value. These ancient boundaries should be protected and carefully managed to sustain their historic and ecological interest.

iii Replanting and strengthening of existing hedgerows, with groups of hedgerow trees, where there are obvious gaps, should be a management priority.

iv Where stone walls are an important local feature they should be repaired and rebuilt using local stone.

v Tree planting, with native species, could be encouraged in association with hamlets, farmsteads, and new farm buildings.

vi The unimproved acidic grassland habitat on Corfe Common is ecologically important and needs special management for its conservation. Threatened by scrub encroachment, management strategies should aim to reduce invasion of bracken and gorse, and sustain a grazing regime.

vii The character of the network of the lanes should be sustained.

viii Military control has protected the Tyneham area from intensive agriculture and development, however the landscape here needs particularly careful management, probably with increased grazing, to maintain its visual character, historic importance and ecological diversity.

Purbeck Limestone Plateau

There is a broad transition from the Corfe Valley to the Purbeck Limestone Plateau. Sloping consistently towards the south and east, the plateau is slightly rolling on the upper slopes, becomes flatter to the south of the Priests Way, and then plummets towards the sea. At Worth Matravers, deep valleys cut down to the coast.

Rough hedgerows on north side of plateau, but minimal tree cover

Smooth, sloping landform

Exposed, isolated buildings

Hedges / stone walls enclose rectangular fields with straight edges

PURBECK LIMESTONE PLATEAU: *Purbeck limestone plateau near Acton.* GR 984788.

The plateau is high, exposed and windswept. The fields are mostly geometric in shape and the relatively flat terrain does not disguise the straight edges. There are hardly any trees and most fields are enclosed by stone walls so the landscape appears stark and quite bleak. Some of the walls are overgrown with bramble and supplemented by thin hedges, which have become established on the lee side. Any vegetation is sculpted into expressive shapes by the prevailing wind, but there is more growth within the deep clefts of the coastal valleys, where ash and sycamore survive. Farming is difficult on the rocky soil, with arable on the higher, flatter, more accessible areas.

The building stone industry has a continuing influence on the landscape. Many fields are littered with small, shallow quarries, surrounded by piles of limestone. Signs, telegraph poles and spoil heaps stand out clearly on the skyline in this open landscape. Those quarries being worked are concentrated along the most elevated parts of the ridge, so they are an obvious component in local views. The villages, and stone walls extending from them, are uncluttered by vegetation and appear crisp, stark and solidly well-built. The continuity of stone features gives the plateau landscape a strong visual unity and the buildings make an important contribution to its character. Langton Matravers extends along the ridgetop road to Swanage, but Worth Matravers has a more clustered form, sited at the head of the deep valley which extends southwards to the coast at Winspit. The tracks and side roads have a straight, north-south alignment and join the principal roads at right angles. An ancient track, the Priest's Way, connects the farmsteads to the south of Langton Matravers, taking the form of a grassy highway, enclosed by stone walls. Traces of Iron Age field systems survive on Smedmore Hill and Kingston Down, and the striking medieval strip lynchets on the coastal headlands are evidence of the expansion of the population in those times, when there was the need to bring even these steep slopes into cultivation.

This is a powerful, unrelenting landscape, which seems stripped to its bare essentials, accosted by the sea, stubbornly resistant, yet sculpted over centuries by the wind. Nothing is soft or pretty. The plateau feels primitive and ancient, a striking contrast to the domestic field pattern of the Corfe Valley to the north and the bustling streets of Swanage to the east.

THE KEY CHARACTERISTIC FEATURES OF THE PURBECK LIMESTONE PLATEAU ARE:–

- Exposed, limestone plateau rising southwards then falling sharply to the sea and incised by deep, narrow coastal valleys.
- Windswept landscape with virtually no trees, a few sparse hedgerows but with a little scrub in the valleys.
- Geometric fields, divided by a network of stone walls.
- Stark stone villages and isolated, exposed farmsteads.
- Landscape is littered with small limestone quarries.
- Extensive views towards the sea and inland over the Corfe Valley and to the Purbeck Chalk Ridge.
- Ancient field systems on many of the unimproved grassland slopes

MANAGEMENT GUIDANCE

i Stone walls make an important contribution to the visual character of the limestone plateau landscape and should be repaired, and rebuilt, to maintain the consistent, stark quality of the field patterns. Local stone should always be used.

ii Signs, fencing and gates are very obvious in this open landscape, especially when they are silhouetted against the sky, and it is important that they have a simple functional style so that the landscape remains uncluttered. Opportunities to remove unsightly features should be taken.

iii The open, grassy verges and tracks, such as the Priests Way, contribute to the special character of the limestone plateau and could be mown or grazed to maintain their appearance and wildlife interest. Bramble should be cut back on a regular basis to prevent excessive encroachment.

iv Areas of unimproved limestone grassland of high floristic value should be protected and maintained by a management regime of controlled grazing.

v Traditional building designs and materials, including roofing materials, should be used to retain the local distinctiveness and character.

vi Hedgerows make a limited contribution to defining the field pattern. Although this network should be maintained and strengthened, opportunities should be sought to build stone walls and replace wire fencing whenever possible.

vii The ancient field systems should be preserved.

viii Woodlands are not a characteristic feature of this landscape and tree planting would generally be inappropriate in this exposed, open, area. Shrub planting should be carefully designed to maintain a low profile.

ix Should the opportunity arise it would be appropriate to restore arable fields to permanent grassland.

West Purbeck Coast

It is the softness of the Kimmeridge Clay, in contrast to the hard resistant limestone, which is fundamental to the character of this area. The clay has been eroded to form a distinctive, raised, undulating coastline, squeezed between the sea and the steep limestone ridge which is a physical and visual barrier separating this coastal vale from the Corfe Valley and Limestone Plateau. It stands as a dramatic horizon, notched at the summits of Swyre Head and Tyneham Cap, and form-

WEST PURBECK COAST: *Kimmeridge, from the slopes of Smedmore Hill.* GR 917797.

ing abrupt crumbling cliff faces where Houns-tout Cliff and Gad Cliff meet the coast. The clays are constantly eroding, giving unstable slopes and landslips in the Kimmeridge area, with an irregular, slumped landform. Chapman's Pool is a small bay, formed by the erosion of soft clays at the foot of Houns-tout Cliff. In Kimmeridge Bay itself the almost horizontal shale beds are clearly exposed, especially at low tide. It is a notable area for marine life, and the site of the first Voluntary Marine Reserve in the Country.

This is a fairly open landscape, with some hidden valleys, and completely enclosed in the north from the rest of Purbeck. The irregular fields and their boundaries constantly curve, as they undulate with the landform. Fragments of woodland occasionally separate the fields but there are relatively few hedgerow trees. The fields around the village of Kimmeridge are predominantly arable but those further east, towards Smedmore House, are mostly pasture and the seaward ridge of Smedmore Hill is rough grazing land. Landmarks are very important in this open landscape, such as the particularly distinctive profile of Gad Cliff, a dramatic, vertical wall of rock, with an abrupt break to a craggy slope below, and Clavell's Tower, a folly built in 1817 on Hen Cliff on the east side of Kimmeridge Bay. Smedmore House is less prominent but stands out as a formal, imposing mansion backed by woodland and a few prominent Scots pines. Constantly the wedge-shaped Isle of Portland is silhouetted in the view south-westwards.

Kimmeridge is a small cluster of buildings, tucked in at the foot of the escarpment, surrounded by patches of woodland with military ranges to the west. The limestone influence continues in the buildings and the boundary walls. The narrow lanes are very limited, connecting Kimmeridge with Smedmore House, and the private track to Kimmeridge Bay.

This is a hidden landscape, with the valleys of Encombe and Chapman's Pool almost seeming to be in another world, visible only from the limestone plateau. The land has a rippling, dynamic quality which contrasts with the solid, steep protective slopes behind. The whole landscape is vivacious, lively and unpredictable, with constantly changing views.

THE KEY CHARACTERISTIC FEATURES OF THE WEST PURBECK COAST ARE:–

- Soft Kimmeridge Clay forms an undulating coastline, cut off from the rest of Purbeck by a dominant curving limestone ridge where Gad Cliff, Tyneham Cap, Swyre Head and Houns-tout Cliff are distinctive landforms.
- Open, windswept landscape, with a mixture of pasture and arable fields, sparse hedgerows, few hedgerow trees, and small, isolated copses, forming sweeping patterns.
- Clavell's Tower is a prominent landmark on the coast.
- Settlements hidden away in hollows or steep valleys under the limestone ridge.
- Relatively inaccessible, with the sea as significant as the land.

MANAGEMENT GUIDANCE

i The distinctive visual structure of this landscape is determined by the scale of its fields and small, fragmented woodlands. Management could focus on sustaining the balance of hedgerows and walls, maintaining the network and reinforcing it along existing alignments.

ii Groups of trees could be planted to supplement existing woodlands or copses but isolated trees would be incongruous.

iii Active management of existing woods, plus a few creatively sited and carefully designed small woods, could continue to emphasise the undulating landform and help to maintain a sense of discovery.

iv Existing hedgerows should be actively managed and enriched with new planting of appropriate local species.

v Stone walls should be repaired, and rebuilt, using local stone.

vi Around the farmsteads and the village of Kimmeridge, the boundary walls and existing planting should be reinforced.

vii The sense of remoteness and quality of wildlife interests contribute to the enjoyment of locals and visitors so the special habitats on land and in the sea deserve positive management to sustain and enhance them. Visitor management and information are likely to be crucial elements in managing the landscape around Kimmeridge Bay.

EAST DORSET AND POOLE BASIN LANDSCAPES

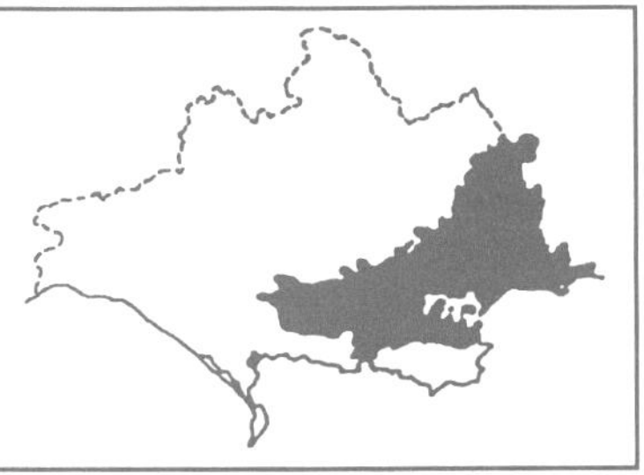

725km^2 27.31%

This zone includes the lowlands of the Poole Basin and east Dorset that are enclosed by chalk on the north, west and south. The transition from chalk to the heathland landscapes consistently follows the same pattern throughout the Poole Basin. The eroded dip-slope margins of the chalk are overlain by the Reading Beds, a combination of clays and sands which produces a gently rolling landscape of woods and farmland.

The Reading Beds separate the chalk from the more acidic and gravelly Bagshot and Bracklesham Beds which occupy the middle of the Poole Basin. Heathland landscapes, which

The View from Dudsbury looking towards Longham. H.S.

are generally associated with these poor, sandy, infertile soils, can be divided into three landscape character areas. The remaining pure tracts of heathland are a distinctive and evocative open landscape. Conifer plantations, which have been planted in large blocks on the heathlands, also have a dominant visual influence and the landscape associated with them is described as a separate character area. The heathland/scrub mosaic is typically a mixture of heathland and woodland thicket which exists in a dynamic balance, depending on the degree of management employed.

These landscapes are drained by four principal rivers: the Frome and the Piddle flow towards Poole Harbour, while the Stour and the Avon drain into Christchurch Harbour. Alluvial deposits smother their shallow valleys, creating flat pastures along the flood plains. The river valley landscape changes in character as it approaches the harbours, where the flood plain is broader and typically very open. There are extensive views which are often influenced by urban development.

The coastline of the Poole Basin was formed relatively recently following the post-glacial rise in sea-level and the breaking of the chalk ridge joining the Isle of Purbeck to the Isle of Wight. The upper reaches of the former Solent River were flooded to form Poole Harbour. This is almost enclosed

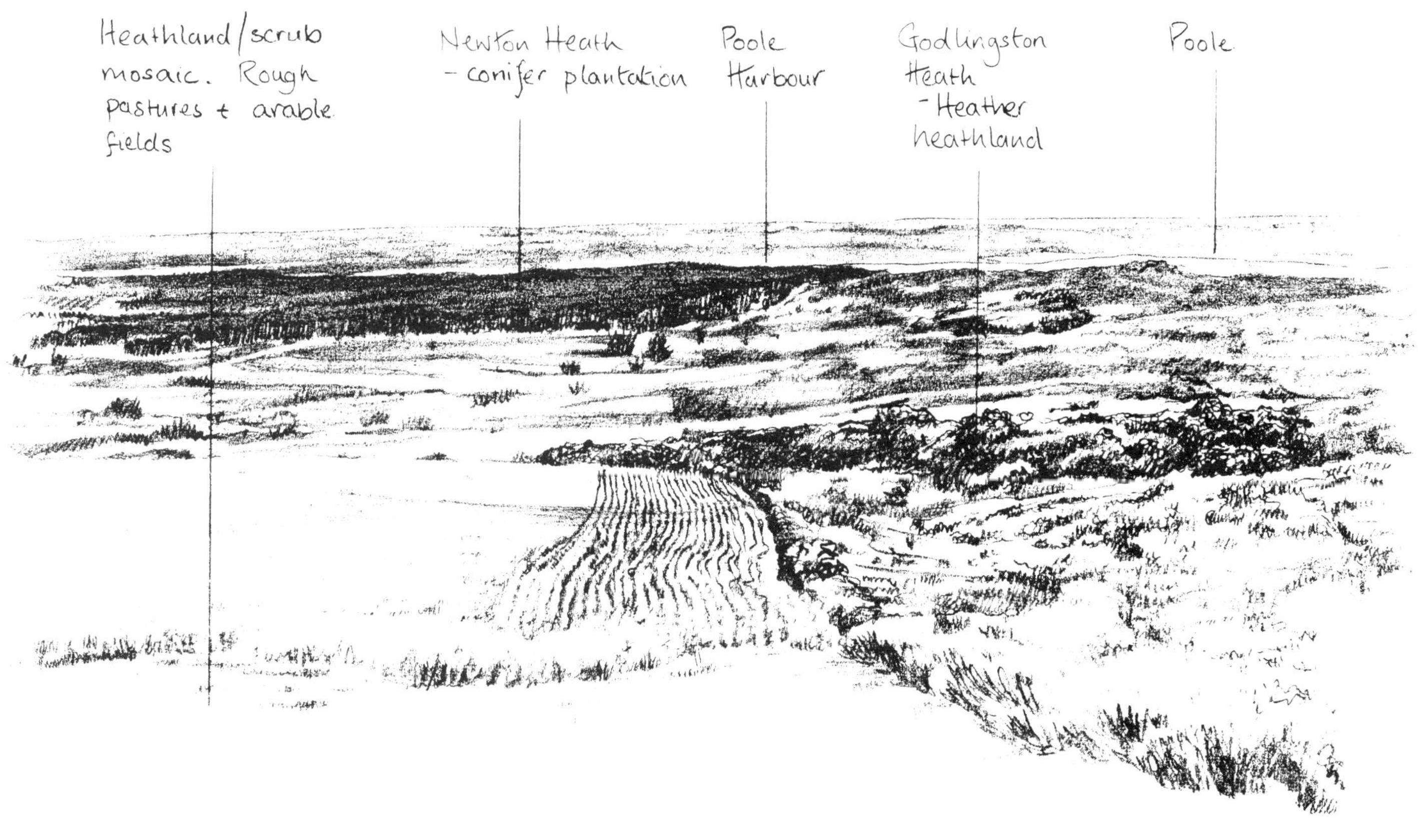

MOSAIC OF HEATHLAND: *Mosaic of heathland landscapes on the north Purbeck lowlands, from Godlingston Hill.* GR 001819.

from the sea by the Studland peninsula which has developed over the past 500 years. The low heathlands are bordered by sand dunes and long-shore drift has deposited elongated sand spits at the mouth of Poole harbour. The deeply-indented, shallow shoreline of the harbour resembles the margins of a huge lake, with wide stretches of still water, mudflats, reed-beds and winding creeks. The islands are remnants of the drowned lowlands which once bordered the former river channel.

The Poole/Bournemouth conurbation is the largest urban area in the county. It has grown rapidly during the present century and has created a landscape all of its own. For this reason it is treated as a distinct landscape character area.

East Dorset and Poole Basin can be divided into the following six landscape character areas (which are to be found at a variety of different localities and are distributed in a mosaic throughout the zone) :

- HEATHLAND
- HEATHLAND/SCRUB MOSAIC
- EAST DORSET WOODS AND FARMLAND
- CONIFER PLANTATIONS
- VALLEY PASTURES
- POOLE/BOURNEMOUTH CONURBATION

Heathland

Heathland landscapes are to be found intermingled throughout the area shown.

Historically extensive heathlands covered much of the Poole Basin and the patches of heather which exist today represent the fragmented remains of this landscape. The heathland is surrounded by the mosaic of scrub/woodland, farmland, forestry plantations and urban and industrial land which extends across the lowlands of eastern Dorset. The context of each piece of heathland is therefore unique, yet very significant from a visual point of view since these tracts of heathland are relatively open and allow long views.

The varied topography of the heathlands of eastern Dorset results from their status as remnants of a more extensive landscape. The tracts of heather have an open, expansive character so even subtle changes in landform are clearly revealed. Minor breaks in slope are often emphasised by variations in the matrix of vegetation which carpets the heathland. The landform is often hummocky but with occasional dramatic high points and eroded patches of silver sand on the steepest slopes.

Several large areas of heathland occur on the lowlands to the north of the Purbeck chalk ridge. Studland Heath, Middlebere Heath and Povington Heath are on gently undulating lowlands, dominated by the dramatic wooded ridge of the Purbeck Hills which loom to the south. Studland Heath has a particularly stunning setting since it extends from the deeply indented coastline of Poole Harbour to the eastern end of the Purbeck Chalk Ridge. Winfrith Heath is an elevated ridge to the south of the River Frome. It is a rugged, open area which stands out clearly from the surrounding mosaic of pasture, scrub and woodland.

The most extensive heathlands to the north of Poole Harbour are Canford Heath and Holt Heath. The former is on the northern fringes of Poole. It is bordered by housing development and roads which, perhaps surprisingly, seem dwarfed by this elevated rugged landscape. Holt Heath has a more rural context with a broad, sweeping landform and long views to the countryside beyond. The urban areas of Ferndown and West Moors are very close but Ferndown is screened from the heathland by the White Sheet plantation and West Moors is out of sight in a valley to the east.

There are smaller fragments of heathland on the margins of many of the conifer plantations in eastern Dorset. These are mostly hidden from long views by the dense woodlands which surround them but where they occur on elevated land as on Black Hill to the east of Bere Regis and St Catherine's Hill near Christchurch, even small tracts of heathland have a significant visual impact.

Heather is always predominant but other species such as gorse and purple moor-grass are intermingled, and the resulting blend of colours and textures is rich and varied. The valley bottoms are often boggy and as the ground gets wetter the colour of the vegetation changes from the darker heathers of the dryer land to the greens of the marsh plants. Thus the colours of the heathland can range from burnt sienna and ochre through vermilion and bright purple to vivid yellows and greens, and their shades reflect and emphasise the undulating landform. The colours alter constantly with changing light conditions and the seasons so the landscape seems dynamic and diverse on a local scale while maintaining an overall harmony and unity.

HEATHLAND: *Holt Heath.* GR 068048.

Superficially heathland has a simple visual structure and a uniform character but towards its margins the landscape becomes more fragmented to form a mosaic of pasture fields and patches of woodland. The fields are only partially enclosed and tend to coalesce towards the edge of the heath, forming a patchy, irregular edge.

The heathlands were created as a result of the clearance of prehistoric woodland, probably beginning in the Bronze Age. The sandy, gravelly soils are highly porous and do not retain water so the loss of tree cover led to the leaching of soil nutrients. Evidence from pollen records suggests that much of the Dorset heathlands were established by 500 BC. During the Middle Ages the heathlands were generally unenclosed but the acidic clays on their margins supported many small, isolated farmsteads while the heathland beyond was used as grazing for ponies, pigs, cattle and sheep. A more valuable asset was turf-cutting and heathlands were managed and maintained by this combination of land uses throughout the medieval period. Since the eighteenth century conifer planting, agriculture enclosure and, more recently, modern development has obliterated extensive areas of heathland. The remaining heaths still feel relatively remote despite their proximity to urban areas. They are often bordered by roads which are typically straight and on slightly elevated land.

Heathland supports few native trees, principally Birch, which can be an important component of the heathlands since large mature specimens support a specialist insect fauna. Formerly the active uses of the heathland restricted expansion of wooded areas, but as these practices have declined the birch has spread, overwhelmed the heather and is sometimes viewed as a pest.

The lowland heathlands are an internationally rare ecological habitat which support a unique community of plants and animals. Those in Dorset have particular value because of their geographical location where the Atlantic type species overlap with continental type species. This means that the Dorset heathlands are on the edge of the range of several important species, including breeding birds, reptiles and also many invertebrates, some restricted to this heathland habitat. All the substantial tracts of heather habitat have SSSI status and many have some protection from planning policies. The *Dorset Heathland Strategy* seeks to supplement these designations with more positive protective policies and to promote the active management of the heathlands.

Even quite small tracts of heather heathland can evoke a strong sense of being close to nature and these feelings are all the more powerful where the heathland is extensive. The weather is always apparent on the heathlands, in summer they are often uncomfortably hot, whilst in winter the converse is often bitterly true. It is an expansive, open landscape which feels exposed and exhilarating because it has

The View from Ramsdown looking towards the Island.

remained untamed and unstructured by man's efforts to cultivate, manage and subdivide. The isolated, dark, Scots pines and gorse have dramatic windblown silhouettes, revealing the power of natural forces on a human scale. The margins of the heathland seem like a refuge from which to view a fairly inhospitable, but attractive landscape.

THE KEY CHARACTERISTIC FEATURES OF THE HEATHLANDS ARE:–

- Undulating, lowland terrain, carpeted by dense tracts of heather with birch trees, occasional stunted pines and gorse bushes.
- Exposed open landscape with a broad, simple scale, often fragmented by patches of scrub and woodland.
- Coloured differently to other Dorset landscapes, brown, purple (in summer) and gold predominate.
- Historically inhospitable terrain which has not supported any settlement, but heathlands are often now juxtaposed against and threatened by urban development.
- Fragile landscape, easily damaged by human activity

MANAGEMENT GUIDANCE

i Much of the landscape character comes from the ecological and wildlife aspects; conserving these aspects will also help sustain the landscape qualities.

ii All existing tracts of heather should be managed for their wildlife interest, as outlined in the *Dorset Heathland Strategy.*

iii Buffer zones should be provided between heathlands and adjacent existing settlements to minimise physical trespass and visual intrusion.

iv Emphasis should be placed on heathland restoration in marginal areas, where there may be opportunities to link existing isolated small tracts of heathland together.

v Areas of acid grassland should be managed and protected from scrub encroachment.

vi The open unspoilt character of the heathland landscape is its most distinctive visual characteristic and it is important that the heathland margins are kept free from intrusive development.

vii Where development on the margins is permitted, it should be adequately screened using native species which thrive in acidic soil conditions.

viii Owing to the closeness of centres of population, and the fragility of the sandy soils, visitor management is essential to minimise path and habitat erosion.

ix Although gnarled, mature pines make a contribution to the visual character of the heathlands, they can constitute a seed source for young pines. Consideration should be given to the individual importance to the landscape of **every** tree. No new pine trees should be planted.

x Birch trees have a positive role, and could be encouraged in certain areas. Care must be taken to prevent birch spreading, particularly after fires.

xi Management strategies for heaths should encompass protection from fire, tipping, vandalism, motorised trespass and path erosion.

Heathland/Scrub Mosaic

Heathland/Scrub mosaic landscapes are to be found intermingled throughout the area shown.

This character area includes a varied range of landscape components from heathland to pastures to dense woody thicket, and the lowland heath/scrub mosaic landscape links the conifer plantations and remnant tracts of pure heather habitat. Any land left untended within the lower Poole Basin will rapidly generate this heathland/scrub landscape type, so it is constantly evident over a wide area, scattered throughout the south-eastern parts of Dorset, and even occurs on roadside verges.

Patches of woody scrub, pasture and heathland form an irregular, small scale, random mosaic and the boundaries between thickets, pastures and heathland are often blurred. Maintenance of both pastures and heathland requires constant grazing or other forms of management, so there can be a tendency for the scrub to encroach onto adjacent land. Gorse bushes are the first stage in this natural ecological succession from open countryside to woodland. They are rapidly followed by birch trees and the edges of the thickets typically show a broad range of vegetation from mature oak trees to gorse bushes and bracken. Small, fragmented patches of heather occur alongside tracks and on open verges. Hedgerows are scanty and often supplemented by wire fencing. They consist of gorse, bracken and birch but also contain mature, stag-headed oak trees and occasionally beech. Holly is a frequent isolated hedgerow species and rhododendron is very common, especially in the Bournemouth area, where they have been planted as an ornamental screen. Groups of Scots pine often form dramatic visual accents along the edges of tracks and in hedgerows.

The confined views mean that attention focuses on the details rather than the structure of this landscape. There is a wide diversity of species and forms and the landscape elements forming the mosaic seem to occur in random, irregular patches.

Much of the Poole/Bournemouth conurbation has expanded onto former heathland which frequently leads to a reduction in management of land adjacent to the urban areas. For this reason the heathland scrub mosaic landscape predominates on the urban fringe throughout south east Dorset. It is an effective visual buffer for many activities since the dense woody thickets are a reliable screen. Pockets of regeneration readily occur whenever there is a verge or piece of land 'left-over' so even large-scale developments can appear dispersed and less visible.

This landscape is enclosed and sheltered and nature seems very close with many different forms and textures along the woodland edges. The wild, untamed tangle of vegetation often forms an impenetrable barrier, with bogs and thorny bushes blocking the way. There are very few opportunities to look across open areas and, despite the frequent proximity of housing developments, there can be a sense of vulnerability and fear as 'danger' cannot be seen, or easily escaped from.

THE KEY CHARACTERISTIC FEATURES OF THE HEATHLAND/SCRUB MOSAIC ARE:–

- Irregular, patchy, mosaic of undermanaged heath land and scrub within farmland where dense regenerating woody thickets are actively encroaching onto adjacent land.

- Views limited by interlinked belts and clumps of dense woodland, screening intrusive land-uses.
- Few dense settlements, but sporadic, linear hamlets and often small-scale industry on urban fringes.

MANAGEMENT GUIDANCE

i The heathland/scrub mosaic landscape should be sustained as an effective visual and ecological buffer between the extensive settlements of eastern Dorset and the fragile, ecologically important heathland habitat.

ii Opportunities should be sought to clear woodland/scrub in areas adjacent to existing tracts of heathland, where these do not have an ecological or visual role, with a view to linking the many isolated fragments of this important ecological habitat and increasing their overall area and recreating some more extensive areas of heathland within the scrub mosaic.

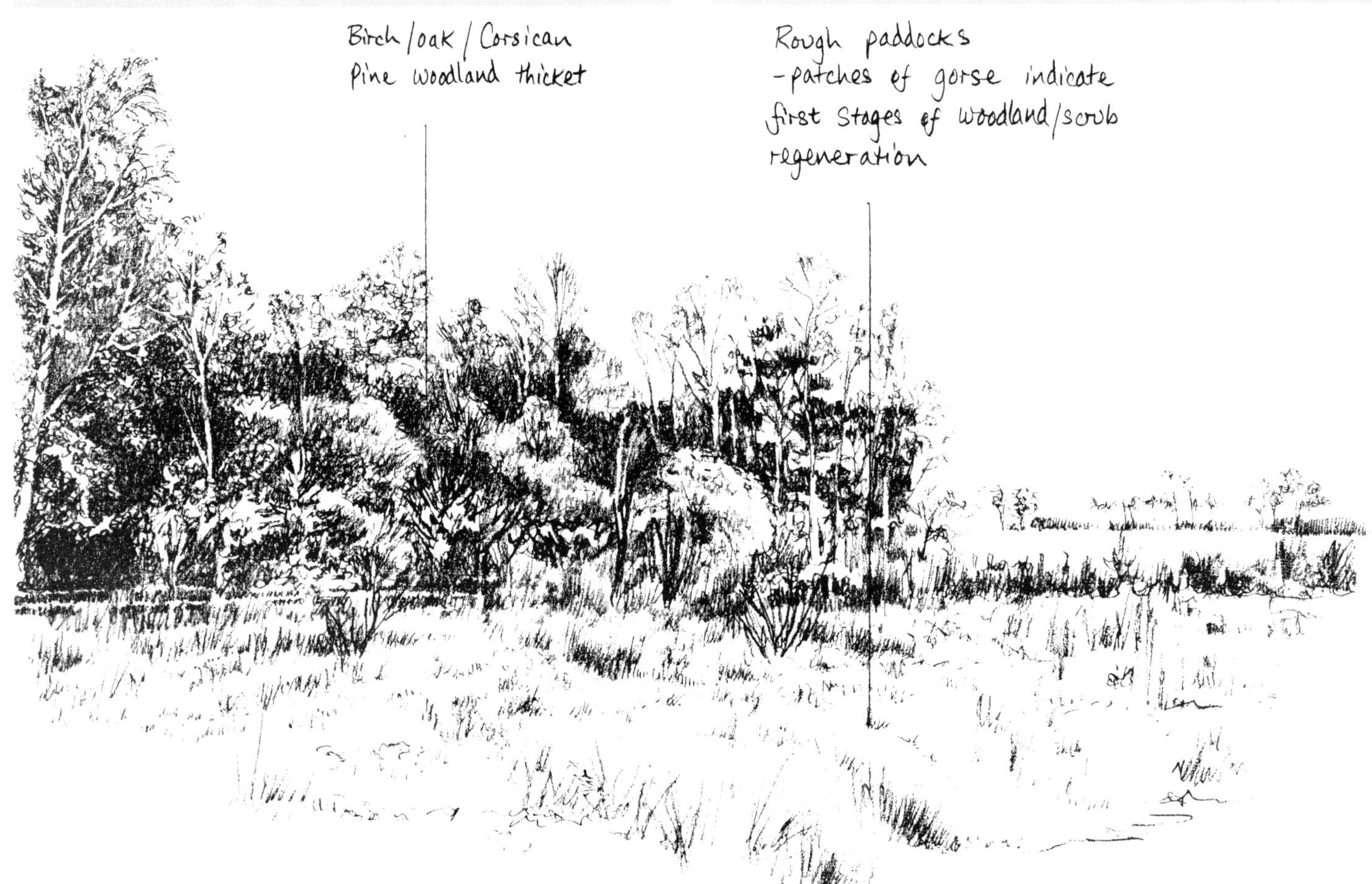

HEATHLAND/SCRUB MOSAIC: *East Parley Common.* GR 095992.

iii The diverse visual structure of the heathland/scrub mosaic should be retained and strengthened by maintaining a local balance between woodland, pasture and heathland.

iv Pasture grazing should be continued to discourage scrub encroachment and maintain acid grassland.

v The heathland/scrub has an unkempt, rough character and care should be taken that any new planting or landscaping around new developments should fit the local character. The desire to 'tidy up' the landscape should be resisted.

vi Particular care should be taken in siting urban fringe developments, such as equestrian centres, golf courses and nurseries, which require extensive parking, and signage. The use of characterless, urban designs should be resisted.

vii Management strategies should include protection from fire, tipping, vandalism, motorised trespass and path erosion.

East Dorset Woods and Farmland

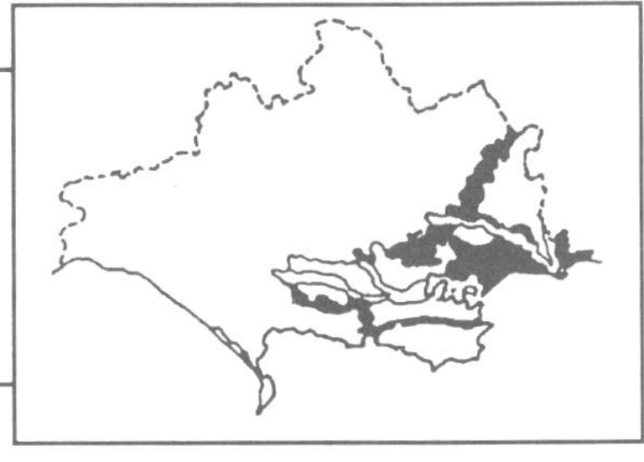

The low rolling hills of this farmland landscape are formed on the sands and clays of the Reading Beds and tend to be a little higher than the chalklands. The numerous small blocks of woodland on these hills make them seem higher than they really are, increasing their visual impact and contrasting sharply with the broader scale of the chalklands. The interface with the chalk is usually well defined although in some places the margins of the Reading Beds are very patchy and indented so there can be outlying low wooded hills amongst the mosaic of sweeping chalk arable fields.

Numerous hedgerow trees

Enclosed landscape with small woodlands and irregular, rough pastures

Conifer plantation forms dense, consistent backdrop - edged with deciduous trees

EAST DORSET WOODS AND FARMLAND: *Woodlands and pastures near East Morden.* GR 923954.

The boundary between the farmland landscape and that of the heathlands is usually less clear. There is a gradual transition to less fertile farmland and corners of fields tend to be abandoned to thickets of regenerating woodland. Even the large coniferous plantations on the heathland blend in with the marginal farmland since the latter includes many small blocks of woodland and the impact of a dominant forest edge is diminished. Areas of this farmland landscape can be found all along the edge of the chalk in eastern Dorset, from the northern slopes of the Purbeck Hills to the countryside around Verwood in the north east of the county.

This marginal farmland has a fairly small scale since long views are prevented by numerous blocks of woodland and the landscape feels well-enclosed and protected. The fields are predominantly pasture but there are occasionally arable fields on flatter terrain. They tend to have irregular shapes and are enclosed by banks and hedgerows, often poorly managed, with numerous hedgerow trees.

On urban fringes this farmland landscape feels less enclosed and is frequently bordered by extensive blocks of suburban housing. Even if housing is not intrusive there is an accumulation of golf courses, equestrian centres and nurseries. Pastures on these urban fringes, such as those bordering the Stour Valley, are in particularly poor condition, often enclosed by wire and pieces of corrugated iron to supplement inadequate hedgerows. Where fields are low-lying, tussocky grass indicates a casual approach of management. There is a general scruffiness in this area and much of the land is devoted to small-holdings and paddocks.

This is nevertheless a well settled landscape with numerous scattered small villages, hamlets and farmsteads. In places it is hard to tell where one village stops and another starts. Most of the older buildings are built of brick since the clays around Verwood formerly supported numerous brick works and pottery kilns. Traces of these industries are still visible in several places. The buildings blend easily into this wooded farmland and provide a focus and point of orientation in most views The many hamlets are connected by an indirect and twisting network of narrow lanes. There are frequent right-angled bends for no apparent reason which suggest that many still follow the alignment of much older tracks and estate boundaries.

There are some areas of ancient deciduous woodland and old hazel coppice. In the Verwood area coppicing is still practised, with the result that some local views will alter dramatically throughout the years of the coppice rotation.

The mixture of woodland and farmland gives the landscape a strong, rhythmic quality and views have a clear sense of direction and depth since the woodland never forms a complete screen. In areas with more steeply undulating terrain, the landscape is highly enclosed and intimate, with an overgrown, unkempt character. The landscape is more secluded and harmonious, yet more varied. The hedgerow/woodland network emphasises the undulating topography and leads the eye into well-composed views. There is a rich profusion of texture and different shades of green.

THE KEY CHARACTERISTIC FEATURES OF THE EAST DORSET WOODS AND FARMLAND ARE:–

- Low, rolling hills with an irregular mosaic of pasture, woodland and well treed hedgerows
- Smaller-scale, more intimate landscapes on undulating terrain
- Generally acidic soils, often of low fertility
- Predominantly pasture, but sometimes large arable fields on flatter terrain
- Numerous small villages and narrow, winding lanes
- Views are typically limited by the many small, dense blocks of woodland.

i The visual structure of this landscape is determined by the scale of its mosaic of fields and woodlands. Future management should ensure that the existing overall balance between fields, hedgerows and woodlands is maintained to retain the characteristic sense of enclosure.

ii The character and quality of the woodland edges are of particular importance. Variations between the solid outlines of the conifer plantations and the softer profiles of the deciduous trees contribute to the diversity of the landscape and additional planting should maintain and reinforce this varied edge structure.

iii The existing deciduous woodlands are visually attractive and important for nature conservation. Emphasis should be placed on their protection and conservation in order to ensure long-term ecological and visual richness. Semi-natural ancient woodlands and coppices are particularly significant and should have priority for sensitive and appropriate management.

iv Traditional pasture grazing should be encouraged in fields which have remained unploughed to retain the important diverse flora associated with unimproved grassland.

v Existing hedgerows and boundary banks should be conserved and maintained. Where possible wire fences should be replaced by new hedgerows.

vi The management of the more recent conifer plantations is particularly important to avoid creating abrupt gaps and harsh edges during routine forestry operations. Such geometric forms would be inappropriate, and visually distracting, in this relatively small-scale rolling farmland landscape.

vii New or recent development, including additional farm buildings, would benefit from associated tree planting so that buildings are always partially screened by trees and blend easily into the composition of woodlands and open fields.

viii The visual quality of many of the small fields adjacent to settlements is decreased by a proliferation of the rough shelters, paddocks and equipment associated with small-holdings and the keeping of horses. Additional planting to integrate and screen such developments is necessary to retain the secluded, character of this farmland landscape.

Conifer Plantations

Conifer plantations are to be found intermingled throughout the area shown.

Conifers are often perceived as an intrusion to the countryside, being angular, vertical rather than spreading, stiff rather than flexible, and planted in straight lines which serve to emphasise these features. Within a plantation it is dark, rather than light, the needles suppress undergrowth in contrast to the rich flora of a deciduous woodland and, with the exception of larch, they retain the same structure, form and uniform dark blue-green colour all year round.

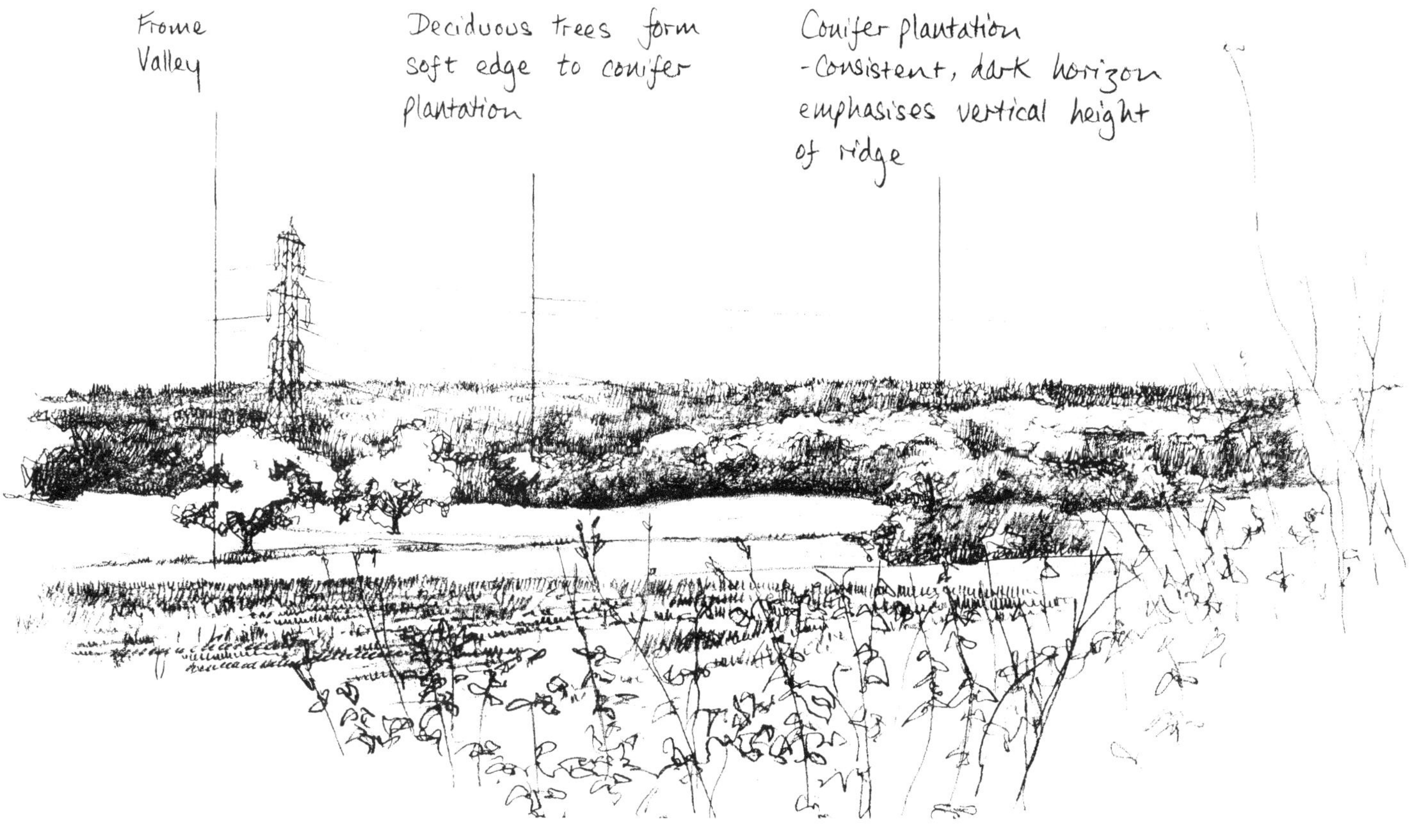

Frome Valley

Deciduous trees form soft edge to conifer plantation

Conifer plantation -Consistent, dark horizon emphasises vertical height of ridge

CONIFER PLANTATIONS *Affpuddle Heath.* GR 805924.

However, plantations are a significant component of the broad mosaic of heathland landscapes, but only those large plantations which form a coherent landscape in their own right have been included within this landscape character area.

Each plantation is composed of a fine-grained mosaic with patches of open pasture, heathland, marsh and deciduous woodland within the overall dominant structure of the conifers. The trees are planted in fairly small compartments so there is a varied age structure within each plantation. Tracts of mature deciduous woodland, mostly beech and oak, remain within the plantations and new deciduous planting on the margins of the woodland is often used to soften the boundary and ameliorate the colour effect between the plantation and the adjacent landscape. Deciduous trees frequently occur along the roads, for example the stands of mature oak and beech trees along the Coldharbour road through Wareham Forest and the road to Pallington through the Moreton Plantation, help to integrate the conifer forests with the surrounding landscape.

It is only on ridgetops, when the trees on the skyline are depleted, that the consistent outline of the plantations begins to break down and the individual silhouettes of the trees become recognisable. This can become distracting in some areas, such as along the ridgetop to the east of Puddletown Forest, where the horizon is notched and irregular, with only a few straggling trees left standing.

The plantations help to reduce the visual impact of the many large-scale developments in south-east Dorset. Bovington Camp, the Atomic Energy Establishment, Wytch Farm oilfields and the extent of the Bournemouth/Poole conurbation are remarkably well camouflaged by the dense evergreen screen.

Views within the plantations are tightly controlled by dense walls of trees. The forest is a powerful microcosm which defines its own sense of scale, rigidly measured by the relative heights of the trees. The interior of a plantation can be disorientating and threatening as there are only snatched glimpses to the surrounding landscape and even the sky seems distant. However, the forests are often on elevated ridges so there are some viewpoints from which it is possible to look out from the woodland to the countryside beyond and appreciate the scale of the mature conifers in relation to their context. The trees evoke a sense of vulnerability while at the same time providing security and protection.

THE KEY CHARACTERISTIC FEATURES OF THE CONIFER PLANTATIONS ARE:-

- Extensive stands of conifers forming bold landscape features blanketing areas of former heathland.
- Small open pastures, marshes and patches of deciduous trees often occur within plantations so they are rarely as dense as their external appearance suggests.
- Plantation borders are varied and frequently striking with sharp edges between cropped areas and differently aged trees.
- Dense visual screens which effectively camouflage many of the large-scale developments in south east Dorset.
- Straight roads, often edged by stands of mature deciduous trees.
- Generally uniform, unchanging dark blue-green colour
- Generally few settlements.

MANAGEMENT GUIDANCE

i Plantation management should aim to avoid unsympathetic straight lines and sharp edges. This is where professional design and management advice would be particularly relevant.

ii The diverse character of the plantation edges could be enhanced by sensitively designed broadleaved planting, in conjunction with small-scale regeneration, which softens the harsh, solid outlines of the conifer trees. These deciduous trees should be allowed to develop to their full, natural profile. They should be left untrimmed so as to minimise the sharp contrasts between the deciduous and coniferous vegetation types.

iii The stands of mature deciduous trees alongside many of the older forest roads should be protected and conserved since they make an important contribution to the visual diversity and ecological richness of the plantations.

iv The varied internal structure of the plantations provides important ecological habitats and forestry management plans should incorporate the principles of the Dorset Heaths and Forest Project to identify opportunities for heathland restoration and the maintenance and expansion of existing heathland communities.

v In particular, opportunities should be sought to reduce heathland fragmentation by maintaining strategic wide bands of open heathland, designed to link existing isolated tracts of heather vegetation.

vi Conifer plantations are visually prominent in the landscape so their overall shape and the character of their outline is of great importance. Plantations should be creatively managed to integrate with landform and other landscape features, creating rich and distinctive characters of their own, which contrast with other landscape types in Dorset.

vii Ridgetop plantations have a significant visual influence and forestry operations and programmes should be designed to ensure that there are either sufficient trees left on the skyline to form a bold silhouette when viewed from the surrounding lowlands or a sufficient area cleared to reveal a substantially open ridge.

Valley Pastures

The valley pastures landscape type occurs on the lower reaches of most of Dorset's major rivers: the Frome and the Piddle flow into Poole Harbour, whilst the Stour and the Avon end at Christchurch Harbour. These rivers all pass through a similar sequence of landscapes, from the chalklands to the heathlands of the Poole Basin. Although the context of the individual river valley changes, the landform remains relatively homogeneous since the alluvial soils, which smother the underlying bedrock, produce a uniform, fairly, flat valley floor. In addition the lower reaches of the Wey around Radipole and the marshes at Lodmoor form a western outlier of this landscape type.

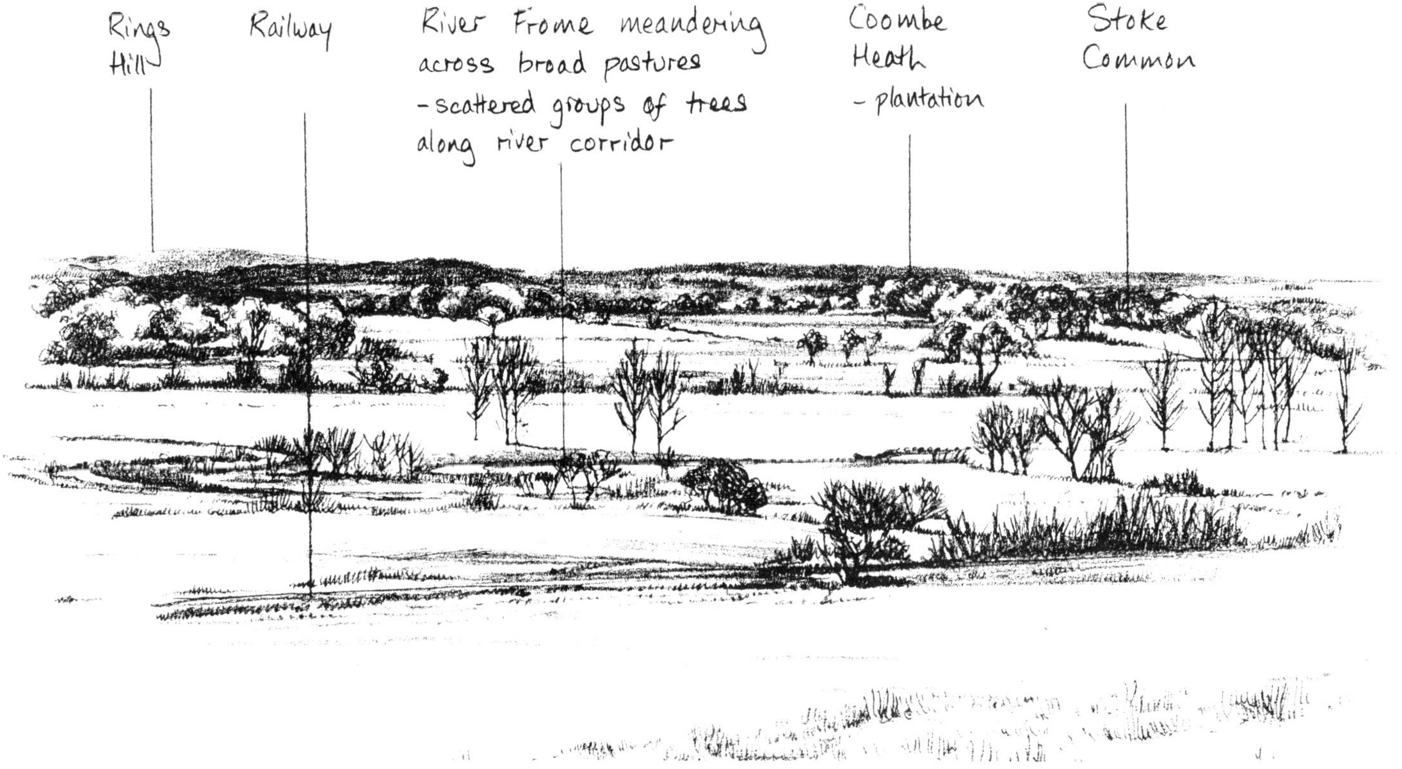

Rings Hill

Railway

River Frome meandering across broad pastures - scattered groups of trees along river corridor

Coombe Heath - plantation

Stoke Common

VALLEY PASTURES: *River Frome near Worget.* GR 902867.

The rivers have meandered over extensive flood plains often leaving river terraces on the edges of the valley. Where there is open farmland, as along the sides of the lower Frome and lower Stour valleys, the layered landform of these river terraces is clearly visible. Whilst the character of the landscape on the valley floor remains constant, variations in its cross section create a sequence of spaces along the valleys. The winding course of the rivers tends to subdivide the valley landscape into a series of visual compartments so views are typically confined to the local context. More extensive views along the valley are possible from the river terraces on the margins, but from within the flood plain they are quite limited and the landscape on the valley slopes forms a visual backdrop and horizon. Land drainage and 'improvements' (deepening and straightening) to the main channel have lowered the water table and cultivation has then produced very large fields, with wider landscapes and longer views, particularly noticeable on the Frome and lower sections of the Stour.

The alluvial soils of the flood plain are mainly managed as improved grassland but there are arable fields on the well-drained, gravelly soils associated with river terraces. The patchwork of fields on the flood plain has an irregular form, although most of the fields are quite large. The fields directly adjacent to the river channel are sometimes smaller and have a rougher, hummocky texture, often with copses in isolated groups within the open fields. Numerous traces of old watermeadow systems can often be found. There are no extensive woodlands on the valley floor and the only dense tree cover occurs in winding belts, along the meandering river corridor, or in irregular small copses which are part of the network of dense hedgerows and small, lush pastures beside the river.

These flat valley landscapes have long been a focus for settlements, although they are necessarily on the slightly elevated land adjacent to the flood plain. Dorchester, Wool and Wareham, for example, along the Frome valley, similarly Shillingstone, Durweston, Blandford and others along the Stour. As the some of these names suggest, they often developed at points where the river could be forded. Others, such as Sturminster Marshall, are the sites of ancient crossings over the river. These old stone bridges, and the causeways which lead up to them across the valley floor, make an important contribution to the local landscape. In addition they provided easy routes for major roads and they are probably the most accessible parts of the county. The roads, like the settlements, are always on the slightly higher land along the valley sides. Also beside the rivers are old water mills. They stand out both because they are often the only building in the area and for their distinctive architecture which reflects their function. Whilst the majority have now ceased to work some have been restored as important historic features. Lines of pylons are a more recent, but frequently an imposing, visually intrusive, landscape component. There are no ancient settlements on the Dorset side of the Avon, the better agricultural land is all on the eastern, Hampshire, side and this is where the people lived.

The open, extensive flat pastures of the valleys in south east Dorset are often dominated by views to urban development, especially when it occurs on the horizon towards the mouth of the river or on the upper terraces within the valley. The northern fringes of Poole are on elevated ridges and where these are well wooded, much of the urban development is obscured. However the lower reaches of both the Stour and the Avon become progressively dominated by urban views as they flow towards Christchurch Harbour.

The wetland corridors generally include a range of habitats with marginal vegetation, patches of wet grassland and marsh. Parts of the river corridors are well wooded and some areas are fringed by groups of willow, alder and poplars. Some wetland areas are important for invertebrates, especially dragonflies and damselflies. The few working watermeadow systems inland also support a small number of wintering wildfowl and waders. The reed-beds and marshes at Lodmoor and Radipole and around Poole harbour are important wildlife habitats as well as being special landscape features.

The valley pastures are generally a very tranquil landscape, there is little feeling of the power of nature other than on the occasions when the rivers flood. It is a landscape where leaning on a gate looking at the view seems the natural thing to do.

THE KEY CHARACTERISTIC FEATURES OF THE VALLEY PASTURES ARE:-

- Relatively flat valley floor, with a meandering river channel, prone to flooding.
- Typically fairly large, open fields, but with a smaller mosaic of fields and dense copses alongside the river channel.
- Hedgerow trees and groups of riverside trees provide a vertical component and are important visual features.
- Predominantly pasture, but with some arable fields on the marginal river terraces.
- Extensive areas of old watermeadow systems.
- Settlements and roads are concentrated along the outer margins of the valley floor, away from the flood plain, usually close to places the river can be crossed.
- Towards the coast, the flood plain widens to form extensive level stretches of pasture, reed bed and marsh.
- Wide horizons and long open views across Poole and Christchurch Harbours, often influenced by urban development.

MANAGEMENT GUIDANCE

i Grazing of the valley pastures should be maintained.

ii Opportunities for the reversion of arable to permanent pasture, with higher groundwater levels, should be encouraged.

iii The care and protection of water quality and the retention of the historic course of the river should be aims of all management plans and activities.

iv There is scope for maintaining and restoring water meadows in some areas. They make a significant contribution to visual character, changing in appearance with the seasons and providing contrasts in colour and texture.

v Old bridges and causeways should be maintained using traditional materials, and causeways should not be widened without overwhelming need.

vi Riverside trees should be maintained and replanted where necessary. Pollards should be managed as such, and new pollards established.

vii Hedgerows and particularly hedgerow trees, are visually important because they provide vertical scale in an otherwise fairly flat landscape. Existing hedgerows should be managed and new hedgerow trees could be planted to strengthen the visual structure of the landscape.

viii Broader belts of trees could be planted to screen intrusive development on the edges of the flood plain.

ix Management should be directed towards the conservation of the sequence of wetland habitats alongside the river corridor. Of particular ecological importance are the marshes, reed-beds and mudflats at the river mouths. Positive management of the reed-beds can also produce a traditional thatching material.

x Where the valley pastures landscape occurs on the fringes of urban development, the fields and hedgerows are poorly maintained, with patches of bramble, thistle and a sense of abandonment. These areas form the viewshed for large urban areas and their visual character would be enhanced by the strategic planting of trees and hedgerows to screen intrusive development, and reinforce the poor visual structure of the landscape.

Poole/Bournemouth Conurbation

The Poole/Bournemouth Conurbation, with a population of 282,228, is amongst the largest urban areas in England and extends 20 kilometres along the coast from the northern side of Poole harbour in the west to Christchurch harbour in the east. The boundary is formed in the north-east by the Stour Valley and in the north and west by Canford Heath, Corfe Mullen and Upton Heath. North of the main area, Ferndown and Merley share many characteristics with the conurbation. The towns of Christchurch and Wimborne do not fall within this landscape type as they have both grown up around historic cores and are similar to other older Dorset towns which tend to sit within a landscape. The conurbation, on the other hand, has created a landscape type of its own.

This urban area is built on a gently rolling landform of Bagshot Beds and Plateau Gravel, rising from the Stour Valley southwards to the sea. On the western side there are a few prominent high spots along the gravel ridges, notably on the southern edge of Canford Heath where a distinctive modern water tower is a prominent local landmark. A low ridge runs round the north-eastern edge of Poole Harbour, and many of the roads which cross this ridge provide fascinating glimpses of the harbour with the Purbeck hills beyond.

The coastline consists of low cliffs of soft sands, clays and gravels. From Poole Harbour to Bournemouth Pier there are several steep sided valleys, or chines, running back from the sea. These are well wooded and, owing to their form, have not been heavily developed. The valleys of the short steams form narrow linear parks, and apart from playing fields the other open spaces are golf courses. East of Bournemouth Pier the coastline is smoother and heavily defended. However, development on the cliff top often screens the sea and its influence is not readily apparent. A visitor to Bournemouth, and especially Boscombe, could be excused for not realising that they were in a seaside town until they stumbled by chance upon the cliff top.

In the nineteenth century Scots and Maritime Pines were planted extensively on the heathlands around Bournemouth, for aesthetic rather than commercial reasons. Indeed the Maritime pine (*Pinus pinaster*) did so well that it received the alternative English name of the 'Bournemouth pine'. These pines, in open spaces and private gardens, give a well wooded impression and make a particularly important contribution to the urban landscape. Pines have also been planted along many of the older residential roads to form impressive avenues. Conversely some open areas surrounded by more modern housing estates still retain fragments of heathland.

Poole is an ancient sea port, justly proud of its maritime heritage, Bournemouth however is of recent origin having been created in the nineteenth century as a holiday resort. In the twentieth century, particularly since the Second World War, the two towns have spread northward to engulf several smaller settlements. These villages, some of considerable antiquity, cling to their identity though in reality they are virtually indistinguishable; each consisting of a cluster of shops surrounded by a sea of housing and industrial estates.

The older parts of Poole, Bournemouth and the surrounding 'villages' all contain some buildings of visual interest. These are, however, isolated fragments within a fairly uniform landscape of relatively uninspired architecture and post war development which contrasts with the few older establishments and some recent taller, more stylish, business buildings.

The hustle and bustle provides an atmosphere nearer to London than Dorset, and the 'anywhere' designs of shops and housing do little to create local character or sense of place. Taller, recent, buildings are more exciting, rising above the grandeur of the stately old pines. Where the land slopes down to the sea in the west there is a clearer and more obvious maritime relationship and tradition associated with Poole and its harbour.

THE KEY CHARACTERISTIC FEATURES OF THE POOLE/BOURNEMOUTH CONURBATION ARE:

- Raised, relatively flat topography with few dramatic changes of level.
- Urban character, influenced by the sea in the west but little maritime feeling with difficult access to the sea east of Bournemouth pier.
- A coast line with extensive views across Poole Harbour, to Swanage, and the Isle of Wight.
- Old pine trees lining many roads and in larger gardens give a wooded appearance.
- Short narrow valleys run through to the coast.
- Occasional small areas of open land retaining fragments of heathland.
- Outside the historic cores of the older settlements there is generally undistinguished post war development.
- Smaller settlements overwhelmed by the developing conurbation losing their separate identities.
- A few innovative modern buildings.

MANAGEMENT GUIDANCE

i Avenues and roadside tree planting should be maintained and enhanced to sustain the local character.

ii Wooded areas should be maintained and replanted when necessary.

iii If pine trees are to be used in planting schemes, then Maritime Pines should be included wherever possible because of their historic links with the area.

iv The contributions of private gardens and playing fields to the sense of space in this urban area should be taken into account in management plans and programmes.

v All remaining areas of heathland should be fully protected and management programmes introduced to maintain them.

vi The settlements surrounding, and incorporated by, the conurbation have lost much of their individual identity. Consideration should be given to ways of enhancing and recreating a separate identity for each of these settlements, by means of, for example, character surveys, design guidance, and varying designs of street furniture, signs, and planting schemes.

vii The coastline is under appreciated and not readily apparent within Bournemouth and Boscombe. Improved signing and other means are needed to overcome this.

NORTH DORSET LANDSCAPES

489km^2 18.42%

There are four landscape types which lie to the north of the chalklands and to the east of Melbury Park. The area includes the rolling foothills to the north of the chalk escarpment, the Oxford Clay of the Blackmoor Vale, the oolitic limestone ridges to the north and west of the Vale and a small section of the Yeo valley west of Sherborne.

A Dorset Farmhouse.

The Northern Chalk Escarpment is bordered by the undulating landscape of the North Scarp Hills, formed from outcrops of Upper and Lower Greensand and Gault. These foothills generally follow the alignment of the escarpment, but in places extend as far northward as Sturminster Newton and East Orchard.

The Blackmoor Vale is a broad clay vale, lush and green in all but the driest summers, flanked by the rolling foothills and the chalk escarpment to the south, and the limestone ridges towards the Somerset border to the north-west.

Fifehead Magdalen.

These limestone ridges themselves have varied landforms ranging from the broad, low ridge near Alweston to the high, lumpy profile of Knighton Hill and the smaller scale scarp and vale landscape to the north of Sherborne.

The broad Yeo valley is formed on the Pennard Sands of the Lower Lias and extends from Yeovil to Sherborne. The northern side of the valley is a broad, open ridge, but to the south the steep, wooded slopes of Knighton Hill and Lillington Hill provide more dramatic enclosure.

It was this area Thomas Gerard described as;

> *Abounding also with verie good Pastures, and Feedeings for Cattell; watered with fine Streames, which take their Courses through rich Meadowes; which Inducements have invited manie of the Gentlemen of these Partes to dwell there: Where neverthelesse in the Winter Season they reape more Profite than Pleasure, for that then this flat Countrie is verie subject to Durt and foule Wayes.*

The moist, and muddy, nature of many parts of northern Dorset is aptly described by one local resident as;

> *Wet and dirty? No, t'as ben rainin' mud!*

The following landscape character types are found in the North Dorset area:

- NORTH SCARP HILLS
- BLACKMOOR VALE
- NORTH DORSET LIMESTONE RIDGES
- YEO VALLEY

North Scarp Hills

The North Scarp Hills form a transitional landscape between the Northern Chalk Escarpment and the Blackmoor Vale. These undulating hills, formed from the Gault clay and Lower Greensand, are similar in character to the farmland landscape of west Dorset but here there are no distinctive Upper Greensand summits and it is the chalk escarpment that forms a continuous prominent ridge, enclosing the hills to the south.

There is a gentle transition between the landscape of the Blackmoor Vale and that of the North Scarp Hills, but there is a more abrupt visual edge at the foot of the chalk escarp-

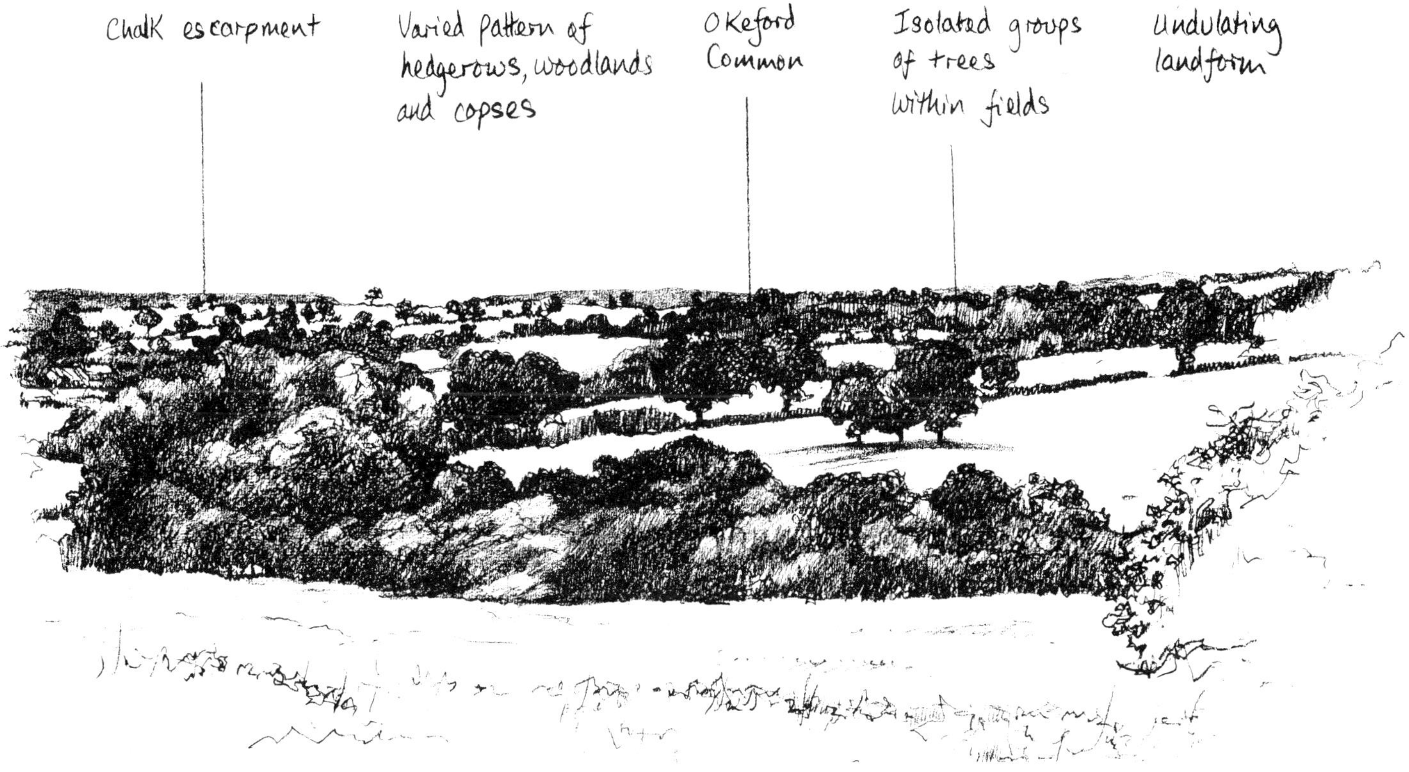

NORTH SCARP HILLS: *Undulating hills near Okeford Fitzpaine.* GR 810119.

ment. Indeed, in places the landscape of the North Scarp Hills continues into some of the indented valleys, which cut into the escarpment. The hills generally become steeper and higher towards the chalk escarpment so the landscape feels more enclosed and protected in this area, although there are many opportunities for long views out over the Blackmoor Vale from the higher points.

The undulating patchwork of predominantly improved pasture, with occasional arable fields, is divided by a varied combination of trees and hedgerows, with dense copses of hedgerow trees, woodlands and isolated trees within the fields. The woodlands are always smaller in scale than those on the chalk escarpment and have a more irregular, organic character. The individual mature hedgerow oak trees, typical of the landscape of the Blackmoor Vale, also occur on the North Scarp Hills but here they tend not to be so visually distinctive as they are surrounded by many other trees in a rich combination of patterns. The patchwork of fields extends across the whole landscape but it is not easy to read clearly since there are so many copses and hedgerow trees to distract from the regular patchwork mosaic. Groups of trees standing alone in the centre of fields are important features which enrich the visual pattern of the agricultural landscape. The fields are in good condition and generally have a smooth, even texture with little evidence of scrub or tussocky grassland, although the landscape is rich in springs and small streams derived from the chalk. The landscape is very verdant and has a strong sense of unity since there are few arable fields to provide a contrasting texture.

There is a concentration of settlements along the foot of the escarpment, with numerous scattered farmsteads and hamlets nestling in the hills. Villages tend to have a clustered configuration and are connected by a twisting network of narrow lanes. The lanes are fully enclosed by hedgerows but they keep to relatively elevated ridges so there are many opportunities for long views.

The landscape of the North Scarp Hills is secluded, with an unspoilt, peaceful rural character. It seems well protected and quite secretive since the landform is undulating and the escarpment provides a further sense of security and enclosure. There are no abrupt edges and the pattern of fields, hedges and trees forms a rich, varied and attractively composed landscape. Views from these foothills out over the Blackmoor Vale often provide a striking contrast and an understanding of their overall context.

THE KEY CHARACTERISTIC FEATURES OF THE NORTH SCARP HILLS ARE:–

- Undulating foothills of the Northern Chalk Escarpment which fall away into the Blackmoor Vale.
- Transitional landscape between the high chalk and low vale.
- Varied, irregular patchwork of small pastures, woodlands and dense hedgerows.
- Northern Chalk Escarpment forms a prominent horizon to the south and east. Longer views out over the Blackmoor Vale to the north.
- Frequent small streams and damp patches, arising from the higher chalk.
- Small villages are typically concentrated along the foot of the chalk escarpment.
- Enclosed, secluded landscape, with no abrupt edges.

MANAGEMENT GUIDANCE

i The diverse pattern of trees and hedgerows should be conserved by the retention and management of all existing hedgerows, hedgerow trees, woodlands and copses.

ii The grasslands and the small field pattern should be conserved by continuing pasture based farming.

iii Streams, marshes and ponds typically occur at the foot of the escarpment and are often fringed with copses and scattered trees. It is important that management is directed towards the conservation of these features.

iv New streamside planting should protect and reinforce the important visual character of the winding wetland corridors.

v The landscape could be reinforced by new planting which should reflect the small-scale and organic character of the undulating patchwork of fields, woodlands and villages, emphasising the contrast with the bolder scale of the escarpment.

Blackmoor Vale

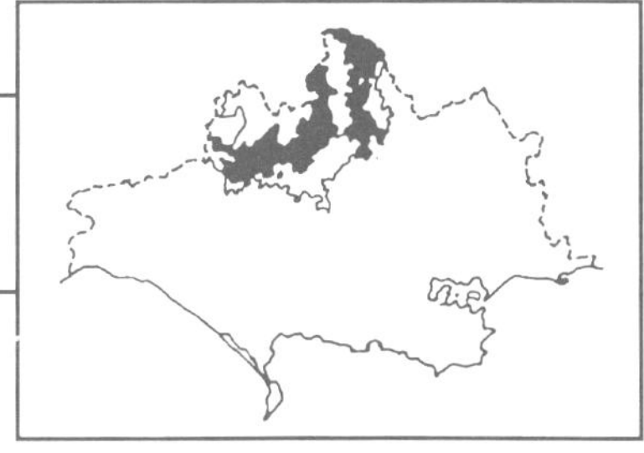

The Blackmoor Vale is a very broad clay vale drained by the River Stour. To the south, the Vale is separated from the Northern Chalk Escarpment by the North Scarp Hills. The Vale is divided in two by the most easterly of the North Dorset Limestone ridges. The western Vale is flanked by the limestone ridges of north-west Dorset and a lower limestone ridge to the east. To the south-west the Vale extends as far as Yetminster, where it is separated from the Halstock valley by another low limestone ridge. This broad western Vale is drained by the River Lydden and the Caundle Brook, which meet the River Stour at Kings Mill Bridge, just south of Marnhull. The eastern Vale, between the limestone ridge and the North Scarp Hills around Shaftesbury is drained by a network of small streams which meet the Stour near Sturminster Newton. These numerous streams probably affect the micro-climate of the Vale which frequently seems to differ markedly from that of the surrounding hills. It is cooler, damper and often mistier, 'a land of mists and mud' as it has sometimes been described. It is certainly lusher than the surrounding countryside, in a dry summer the Vale remains green whilst the surrounding grassland is parched and dry. This is certainly not due to local rainfall as the Vale generally has a lower rainfall than the hills to the south and east. This was most pronounced in 1995 when one rainfall station in the Vale recorded only 759 millimetres, whilst a similar station five kilometres away on the downs recorded 1326 millimetres! This green, lush aspect has been a feature of the Vale for many years, as Thomas Hardy noted in *Tess of the D'Urbervilles*:

> *Here, in the valley, the world seems to be constructed upon a smaller and more delicate scale; the fields are mere paddocks ... Arable lands are few and limited; with but slight exceptions the prospect is a broad rich mass of grass and trees, mantling minor hills and dales within the major. Such is the Vale of Blackmoor.*

The Vale has a gently rolling landform which becomes progressively flatter towards the east and towards the broad River Stour corridor. The numerous small streams within the Vale tend to be very narrow and cause only very minor ripples in the landform. The chalk escarpment forms the horizon and backdrop for all views to the south from within the Blackmoor Vale. Melbury Hill, Fontmell Down and Nettlecombe Tout are examples of distinctive escarpment summits which are important landmarks for orientation, and are an echo of the hills surrounding the Marshwood Vale. The Blackmoor Vale has a finely-grained landscape which forms a highly-patterned, complex mosaic when viewed from the escarpment to the south.

There is mixed farming, but pasture predominates overall. The fields are enclosed by straight hedgerows but have irregular shapes, even though they are all of similar scale. Mature, individually spaced hedgerow oak trees are a regular, distinctive feature of the Blackmoor Vale landscape. They give the Vale a speckled appearance and an overall unity when viewed from the escarpment ridge. These hedgerow oak trees have dramatic, contorted spreading silhouettes and often frame views within the Vale. They are all of similar age and many are becoming stag-headed and broken. The hedgerows are overgrown, bushy and often in poor condition; they have a rich variety of species, including hazel, ash, field maple and blackthorn but there is little evidence of regenerating oak trees. The ash trees are likely

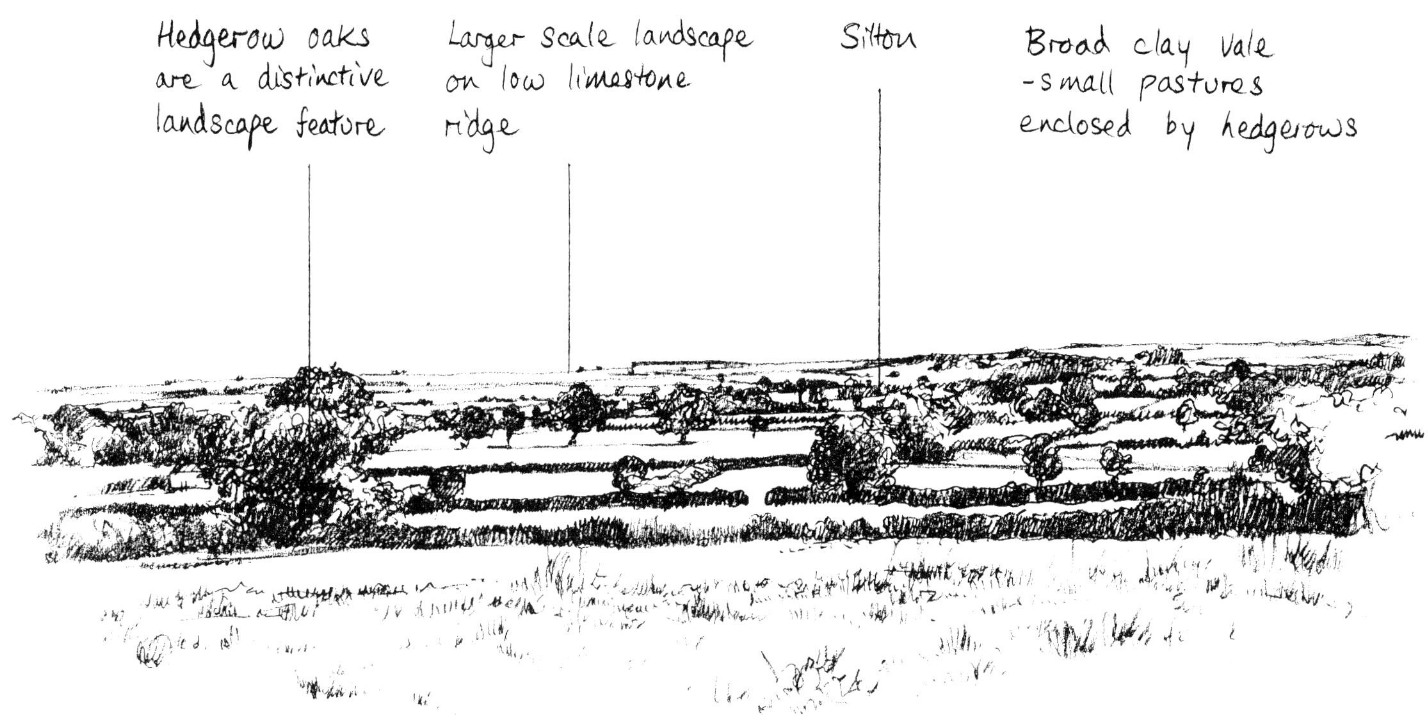

BLACKMOOR VALE: *Looking south-west across the Blackmoor Vale near Silton.* GR 788300.

to become progressively more dominant unless a new generation of hedgerow oaks is planted.

The landscape seems more open in the fields beside the River Stour and there are often long views across the Vale to the higher ridges beyond. The river itself is a visual focus as it meanders across the pastures and the historic bridges, such as those at Sturminster Newton and Kings Mill, are beautiful landmarks. There are often willow trees alongside the narrow tributary streams and their sporadic presence in hedgerows indicates the point at which a stream crosses the road.

The clays of the Blackmoor Vale provide the typical red bricks for the numerous small villages and hamlets which form small nuclei within the landscape patchwork of fields, hedges and small woodlands. The villages tend to be very small and of a similar size - many are tiny hamlets or extended farmsteads. They are often surrounded by patches of woodland so the buildings are partially screened. These villages and farmsteads are connected by twisting, narrow lanes, forming a dense, contorted network across the Vale. The Blackmoor Vale landscape is characterised by subtle, small-scale variations of field shape and texture, a gently undulating landform, glimpsed views of hamlets and the spreading silhouettes of ancient oak trees.

There are occasional areas of surviving acid grassland, of which Lydlinch common is the most important example. This common is also a rare survival of a pre-enclosure landscape, open rough grazing and scattered scrub, with cottages scattered round the edge to take best advantage of their Common Rights.

These small villages, twisting lanes and broad scale of the Blackmoor Vale make it seem bigger than it actually is. The Vale has a relaxing, slow pace and feels slightly disorientating. There are no abrupt edges or sharp contrasts. The Blackmoor Vale has a comfortable, settled atmosphere which feels familiar, peaceful and undemanding. The subtle, undulating landform, the irregular shape of each field and the character of the settlements provide sufficient diversity to give the landscape interest and charm.

THE KEY CHARACTERISTIC FEATURES OF THE BLACKMOOR VALE ARE:-

- Very broad, gently rolling damp clay vale, drained by the River Stour and its dense network of tributaries.
- Fine-grained, irregular mosaic of lush green pastures, villages and small woodlands.
- Woodlands and fields form an irregular patchwork strongly defined by hedgerows
- Distinctive mature hedgerow oak trees.
- Domestic, farmland landscape linked by a network of narrow, twisting lanes.
- Long views are typical along and around the water courses where the Chalk Escarpment forms a prominent backdrop to the south and east.
- Small villages, hamlets and farmsteads are scattered evenly throughout the Vale.

MANAGEMENT GUIDANCE

i Management should focus on sustaining the diversity in the vegetation pattern of the Blackmoor Vale landscape, with its many combinations of field, woodland, copses and hedgerow trees.

ii The fine, rich, ancient hedgerows should be protected and carefully managed to ensure their important contribution to the Vale's character is maintained.

iii Opportunities should be sought to restore mixed species hedgerows where loss is apparent.

iv Hedgerow oaks make an important contribution to the character of this landscape. Most existing specimens are now mature and stag-headed and a new generation of oak trees could be regularly planted throughout the Blackmoor Vale. The trees should be spaced at intervals of 30-70 metres along the hedgerows so that each tree is able to develop a full, spreading crown.

v Opportunities should be sought to restore traditional grazing meadows and create flower-rich grasslands in association with stream corridors and adjacent to hedgerows.

vi The many attractive, small winding streams make an important contribution to the landscape character of the Vale. Water quality should be protected along with the character of the streams. Groups of willows, open pastures and dense copses are typical along the edges of the streams and these diverse features should be conserved, while seeking to establish broader wetland corridors, with a rich assemblage of stream-side habitats.

vii The remaining acidic grassland sites on the historic commons, such as Lydlinch, are ecologically important species-rich habitats and should be protected and managed to control the encroachment of scrub and woodland.

viii The few remaining small semi-natural ancient woodlands should be a priority for nature conservation and sensitive management.

ix Small copses are particularly appropriate in the vicinity of hamlets and farmsteads. Some new farm buildings would benefit from screen planting.

x The character of the network of the lanes should be sustained.

North Dorset Limestone Ridges

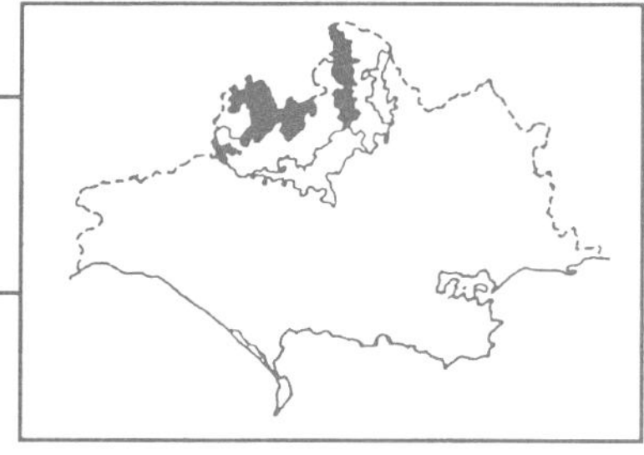

The landscape of the limestone ridges occurs in three separate parts of north Dorset, each with a slightly different landform.

The landscape in the Sherborne area of north-west Dorset is characterised by complex, broken relief, with high rounded hills, small limestone escarpments and deep, branching valleys derived from an involved geological structure. To the north, a limestone escarpment which runs from Poyntington Down to the village of Stallen, forms a bold, steep visual edge in an area of low relief, underlain by the shelly limestone deposits of Ham Hill Stone and Yeovil

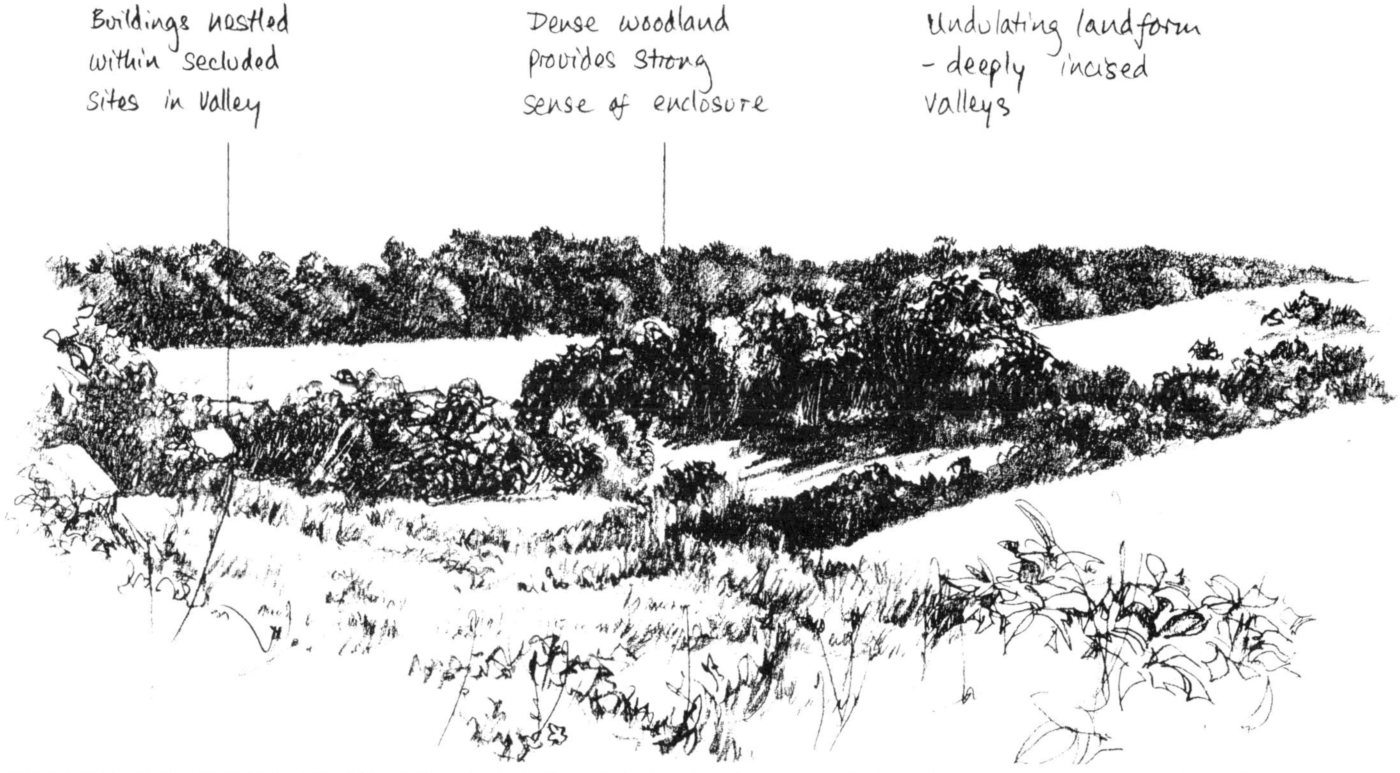

NORTH DORSET LIMESTONE RIDGES: *Secluded undulating landscape at Nether Compton, to the west of Sherborne.* GR 600170.

Sands. Open grassland and patches of scrub give the steep slopes a strong, untamed character which contrasts with the surrounding farmland. To the south of this scarp, a more gentle dip slope falls towards the Yeo valley and the town of Sherborne. Further south and east there are more degraded limestone ridges, with a simple low, rounded profile, separated from the more elevated cluster of hills and ridges by the clay vales of the River Stour and the River Yeo. Finally to the south of Sherborne, the landscape has a larger scale and the landform becomes more rolling and irregular. A cluster of hills, formed on varied combinations of Forest Marble Limestone and Cornbrash, is divided by winding valleys, containing streams which drain towards the Blackmoor Vale.

To the west of the River Stour, a low, rounded limestone ridge extends north-south from Bourton, on the border between north Dorset and Somerset, and divides the Blackmoor Vale into separate east and west sections. Continuing to Sturminster Newton, the ridge has a shallow, rounded profile, broken only by the valley of the River Stour to the north of the village of Marnhull. There is generally a gentle transition between this limestone ridge and the eastern part of Blackmoor Vale, but the west side of the ridge has steeper slopes and a stronger visual presence.

A similar, though slightly smaller limestone ridge divides the Blackmoor Vale from Halstock valley to the west. This ridge runs from Melbury, on the chalk escarpment, to Ryme

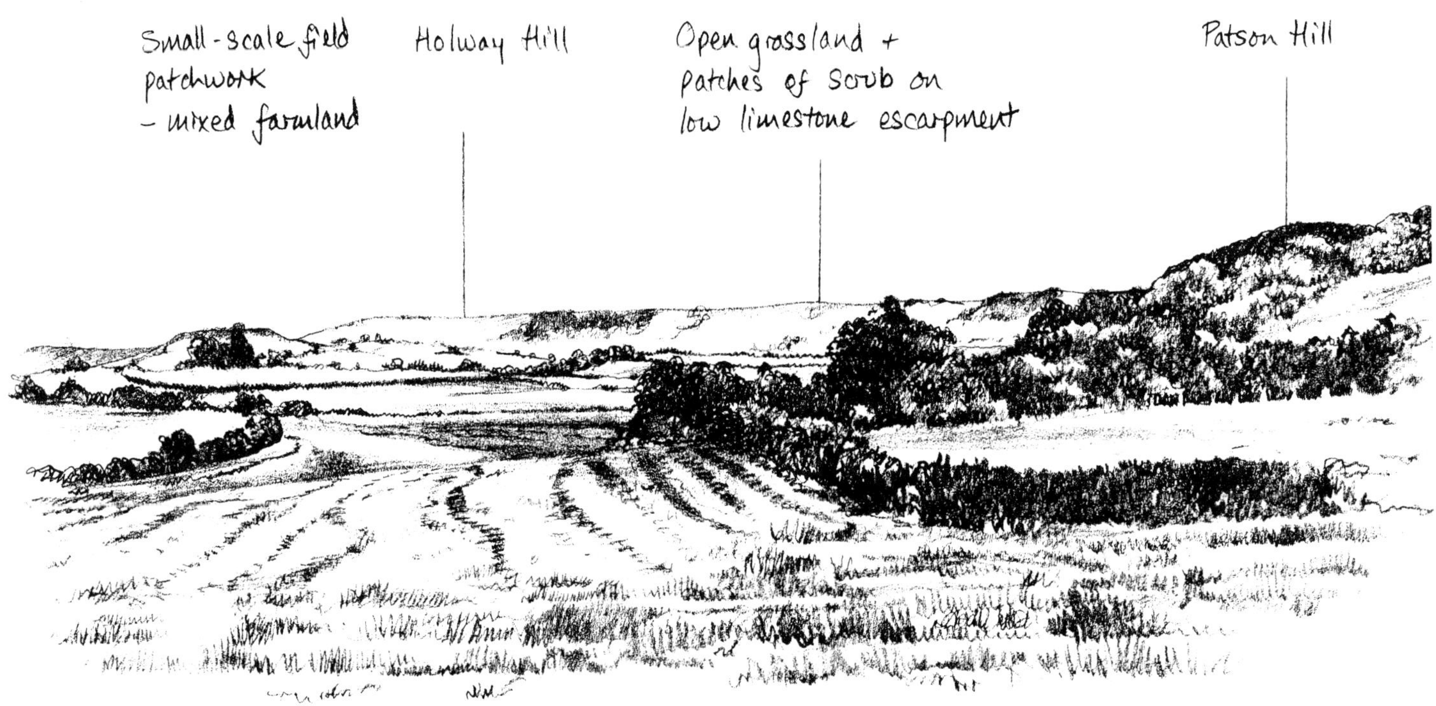

NORTH DORSET LIMESTONE RIDGES: *Limestone scenery to the north of Sherborne: looking north-east towards Holway Hill.* GR 612191.

Intrinseca and Yetminster, where it is divided from Knighton Hill by a valley containing a tributary to the River Yeo.

The varied relief of these limestone hills is matched by a diverse landscape structure. The fields tend to be fairly large and are used as both arable and pasture, with a higher proportion of pastureland on the steep slopes of the hills and valleys near Sherborne. Many of the fields are fully enclosed by hedgerows containing groups of hedgerow trees. There are noticeably fewer hedgerow trees on the more elevated ridges but large blocks of woodland often occur on the steeper slopes and occasionally on the ridgetops. These woodlands tend to emphasise the vertical height of the ridges and the sharp break in slope at the top of the slope. The fields on the shallow ridges within the Blackmoor Vale are typically larger than those in the clay vale below and there is a higher proportion of arable fields.

There are numerous villages and farmsteads, strung out along the low limestone ridges, such as Yetminster, on the western ridge and Marnhull on the ridge to the east. These settlements have an open, sporadic character and are connected by ridgetop roads, with long views out over the surrounding lowlands. The more elevated limestone landscape around Sherborne has a different settlement pattern. Here villages such as Poyntington and Nether Compton are clustered within deep valleys and the town of Sherborne is on the slopes of the Yeo valley. Fine manor houses, picturesque limestone villages and stately homes such as Stalbridge Park and Sherborne Park are characteristic of this limestone scenery. Walls, built of the local faded yellow stone, and church towers are also important landscape features.

The limestone landscape around Sherborne has an overall harmony and unity despite its varied topographic structure. The ridgetops have long, expansive views but there are also undulating areas where the landscape feels more enclosed, and deep valleys where it is secretive, with an intimate scale. There are numerous topographic and cultural features to provide a visual focus and views generally are pleasant, visually-balanced and well composed. The lower limestone ridges have a less varied structure and scale, the landscape too is less impressive and interesting here. The scattered villages, together with their surrounding gardens and paddocks, often provide a distracting foreground for long views across the Vale.

THE KEY CHARACTERISTIC FEATURES OF THE NORTH DORSET LIMESTONE RIDGES ARE:–

- Northerly or north-easterly orientation, higher and drier than adjacent vales.
- Variable landform; with the ridges sometimes broken and complex, elsewhere low.
- Diverse scenery with mixed farming, dense hedgerows, stone walls, and some steep wooded slopes.
- Expansive, fairly open landscape, but with some deep, enclosed valleys.
- Numerous scattered villages and farms frequently built of local faded yellow stone which imports a warm colour to this landscape.

MANAGEMENT GUIDANCE

i The network of walls and hedges should be conserved and reinforced along existing alignments, following contours and emphasising the landform in open ridgetop areas and within the smaller-scale valley landscapes.

ii Some of the existing woodlands and hedgerows are ancient semi-natural ecosystems, which are biologically diverse and significant for nature conservation. These habitats should have priority for sensitive and appropriate management.

iii Care should be taken to ensure that the ridgetops retain their character by maintaining a consistent silhouette against the skyline. Abrupt harsh edges and gaps should be avoided.

iv Stone walls should be maintained and repaired and rebuilt where necessary, using local stone.

v There are some opportunities for belts of hedgerow trees and smaller copses. Any new woodlands should use only local species. Woodland edges should have organic shapes which connect into the existing patchwork of fields and hedgerows, with some belts of trees extending out from the woodlands along the alignment of the hedgerows.

vi To sustain the character and colour of the landscape local materials would help to integrate new developments and farm buildings, as would strategically sited screen planting.

Yeo Valley

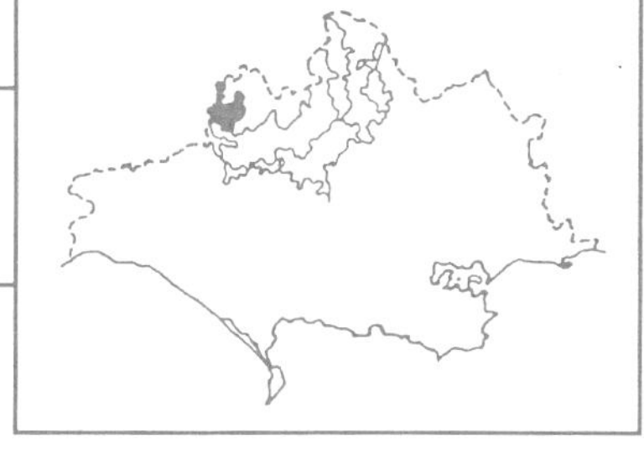

The River Yeo flows westwards from Sherborne Park, just south of the town of Sherborne, to Bradford Abbas, where it turns due north to flow into Somerset. Between these settlements the Yeo valley has a broadly sloping landform and a very wide, flat valley floor. The north side of the valley has a smooth profile, but to the south the slopes are much steeper and more wooded. As the River Yeo turns northwards, the valley narrows slightly before broadening out to form a wide vale in south Somerset.

The geology of the area is complex. The valley from Sherborne Park to Bradford Abbas is formed of Jurassic Clays and Fullers Earths, to the north lies a ridge of Inferior Oolite, on which the town of Sherborne is largely built. To the south the clays lead up to an area of Forest Marble and Cornbrash. When the Yeo turns northwards at Bradford Abbas it flows across the Yeovil Sands into Somerset.

The slopes of the Yeo valley are predominantly large arable fields, divided by neat, narrow hedgerows. There are few hedgerow trees and none at all in some areas. The patchwork of arable fields extends right up onto the limestone ridges to the north and west of Sherborne. Pastures are more common on the steeper, undulating valley slopes to the

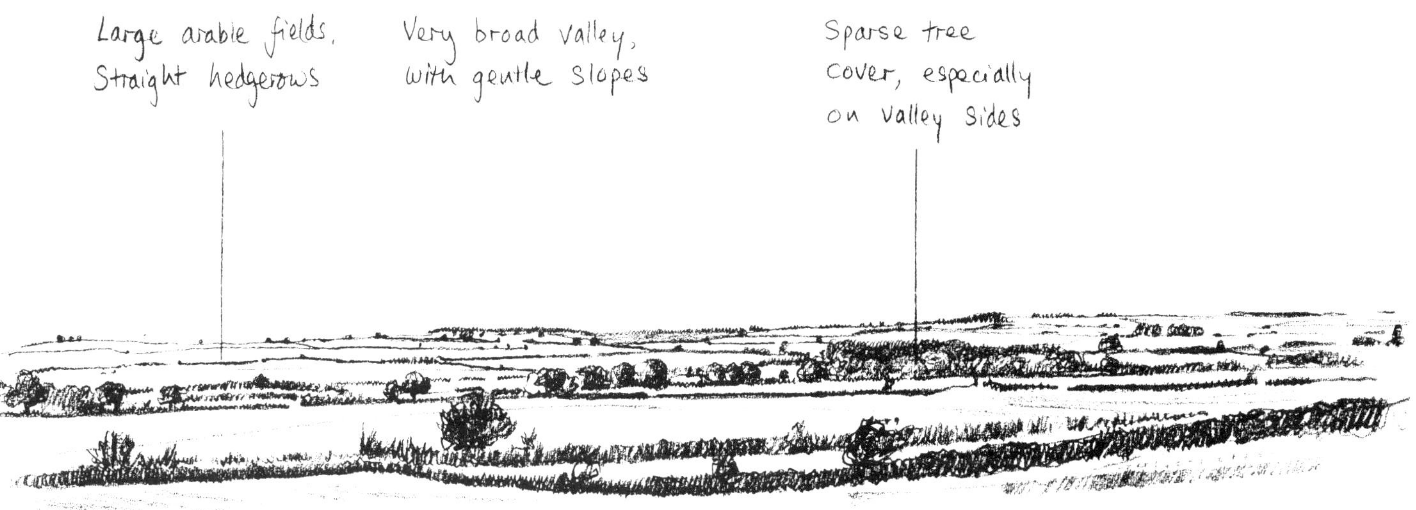

YEO VALLEY: *Looking north across the Yeo valley from Thornford. GR 596128.*

south of the village of Thornford and to the west of Trent. Here there are more hedgerow trees, copses, and on the northern slopes of Knighton Hill, extensive woodlands. Between Thornford and Bradford Abbas the valley floor is dominated by arable fields, enclosed by thin, gappy hedges and wire fences. Further north, on the margins of the broader vale, the valley floor has more pasture fields, a denser network of hedgerows and many scattered hedgerow trees. There is an abrupt contrast between the broad arable fields of the Yeo valley and the more intricate farmland patchwork of the Blackmoor Vale to the south of Thornford.

Settlements tend to have a clustered form and are towards the margins of the valley floor and on the valley slopes. The villages of Thornford and Bradford Abbas have few trees and seem very exposed. The Somerset town of Yeovil also has a higher exposed site and is dominant in views to the west. Further north, on the borders of the vale, the villages are smaller and more sheltered and there are many scattered farmsteads.

The valley seems bleak, exposed and quite windswept in the Bradford Abbas area, where it is dominated by broad arable fields. Further north, it is more verdant but the valley rarely feels secluded or sheltered since views are so dominated by the town of Yeovil.

KEY CHARACTERISTIC FEATURES

- Broad valley, with a flat valley floor.
- Open character and expansive scale.
- Patchwork of large arable fields extends up onto surrounding broad limestone ridges.
- Villages, with a clustered form and exposed character, on lower valley slopes.

MANAGEMENT GUIDANCE

i Much of the landscape character relates to the open valley floor so this should be maintained whilst there may be opportunities to broaden wetland corridors and provide a richer variety of stream-side habitats.

ii Existing hedgerows should be conserved and new hedgerows established in areas where they have been removed or depleted.

iii Natural regeneration of hedgerow trees could be encouraged and new hedgerow trees planted, especially on the wide valley floor to the south of Bradford Abbas, where the valley landscape could have more continuity with the patchwork of fields, hedgerows and trees of the Blackmoor Vale.

GUIDING PRINCIPLES FOR LANDSCAPE MANAGEMENT

County-Wide Principles for Landscape Management

The Management Matrix on pages 134-5 draws together the broad range of landscape management advice proffered for each of the landscape character areas. Although an assessment of this guidance can lead on to the formulation of topics and programmes for action there are additional matters that it is wise to consider first.

They are those significant aspects and principles of landscape management, partly specific to Dorset and partly 'second nature' to a professional landscape manager, that apply generally across the county. These broad themes apply consistently across different character areas, and relate to features that occur irregularly in a variety of landscape character areas. Furthermore, having derived the management advice at a broad county scale, there may be more detailed and particular elements, or specific localities, that are not covered by the key characteristics or management guidance for a particular character area. Those situations can, nevertheless, be handled adequately by applying the following basic concepts and principles.

The Skills and Special Situations

There are many situations where the commonsense and experience of a countryside manager will lead to appropriate landscape management solutions. It is, however, vital to look around, identify the key characteristics, the local distinctiveness, the local materials and local species that contribute to the particular sense of place. In all cases it is as well to bear in mind the dictum, carved on to the cliffs at Durlston, 'Look around and read great Nature's open book'. The more complex situations will require the skills and experience of a professional landscape architect or landscape manager. For example, the unenclosed landscapes can be especially difficult to handle, such as extensive woodlands, downlands, cliff tops or heathlands. Furthermore, the urge to replace like with like after storms or disasters may not be an adequate solution, as was demonstrated by the onslaught of Dutch Elm Disease. Then many old trees were lost, and visual barriers were removed from formerly close and enclosed landscapes. Some wider and more open landscapes, with tantalising longer views, were created by this disaster. The opportunities for positive change, or the restoration of an under-managed landscape, should be considered in the wake of tempests such as those of October 1987 and January 1990.

Wildlife Habitats

Dorset is rich in both wildlife and semi-natural habitats. They are significant features of the landscape and contribute positively to the quality and enjoyment of it. The protection and enhancement of such sites are just as important in landscape management as the conservation of other landscape features. Indeed, in many areas, such as the heathlands, management for wildlife and for landscape are very similar, so there are likely to be few disagreements between land-

MANAGEMENT MATRIX

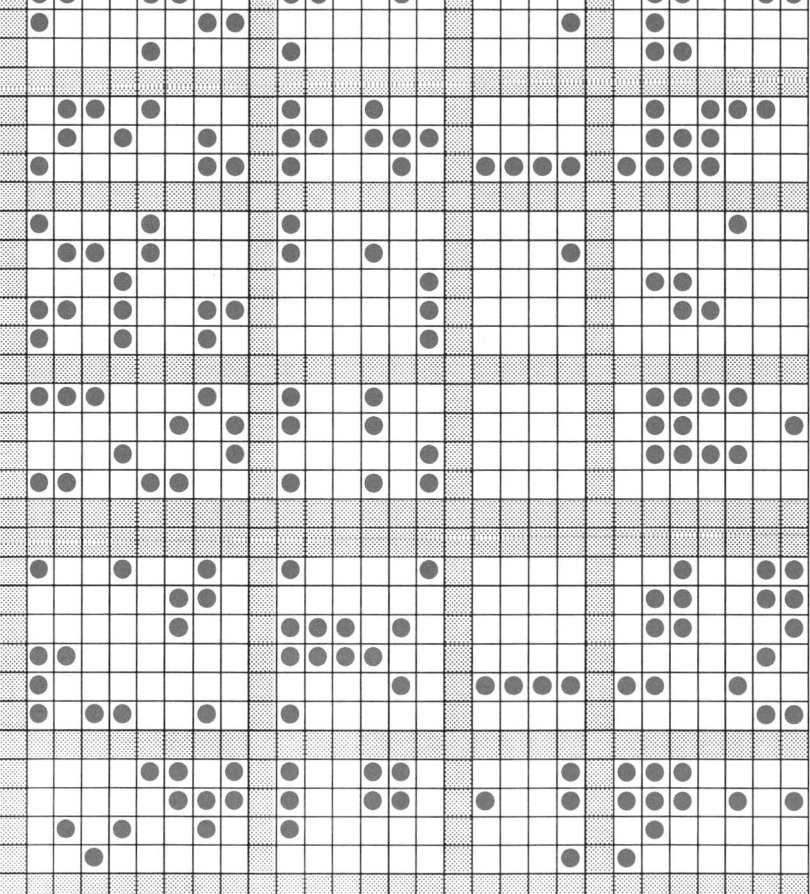

Landscape	GENERAL	Special management study and/or design advice	Manage hilltops and skyline	Maintain open vistas/fine views	Control intrusive features	Reflect scale/variations of scale	Maintain balance of fields, hedges, woods	Maintain special structure/appearance & texture	Conserve ancient field patterns	WOODLANDS	Active management of trees and/or woodlands	Increase broadleaved/decrease coniferous trees	Maintain character & quality of woodland edges	Modify woodlands to respect landform	Pollarding and/or coppicing	Tree planting not always appropriate	WATER	Maintain water quality	Water level management	Maintain and restore watermeadows	Maintain streamside corridors of native trees	HABITATS	Establish streamside wetland habitats	Maintain traditional pasture grazing	Control scrub encroachment	Limestone and chalk grassland conservation	Conversion of arable to grassland	Heathland protected, managed and restored	Acidic grassland management
WEST DORSET LANDSCAPES																													
West Dorset Farmland		●	●			●	●				●	●			●									●	●			●	●
Marshwood Vale		●						●	●												●			●					
Powerstock Hills						●					●													●	●				
CHALK LANDSCAPES																													
Chalk Uplands			●	●		●					●			●										●		●	●	●	
Chalk Escarpment			●		●			●			●	●		●	●	●								●	●	●			
Chalk Valleys		●						●	●		●				●			●	●	●	●		●	●	●	●			
SOUTH DORSET LANDSCAPES																													
Weymouth Lowlands		●				●					●																●		
Bride Valley			●	●		●					●			●							●								
Coastal Grasslands					●											●								●	●				
Isle of Portland		●	●		●			●	●							●									●	●			
Chesil Beach		●			●			●								●													
ISLE OF PURBECK LANDSCAPES																													
Purbeck Chalk Ridge		●	●	●				●			●			●										●	●	●	●		
Corfe Valley							●		●		●			●										●	●				●
Purbeck Limestone Plateau					●				●							●								●	●	●	●		
West Purbeck Coast		●	●			●	●				●			●		●													
EAST DORSET AND POOLE BASIN LANDSCAPES																													
Heathland		●			●			●			●					●									●			●	●
Heathland/Scrub Mosaic							●	●																●	●			●	●
East Dorset Woods and Farmland							●				●	●	●		●									●	●				●
Conifer Plantations		●	●								●	●	●	●														●	
Valley Pastures		●													●			●	●	●	●		●	●			●		
Poole/Bournemouth Conurbation		●		●	●			●			●																	●	●
NORTH DORSET LANDSCAPES																													
North Scarp Hills						●	●		●		●			●	●						●		●	●	●				
Blackmoor Vale							●	●	●		●			●	●			●			●		●	●	●		●		●
North Dorset Limestone Ridges			●		●			●			●													●					
Yeo Valley				●																	●		●						

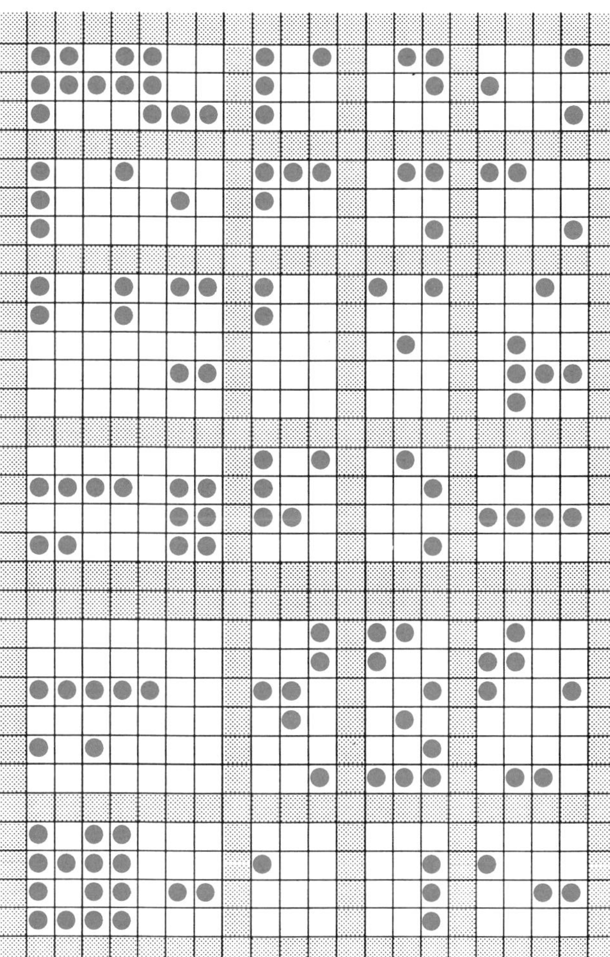

	BOUNDARIES	Hedge management	Hedge replanting	Plant hedgerow trees	Cease hedgerow removal	Boundary bank management	Maintain stone walls	Replace/recreate stone walls	ACCESS	Maintain character of lanes	Maintain verges of roads and tracks	Control path erosion by appropriate management	AMELIORATIONS	Maintain buffer zones	Protect and manage open space	Plant screens of trees & woodland	MATERIALS/FORM/DESIGN	Scale & form of domestic & agricultural buildings	Use simple designs for signs/parking/fences	Strengthen or recreate local distinctiveness	Use traditional building styles and materials
WEST DORSET LANDSCAPES																					
West Dorset Farmland		●	●		●	●				●		●			●	●					●
Marshwood Vale		●	●	●	●	●				●						●		●			
Powerstock Hills		●				●	●	●		●											●
CHALK LANDSCAPES																					
Chalk Uplands		●			●					●	●	●			●	●		●	●		
Chalk Escarpment		●					●			●											
Chalk Valleys		●														●					●
SOUTH DORSET LANDSCAPES																					
Weymouth Lowlands		●			●		●	●		●				●		●				●	
Bride Valley		●			●					●											
Coastal Grasslands															●				●		
Isle of Portland							●	●											●	●	●
Chesil Beach																			●		
ISLE OF PURBECK LANDSCAPES																					
Purbeck Chalk Ridge										●		●			●				●		
Corfe Valley		●	●	●	●		●	●		●						●					
Purbeck Limestone Plateau							●	●		●	●							●	●	●	●
West Purbeck Coast		●	●				●	●								●					
EAST DORSET AND POOLE BASIN LANDSCAPES																					
East Dorset Woods and Farmland												●		●	●				●		
Valley Pastures												●		●				●	●		
Heathland		●	●	●	●	●				●	●					●		●			●
Heathland/Scrub Mosaic											●				●						
Conifer Plantations		●		●												●					
Poole/Bournemouth Conurbation												●		●	●	●			●	●	
NORTH DORSET LANDSCAPES																					
North Scarp Hills		●		●	●																
Blackmoor Vale		●	●	●	●					●						●		●			
North Dorset Limestone Ridges		●		●	●		●	●								●				●	●
Yeo Valley		●	●	●	●											●					

scape and wildlife management that cannot be settled amicably. However, whilst the major wildlife habitats are easily recognisable, care must be taken to protect smaller sites, such as particular road verges where rare flowers are found. These can be just as valuable, both to individual species and the landscape character of a locality. Information on habitats, wildlife, and local Sites of Nature Conservation Interest can be obtained from the Dorset Environmental Records Centre. Management plans and activities must take account of these sites and species both within and adjacent to the land involved, and if protected as Sites of Special Scientific Interest, or specially protected species are involved, then English Nature must be consulted.

Geology and Landform

THE INTEGRATION OF DEVELOPMENT AND CHANGES IN LAND USE

Positive landscape management need not prevent development. It does, however, mean that proposals should always respect the landform and seek to integrate development within the landscape rather than impose upon it. Equally, changes in land use should respect the landform. The locally distinctive characteristics and sense of place should be identified so that they can be sustained and echoed in new proposals. The focus should be on working with the landscape, supporting and enhancing local features and styles. For example, local stone should be used, rather than just 'natural stone', as a Purbeck or Portland building in western Dorset can be almost as out of keeping with local styles as a concrete building. Anonymous, bland, 'anywhere designs', lacking appropriate locally distinctive features and materials, should be avoided. Boundaries often emphasise and reinforce landforms and shapes, so careful consideration should be given to the impact of removing, changing, or creating hedges, fences and walls, as well as their individual details for a particular part of the county.

COASTAL SCENERY

The geology and geomorphology of Dorset are most readily appreciated at the coast. There are scientifically important type sections on the cliffs and internationally known shingle and dune features. The essence of the coast, even in the urban areas, is the exposure of the geology. The coastline of Dorset is, moreover, the backbone of the tourist industry. Management issues are the retention of the open features, the containment of development, the protection of the wild unspoilt character, and the balancing of recreation demands with the sustaining of the conservation interests.

The coast has great variety, from the soft, low lying muds and sands of, for example, Poole Harbour and Studland, to the tall robust limestone cliffs of Purbeck and Portland. In addition there are the unstable clay cliffs of western Dorset, the softer chalk cliffs, and the shingle beaches. Virtually all is highly prized either for its natural undeveloped character or its tourism value. In both cases quality is the key attribute in coastal landscape management.

Different localities have their individual character, and management should focus on sustaining and enhancing the local landscape characteristics. That is likely to involve limiting the scale of unsightly facilities, such as car parks, in relation to the quality of the area and its capacity to accommodate them. Signs and other information should be co-ordinated in both form and style to fit in with the local coastal scene, avoiding urban designs that detract from the undeveloped character. Existing uses, for example, caravan and camping sites in prominent places, can be softened and better integrated into the scene by internal and external screen planting, the use of appropriate colours, and adjusting the layout. In coastal situations extra care is necessary to ensure that any new tree and shrub planting survives. Native species that are both resistant to exposure from wind and salt spray should be chosen, in addition such planting needs to be well protected initially. Other major works, such as coast protection, should be rigorously assessed to determine their impact on the coastal landscape and whether there are other options. They should be designed in sympathy with the existing scene, using compatible materials, and executed with care and respect for the coastal environment.

Paths and surfaces need individual consideration, as some wear on a rocky route may be acceptable but further formalising with kerbing and tarmac would not. Boardwalks may be necessary in soft or sensitive areas. The routing and signing of paths to avoid steep slopes is crucial in minimising wear and erosion. On the other hand, in lightly used areas it may be necessary to cut back the plant growth to keep routes open!

Farmed Landscapes

BOUNDARIES AND NOVEL CROPS

These two aspects have a quick and rapidly changing impact on the colour and character of any landscape. Not only is there seasonal change but new crops bring new colours, and plant breeding has brought green overwintering crops to previously brown ploughed scenes. Boundaries create a sense of enclosure, linkage, and unity. Whilst there may be occasions where the removal of a boundary can create a sense of space, that needs to be considered in relation to the scale of the immediate landscape around. Indeed there may be some situations, such as the open downlands and heathlands, where formal boundaries argue with and interrupt the scene, and are inappropriate. Boundaries do need management and any replacements should be in keeping with the locality. This means that urban styles, designs or materials should not be introduced into a rural scene, even beside a road. Post and wire fences are generally less appropriate than a well maintained hedge or wall. Where a wire fence is necessary, the form, colour and texture of one with pressure-treated round timber is much more appropriate than one of square concrete materials. Sawn timber may be appropriate in a more formal or village setting, and stone walls should be maintained where they are the main form of boundary.

HEADLANDS AND HEDGE MANAGEMENT

There is a wealth of information in the ecological literature and in the work of the Game Conservancy about the importance to wildlife of the management of hedges and the strips of land adjacent to them. Whilst tall bushy open hedges have some value, they are frequently too open to provide protection and nest sites. Tightly trimmed narrow hedges, although appearing neat and tidy, are often as sterile as fences. Ideally, grown-out hedges should be laid and regularly trimmed thereafter or laid again on a cyclical basis. Trimming should be with a sharp, well maintained machine to ensure clean cuts, avoiding broken and battered stems. Hedge profiles should be an inverted U or an A shape giving a thick base that is both stockproof and a good habitat. The grassy headlands adjacent to hedges and the verges of trackways frequently retain relicts of interesting vegetation, relatively unaffected by the intensification of agriculture. Fertilisers and pesticide sprays should not be used in these situations, thereby retaining the natural nutrient levels and providing crucial food sources for wildlife at critical seasons. As well as being a rich habitat, hedgerows also act as 'corridors' allowing the passage of wildlife across the countryside, frequently linking up areas of woodland. The wildflowers and insects of the hedges and headlands contribute significantly to the character and local distinctiveness of individual areas of the county.

ROADS AND VERGES

Roadside hedges also need regular management, not just for safety and to control growth overhanging the carriageway but also to retain the openness of the verges, which, in themselves, contribute to the character of a locality. The lanes vary throughout the county from twisting narrow ones with high hedgebanks, or open straight roads with broad verges. Furthermore most people experience Dorset's landscapes from the roads, in their cars or on bicycles, so the maintenance of the roadsides and their boundaries is fairly important when it comes to viewing and appreciating the countryside. Care should therefore be taken in any road improvement scheme to try and maintain the local style as far as possible.

Verges vary widely in width and form, and can provide refuges for many plants and insects. Downland flora survives on some road verges where the adjacent fields have long been arable. Verges are, nevertheless, managed habitats, having been grazed, cut, or even treated with weed-killers over the years. As a result of criticism, and as a cost-cutting measure, many authorities reduced the level of cutting, but now this has gone to the other extreme, with verges getting overgrown with scrub. Verges, like headlands, should be treated as grassland, and managed to keep scrub encroachment in check.

FARM BUILDINGS

This topic has been discussed recently in the Countryside Commission's publication *Design in the Countryside*. The maintenance of traditional farm buildings, in harmony with the locality, can contribute greatly to the character and sense of place of a landscape. On the other hand, industrial type buildings, concrete access roads, and galvanised metal gates and fences are alien features in many landscapes. The siting, form, and colour of new or replacement farm buildings should be considered in relation to the landform, the scale of the landscape and the integration of the development with the landscape. That may mean considering locations or routes that are not immediately obvious, and using special designs, forms, materials and colours.

URBAN FRINGE

The intensive use of fields on the edges of towns often leads to an atmosphere of scruffiness and a lack of management of the key landscape features. Particular problems deserving positive attention are the lack of boundary maintenance, the dilapidated and ill-sited sheds, the harshness of the urban edge, and the general lack of care resulting from trespass and fly tipping.

Woodlands and Trees

TREES

To sustain landscapes where trees are significant features requires special assessments of the health and longevity of those trees. Pollarding and coppicing may be positive options in some situations, particularly where there are old pollarded trees in the locality or where the woodland shows evidence of formerly having been coppiced. It should be remembered that woodland will naturally develop on ground left untouched, but this young woodland is often dismissed as 'scrub'. To clear 'scrub' and plant trees, as is sometimes done, could therefore be considered a waste of time, effort and money. When replacement or new planting is needed species and varieties native to Dorset and adjacent counties would be the most appropriate. It should, however, be remembered that trees are rarely the major component of a landscape so the planting of trees is <u>not</u> automatically the best option. The planting of trees in hedgerows or field corners can be considered where it reflects the local pattern and tradition of planting. In establishing native trees, care should be exercised to ensure that the trees are not obscuring or shading out another important habitat or landscape feature. Where trees have grown from self sown seed there will be little management needed apart from protection from grazing animals. Planted trees, however, will initially need constant care whilst they establish a viable root system. Where trees are planted to create enclosure or as a visual screen, it must be remembered that deciduous trees loose their leaves in the winter. This is frequently forgotten, and a well-screened development in July can be clearly visible in November. This should not, however, be an excuse for planting conifers in inappropriate places.

WOODLANDS

Although there is a place for conifers as a crop and a nurse in commercial forestry, there are many situations where the harshness of form, shape, texture, and colour of conifers are less appropriate than those of broad-leaved trees. Indeed, there are situations, such as heathland and downland, where establishing a woodland is inappropriate and jeopardises other particularly valuable habitats. Even though trees appear to grow slowly, woodlands usually need regular and timely management, preferably based on long term plans with regular reviews of their health and growth rates. Coppices and withy beds, for example, need regular cutting to produce a usable product and to sustain the cycles of light and shade, short and tall growth, protection and exposure, which are vital to continuance of the wildlife and the particular character of these features.

Water Landscapes

PONDS AND SMALL LAKES

Ponds are very uncommon in Dorset, indeed Oliver Rackham, in one of the few modern studies of ponds (1986), considers Dorset to be one of the 'driest' counties in England. The ponds that do exist fall into several categories. The largest are the artificial lakes such as those at Sherborne or Moor Crichel created as landscape features; then there are relics of mineral extraction such as the Blue Pool and, rarest of all, a duck decoy at Morden. Smaller ponds can be either natural or artificial, but all are valuable either as a landscape or historic feature, or for their wildlife. The combination of reflections and movements provided by water give a unique added dimension to any landscape. Opportunities to maintain dew ponds, and open water free from pollution, with associated fringing vegetation, should be grasped. In particular, reed-beds have a special character and wildlife value that is dependent on the maintenance of the water level and a regular cutting regime.

RIVERS AND STREAMS

Dorset is renowned for its chalk streams. The moving water is a unique attraction in the scene, and the water supports a lush green corridor in all but the driest season. Many of the streams are seasonal winterbornes which dry up in summer. They are valuable wildlife features and corridors, are sensitive to pollution and water extraction, and are often associated with historic features such as old mills, water meadows, or watercress beds. The purity and seasonality of flow, together with maintenance of water levels in winter, are key management topics.

HARBOURS AND THE FLEET

The 3 main, naturally enclosed, tidal areas are Christchurch Harbour, Poole Harbour and The Fleet. All provide a foil to their surrounding landscapes, having their individual open and wild character. They are all particularly valuable for bird and marine wildlife, as well as being a focus for recreational activities so key management issues are, therefore, the maintenance of the open character, the prevention of pollution, the protection of the wildlife, and the balancing of the recreational demands with the conservation interests.

Historical Landscape Features

PARKLANDS AND HISTORIC LANDSCAPES

The extent of these landscape elements, and their contributions to wider landscapes, are easily underestimated. Parklands have been created in all the main landscape types, often with different characteristics and have a much more managed, designed or domestic atmosphere than the surrounding areas. Some reflect a carefully chronicled, long term, commitment by successive generations of a land owning family, whilst others reveal the variety of tastes of former owners. The personal wishes and influence of the larger landowners and estates, sometimes in the vanguard of agricultural technology, at other times creating woodlands and copses for sporting purposes, have also had a significant impact on the wider landscapes around the more formal parklands. These more private places often have a fringe of woodland around them, both to contain the scene within and to keep prying eyes out! As such, they can be seen as islands within a particular landscape character area or as a particular landscape style imposed upon a landform.

Dorset is blessed with a richness of large and small historic features that provide a special scale and 'sense of place' to an individual locality. Generally, therefore historic landscapes and parklands need specialist research and professional skills to manage them effectively. The urge to plant, fell, build or restore should be resisted until that research has been done. The protection of earthworks may be necessary and the historic means of management may have to be replaced by modern alternatives. The recycling or regeneration of parkland and historic features may involve both the clearance of scrub resulting from the lack of earlier management and new planting with special techniques or protection.

ARCHAEOLOGICAL AND HISTORIC SITES

It must not be thought that historic features are only to be found in 'historic landscapes'; indeed, owing to the degree to which the landscapes of Dorset have been adapted by people over the millennia, there are traces of past human activity to be found in virtually every field. These features can give a remarkable sense of the ever-present past, for example the chalk escarpment east of Portesham is heavily terraced and even to the untutored eye it is clear that the 'ancient chalk grassland' is covering a man-made landscape. Whilst the larger sites, such as hill forts, barrows and lynchets can be obvious, care must be taken not to damage the smaller sites which may have an equally interesting story to tell, and regard had to features which may appear of little or no immediate interest. The remaining Second World War defences are now being studied as sites of historic interest, though it is not many years since conservation organisations were removing them as 'eyesores'. Information on the known archaeological sites can be found through the County's Sites and Monuments Record who can also advise on the likelihood of there being undiscovered archaeological material within the area. Management plans and activities must take account of these sites, and if protected as Scheduled Ancient Monuments, then English Heritage must be consulted.

ACHIEVING LANDSCAPE MANAGEMENT

Although it is easy to look in the direction of the landowner to undertake management, some responsibility rests on society generally if it really wants positive landscape management. In addition, there are Governmental and Local Authority responsibilities for publicly owned landscapes. Fiscal changes linked to agriculture and forestry often influence landscape management, and this can be seen through the Forestry Commission's woodland planting and management grant schemes, and the Ministry of Agriculture's Set-aside, Environmentally Sensitive Area payments, and Countryside Stewardship programme. Indeed, detailed landscape assessments exist for the South Wessex Downs and Avon Valley Environmentally Sensitive Areas which both cover parts of Dorset.

These schemes, and the numerous Countryside Stewardship sites, are targeted specifically at adjusting agricultural management activities to benefit the landscape. English Nature and English Heritage management systems contribute to the overall picture, tending to be directed primarily at specific wildlife and historic interests.

All these approaches to landscape management adopt a similar style. Working through the medium of a visionary and professionally prepared management plan, with clearly stated targets and objectives, annual programmes of tasks are set out.

Progress towards the aims are annually reviewed and assessed. Activities are adjusted, if necessary, for subsequent years in response to the monitoring and experience gained from similar projects.

Local distinctiveness and sense of place can be recorded by anyone or any community, through, for example, the village map scheme, which can, in turn, highlight features valued and indicate areas for management. Local people and voluntary organisations often undertake amenity and conservation tasks with the agreement of landowners and with the help and guidance of the professional countryside staff of local authorities.

Through the Inheritance Tax arrangements, and also frequently because of a genuine concern for the health of their landscapes, the major estates undertake significance research, survey and management work. So, as landscapes are all around us, it is possible for us all to contribute in some way or another to sustaining them.

APPENDIX

A Use of Landscape Assessments
(AN EXAMPLE)

Working on the basic premise of integrating, rather than imposing, changes on the landscape we have considered how the individual landscape character areas, with their different attributes, could accommodate, cope with, or absorb land use and management changes or absorb development. Some activities are entirely within the scope of the land manager, others are encouraged by grant aid and management agreements, and significant changes are controlled by licences, orders, and the formal landuse planning processes. Clearly the latter controls, with legal and democratic support, include landscape matters as major items to be weighed in the balancing processes involved in developing policies and granting (or refusing) licences and planning permissions. There are, however, many elements of good practice in landscape management that should be considered both in those processes and in addition to any requirements to comply with legally supported policies and controls. They relate particularly to the character, scale, local distinctiveness, and sense of place of landscape zones and areas. We have therefore sought to make a contribution to the debate on the capacity of the landscape to handle changes, without suffering significant or unacceptable alteration.

The approach we have taken is to focus on the key characteristics of each landscape type and then to consider, on the basis of professional experience, whether development could be accommodated and the capacity for it. As is the case with any value judgement this is a personal view and, although others may come to slightly different conclusions, the important element is the landscape assessment. The process does lend structure to the discussion and helps to test whether the concept of capacity has any validity when applied to landscapes.

The key characteristics and aspects of the landscape areas, with an opinion on what might, or might not, be capable of absorption in the area are set out as an example of the process. **They do not, nor are they intended to, override established planning or related policies which seek to control development for other reasons or purposes.**

WEST DORSET LANDSCAPES

West Dorset Farmland:
A mixed, domestic landscape, with diverse, small scale topography. The importance of attention to scale, form, and unspoilt qualities would limit development opportunities to those that are small scale and associated with existing settlements.

Marshwood Vale:
Essentially a rural bowl with a positive hedgerow pattern, very little existing development (mainly isolated farmhouses), and clearly visible from surrounding countryside. Narrow lanes limit access, and any significant development would change the remote feel of the area.

Powerstock Hills:
Has an intimate scale of conical hills and narrow twisting lanes through steep valleys with an enclosed atmosphere.

Difficult access and topography limit development opportunities.

CHALK LANDSCAPES

Chalk Uplands:

Covering a large part of the county, these are open, expansive, with large fields and minimal boundaries, therefore any development is likely to be easily visible for great distances. The angular shape and vertical emphasis of buildings would contrast with the long gentle curves of the landform.

Chalk Escarpment:

The slope towards the lower ground makes all features on the escarpment very visible, both from the higher land and the valleys. Scope for development seems to be extremely limited.

Chalk Valleys:

The patchwork of smallish fields and woodlands limits visibility, so some development could be absorbed but any development should conserve that patchwork. There are, however, potential problems of visibility from the higher chalk uplands and chalk escarpment.

SOUTH DORSET LANDSCAPES

South Dorset Lowlands:

Gentle landscape of east-west ridges, with mixed farming, clearly managed with largish fields. Wide views from many angles. The Bride Valley has a remote atmosphere and existing modern farm buildings jar and argue with the rural scene. The encroachment of Weymouth already bites into the gently rolling view. Very careful attention needed to location, style, form and materials if further development is to be contemplated.

Coastal Grassland:

Exposed, windswept, no trees, stunted hedgerows, with a wild character. Long views from surrounding higher ground. Any development would be clearly visible and intrusive.

Isle of Portland:

Hard, rocky, exposed and a little untidy, with little vegetation cover, but strongly influenced by low walls and low stone buildings. Development should be organic rather than formal, low in scale, utilising traditional materials. The quarries provide an opportunity to conceal taller or industrial development.

ISLE OF PURBECK LANDSCAPES

Purbeck Chalk Ridge:

High ridge, clearly visible from surrounding areas. Any development is likely to be clearly visible and intrusive.

Corfe Valley:

Intimate landscape, gently rolling, with hedgerow trees and small woods. Existing small scale development blends into the landscape so any new building would have to have particular regard to scale, materials, limited access, and balance with existing, long established, landmarks.

Purbeck Limestone Plateau:

Exposed, windswept, with wide fields bounded by stone walls, strongly influenced by the presence of the sea. Existing villages tend to fit in the hollows, seeking protection from the wind, and are robustly made of local stone. Any new development would be difficult to integrate, without creating visual intrusion, and would need to respect the traditional proportions, style and materials for buildings.

West Purbeck Coast:

Remote, small scale, tucked under the limestone ridge, and exposed to the south west. Visible from the surrounding high ground, particularly from coastal viewpoints. This, coupled with very limited access, means that opportunities for development in sympathy with the landscape are minimal.

EAST DORSET AND POOLE BASIN LANDSCAPES

Heathland:
Open expansive character, with special wildlife significance. Development inappropriate, and buffer zones should be encouraged between existing developments.

Heathland/Scrub Mosaic:
Irregular, patchy, mosaic of apparently unmanaged heathland, woodland, and farmland. Limited views, hamlets, and some industry on urban fringes. An unkempt, rough character. Any development should retain the mixture of elements and close character whilst seeking, wherever feasible, to revitalise the heathland.

East Dorset Woods and Farmland:
Low, patchwork of pasture and woodland with dense hedgerows and numerous villages, with evidence of many of the same urban fringe pressures as the Heathland/Scrub mosaic. Covering a diverse area of the county with short and limited views due to the small blocks of woodland. Where planning policies permit, retaining the patchwork of hedgerows and woodlands could provide development opportunities in scale with the existing villages and their particular character.

Conifer Plantations:
Dense visual blocks capable of hiding any new development permitted under planning policies so long as the remaining plantations are managed to provide a substantial continued curtain of trees. Opportunities exist for removing trees to recreate views and valuable habitats.

Valley Pastures:
Flat valleys, predominantly pasture, some trees, prone to flooding, with long views both along and across the valleys. Very little existing development is actually in the valleys and any new development would be readily visible and change the undeveloped character of these green ribbons.

Poole/Bournemouth Conurbation:
The most urban part of the county. Any new development should respect and enhance existing open areas, and opportunities should be sought for recreating local distinctiveness within, and between, the old settlements engulfed by the conurbation.

NORTH DORSET LANDSCAPES

North Scarp Hills:
Undulating foothills of the chalk lands, with varied irregular patchwork of pasture, woodland, and hedgerows. Visible from the higher ground, with difficult access, and the unspoilt rural character should be respected. Development opportunities are, therefore, limited.

Blackmoor Vale:
Broad clay vale, with longish views, with lush fields and hedgerows providing an irregular pattern. Development would need to pay particular attention to the scale and form of existing settlements and buildings, whilst sustaining the existing character of the Vale.

North Dorset Limestone Ridges:
Open landscape, with deep secluded valleys, with a Cotswold atmosphere. Access is difficult due to the terrain and development opportunities limited, particularly by the intervisibility of localities.

Yeo Valley:
Broad, open, with large arable fields, sporadic trees, leading to the Somerset levels. Any development is likely to be clearly visible and intrusive.

BACKGROUND AND FURTHER READING

Austen, Jane 1818 *Persuasion*

Barber, K. ed. 1987 *Wessex and the Isle of Wight. Field Guide* Quaternary Research Association. Cambridge.

Betty, J.H. 1996 *Man and the Land. Farming in Dorset 1846-1996* Dorset Natural History and Archaeological Society

Cambridgeshire County Council 1991 *Cambridgeshire Landscape Guidelines* Cambridgeshire C.C. & Granta Editions.

Colebourn, P. and Gibbons, R. 1978 *Britain's Natural Heritage* Blandford Press.

Coker, J. 1732 *A Survey of Dorsetshire* London. (This book was in fact written by Thomas Gerard in about 1625, but when published a century later attributed to the Reverend John Coker)

Countryside Commission 1993 *Design in the Countryside* CCP 418

Countryside Commission 1993 *Landscape Assessment, New Guidance* CCP 423

Countryside Commission 1993 *The Dorset Downs, Heaths and Coast Landscape* CCP 424

Countryside Commission 1995 *The Cranborne Chase and West Wiltshire Downs Landscape* CCP 465

Countryside Commission, Dorset County Council, Landscape Design Associates & Purbeck District Council. 1994 *Dorset Landscape Character Map*

Davies, Peter 1987 *Art in Poole & Dorset* Poole Historical Trust.

Defoe, Daniel 1724 *A Tour Through the Whole Island of Great Britain*

Devon County Council 1994 *The Devon Landscape: A Draft Strategy*

Dorset County Council 1996 *Dorset County Structure Plan; Deposit Plan* CSP 21

Dorset Heathland Forum 1990 *Dorset Heathland Strategy* (obtainable from Dorset County Council.)

Fiennes, C. ed. Morris, C. 1982 *The Journeys of Celia Fiennes* Webb & Bower. Exeter.

Good, R. 1948 *A Geographical Handbook of the Dorset Flora* Dorchester

Good, R. 1966 *The Old Roads of Dorset* Commin, Bournemouth.

Good, R. 1979 *The Lost Villages of Dorset* Dovecote Press, Wimborne.

Hampshire County Council 1993 *The Hampshire Landscape*

Hardy, Thomas 1878 *The Return of the Native* Macmillan

Hardy, Thomas 1880 *The Trumpet Major* Macmillan

Hardy, Thomas 1891 *Tess of the d,Urbervilles* Macmillan

Hawkins, D. 1983 *Cranborne Chase* Victor Gollancz. London.

Hinton, R.F. 1977 *The River Systems of Dorset* M.Sc. Thesis, University College London.

House, M.R. 1991 'Dorset Dolines: Part 2, Bronkham Hill' *Proceedings of the Dorset Natural History and Archaeological Society* 113 105-6

Jones, C.A. 1972 *The Conservation of Chalk Downland in Dorset* M.Sc. Thesis, University College London.

Kerridge, E. 1967 *The Agricultural Revolution* Allen & Unwin, London.

Landscape Design Associates. 1993 *Dorset County Landscape Assessment*

Le Pard, G.F. 1992 'Two Dorset drawings of Heywood Sumner' *Proceedings of the Dorset Natural History and Archaeological Society* 114 264-5.

Ministry of Agriculture, Fisheries and Food. 1994 *Avon Valley Environmentally Sensitive Area; Landscape Assessment*

Ministry of Agriculture, Fisheries and Food. 1994 *South Wessex Downs Environmentally Sensitive Area; Landscape Assessment*

Morris, J. & Draper, J. 1995 ' The 'Enclosure' of Fordington Fields and the Development of Dorchester, 1874-1903. *Proceedings of the Dorset Natural History and Archaeological Society* 117 5-14

Muir, R. 1989 *Portraits of the Past; the British Landscape through the ages* Michael Joseph. London.

Muir, R. & Muir, N. 1987 *Hedgerows: their history and wildlife* Michael Joseph. London.

Muir, R. & Muir, N. 1989 *Fields* Michael Joseph. London.

Paxman, D.. 1995 'Dorset Rainfall 1995' *Proceedings of the Dorset Natural History and Archaeological Society* 117 158-62

Potter, B. 1930 *The Tale of Little Pig Robinson* Warne. London.

Rackham, O. 1986 *The History of the Countryside* Dent. London.

Simpson, R.H. 1975 *The Conservation of Agricultural Land in Dorset* M.Sc. Thesis, University College London.

Stanier, P.H. 1993 'Dorset Limekilns: a first survey' *Proceedings of the Dorset Natural History and Archaeological Society* 115 33-50

Stanier, P.H. 1995 'More Dorset Limekilns' *Proceedings of the Dorset Natural History and Archaeological Society* 117 91-4

SWRPC 1994 *The Landscape, Coast and Historic Environment of the South West* South West Regional Planning Conference (obtainable from Somerset County Council).

Sumner, H. 1910 *The Book of Gorley* Chiswick Press, London.

Tavener, L.E. 1940 *The Land of Britain, The report of the land utilisation survey, Part 88 Dorset*

Thomas, J. 1992 'Building Stones of Dorset - Part 1. The Western parishes Upper Greensand Chert and Lower Lias' *Proceedings of the Dorset Natural History and Archaeological Society* 114 161-8.

Thomas, J. 1993 'Building Stones of Dorset – Part 2. Chideock to Broadwindsor – Middle and Upper Lias' *Proceedings of the Dorset Natural History and Archaeological Society* 115 133-8.

Thomas, J. 1994 'Building Stones of Dorset – Part 3. Inferior Oolite, Forest Marble, Cornbrash and Corallian Limestone' *Proceedings of the Dorset Natural History and Archaeological Society* 116 61-70.

Thomas, J. 1995 'Building Stones of Dorset – Part 4. The northern parishes which use Forest Marble and Cornbrash limestones' *Proceedings of the Dorset Natural History and Archaeological Society* 117 95-100.

Trades Union Congress 1934 *The Book of the Martyrs of Tolpuddle*

Treves, Sir Frederick 1906 *Highways and Byways in Dorset* Macmillan, London.

Turnbull, M. 1994 *The Dorset Coast Today* Dorset County Council.

Rippey, B.H.R.T. 1973 *The Conservation of the Dorset Heaths – a factual study* M.Sc. Thesis, University College London.

Warren, M.S. 1976 *The Dorset Woodlands – their history and conservation* M.Sc. Thesis, University College London.

Woodell, S.R.J. ed. 1985 *The English Landscape; Past, Present and Future* Oxford University Press

Wordsworth, D. ed. de Selincourt, E. 1941 *The Journals of Dorothy Wordsworth* Macmillan

Ordnance Survey Landranger Maps. 183,184,193,194,195.

INDEX OF PEOPLE AND PLACES

D

E

F

G

H

W

Y

THE AUTHORS

Richard Burden and Gordon Le Pard have over forty years' combined experience of working with and interpreting the Dorset landscape.

Richard Burden is a Fellow and Vice-President of the Landscape Institute. He became involved with landscape appreciation at Sheffield University after studying biology and conservation at Sussex and London Universities in the late 1960s. Moving to Dorset in 1971, he established countryside management projects and teams with the philosophy of 'Conservation for Public Enjoyment', as well as helping to integrate essential developments into the landscape. Working at a county and regional level, as part-time Countryside Policy Officer, he is bringing greater awareness to Areas of Outstanding Natural Beauty and has particular expertise in evaluating and managing human impact upon sensitive and heritage landscapes.

Gordon Le Pard was brought up in the New Forest where he developed a practical interest in archaeology and the wider countryside before he studied zoology and education at Bristol and Exeter Universities. He worked for eight years as a country-side ranger in Dorset and is now with the County Council's Coast and Countryside Policy Unit. He has particular interest in landscape history, the life of the artist and archaeologist Heywood Sumner, and the wider influence of the Arts and Crafts Movement in Dorset. In his spare time he lectures and writes on these subjects.